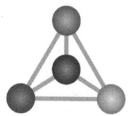

CONNECTING THE DOTS™

www.PragmaticEA.com

Enterprise Transformation

A Pragmatic Approach Using POET

v2021
Kevin Lee Smith

First published: August 2014
Last updated: January 2021

ISBN 978-1-908424-06-8 (hardback)
ISBN 978-1-908424-07-5 (paperback)
ISBN 978-1-908424-08-2 (ebook)

Published by:
Pragmatic365 Ltd
25 Buttermere
Great Notley,
Essex CM77 7UY
England

www.Pragmatic365.org

Currently Available Reference Books	ISBN	Pre-requisites
The Pragmatic Family of Frameworks A Pragmatic Introduction	978-1-908424-42-6	
Enterprise Fundamentals A Pragmatic Approach Using PEFF	978-1-908424-42-6	
Enterprise Transformation A Pragmatic Approach using POET	978-1-908424-07-5	PEFF
Enterprise Architecture A Pragmatic Approach using PEAF	978-1-908424-10-5	POET

Currently Available Focus Books	ISBN	Pre-requisites
PEAF 4 TOGAF Kick-start Your TOGAF Adoption. Pragmatically	978-1-908424-25-9	
Transformation Governance A Pragmatic Approach using Transformation Debt™	978-1-908424-48-8	
Enterprise Architecture Tools A Pragmatic Approach to EA Tool Selection and Adoption	978-1-908424-54-9	
What is EA A Pragmatic Explanation	978-1-908424-57-0	
Transformation Culture The Inconvenient Pragmatic Truth	978-1-908424-59-4	
Transformation Maturity Assessment A Pragmatic Approach using the PTMC	978-1-908424-63-1	
Connecting the DOTS™ The Death of "The Business" & "IT"	978-1-908424-68-6	

Coming Soon	ISBN	Pre-requisites
Enterprise Direction A Pragmatic Approach using POED	978-1-908424-16-7	PEFF
Enterprise Operation A Pragmatic Approach using POEO	978-1-908424-19-8	PEFF
Enterprise Support A Pragmatic Approach using POES	978-1-908424-22-8	PEFF
Enterprise Engineering A Pragmatic Approach using PEEF	978-1-908424-13-6	POET

This work was inspired by all those who seek to make the world a better place, rather than those who seek to own it.

"We cannot solve our problems,
with the same thinking we used when we created them."

Albert Einstein

"Sometimes it is the people who no one imagines anything of,
who do the things that no one can imagine."

Alan Turing

"Computers are useless.
They can only give you answers"

Pablo Picasso.

"You cannot 'cost justify' Architecture"

J. A. Zachman

"We have seen the enemy,
and the enemy is us (management)."

W. E. Deming

"If I have seen further,
it is by standing on the shoulders of giants."

Isaac Newton

Acknowledgements

The author would like to acknowledge the extensive help and advice provided by Murphy to get this book to market, particularly for the constant companionship and irritating interruptions (which provided much needed relief although I didn't know it at the time) and a chance for mutual tummy tickles.

I would also like to thank my wife, Virginia, for her moral support and the constant supply of Marmite on toast.

Please note that, to preserve commercial and personal confidentiality, any stories and examples in this book will usually have been adapted, combined and in part fictionalised from experiences in a variety of contexts, and do not and are not intended to represent any specific individual or Enterprise.

Registered trademarks such as PEAF, Zachman, TOGAF, ITIL, COBIT etc are acknowledged as the intellectual property of the respective owners.

Pragmatic thanks the following people who have contributed their ideas.
(In country alphabetical order)

If you would like to contribute ideas or have any comments or suggestions for improvements or corrections, please contact us .

| Australia | Hungary | New Zealand | United Kingdom | United Kingdom | United Kingdom | United States | United States | Zimbabwe |

Contributor	Area of Contributions
Taiss Quartapa Interim Executive Enlightened Interest Group **Australia**	Exploring the impossible is my calling. Whether that means working on the Enterprise Architecture, reinventing the internal processes of a global company or creating a new, innovative approach for the retail experience, solving the impossible is what I seek to do. I'm driven to deliver impactful results which enhance aspects of people's lives. POET > Culture > Slaves-to-Psychology > The-Dunning-Kruger-Effect
Tamás Nacsák Senior Enterprise Architect Telcotrend **Hungary**	Tamás Nacsák, is a Senior Enterprise Architect, worked twenty plus years in IT mostly in the telecommunication industry; the last twelve dedicated to Enterprise Architecture. He is currently working as Enterprise Architect on several Telco companies and at Hungarian State Tresury. POET > Culture > The-Architect > The-Pragmatic-Architect-Creed
Brendan S. McEnroe Chief Technology Officer // Enterprise Architect Trade Window Limited **New Zealand**	Brendan is a Certified Enterprise Architect, technology thought leader and start-up founder with 30 years' experience. He has a demonstrated history of digital strategy, innovation and leading high performing teams on large scale technology projects, across UK and NZ organisations. PEFF > Adoption > Measures > PTMC > Tools
Gareth Llewellyn Enterprise and Solution Architect Freelance **United Kingdom**	Over 28 years, Gareth has been a trusted advisor to executives and key decision makers. He has architected strategic transformations for medium to large commercial organisations, and to federal, state and local government across the UK and Australia. Gareth uses design thinking to transition businesses to their target operating model, delivering profound outcomes while reducing cost & risk. POET > Culture > The-Architect > What-Does-An-Architect-Do
Amber Smith Trainee Cabinetmaker Humphrey Munson **United Kingdom**	As someone who likes to learn, and loves a challenge, I have tried working in many different industries, some of which I loved, some I absolutely hated. I have come to know myself through trying new things. Recently, I have attained a job which I absolutely love, and aspire to turn into my career. Cabinetmaking allows me to be practical, creative, and keeps me on my toes! POET > Culture > Slaves-to-Psychology > The-Dunning-Kruger-Effect
Abdul Aziz Business Architect and Cybernetician Vanga Limited **United Kingdom**	A passionate strategist, enterprise architect and business change leader endeavouring to help executives, managers and operatives navigate complexity with principles and values that enable their organisational purpose. Abdul has over 20 years' experience in all aspects of "changing the business" across multiple industries holds an MBA with distinction from the Alliance Manchester Business School. POET > Culture > Architecture-and-Engineering > Fundamentals

James McGovern
Research Director
Gartner
United States

Over twenty years of experience applying technical, process, and people skills to improve individual, team, and organizational performance and overall efficacy. Advanced knowledge of enterprise architecture and enterprise security with a focus on high-profile customer-facing applications. An impassioned leader who mentors with purpose and understands that strong working relationships create great

PEAF > Culture > Roles > EASG-Enterprise-Architecture-Steering-Group

Pedro M. Correa
Harbinger of things to come
Papyrus Software
United States

Regional IT industry leader with SMET background and 25+ years of international experience in the Americas. Award winner for: leading regional sales and service delivery CoE while working as CTO (EDS), for Regional LATAM Sales/Marketing Director (Texas Instruments) and for Business Analyst/PMP (IBM)

PEAF > Methods > Phases > Roadmapping > Intermediate-Journey

Murambwa Clever Haparari
Technology Lead and Design Authority
FBC Holdings
Zimbabwe

Technology Innovation and Enterprise Architecture Leader with a vision to become an Enterprise Transformation leader driving Enterprises for the consistent achievement of their Strategic goals of Effectiveness, Efficiency, Agility and Sustainability of both the Operations and Transformation capabilities through appropriate adoption of the Enterprise Architecture Paradigm.

PEAF > Artefacts > Meta-models > Structural

Contents

FOREWORD

Enterprises have been and will continue to live in a state of flux. A never ending sea of change that buffets them and blows them around, seemingly at random, in an unending churning ocean. Even when it is calm, a storm can blow up "out of the blue" and literally sink the ship at a moment's notice. Most Enterprises invest huge amounts of time and effort in battling the storms. Very few spend any resources on preparing the ship. Instead the call is "all hands on deck" to land the next catch and set the next net. Without proper preparation, every Enterprise is sailing full speed into their own perfect storm.

If we are to sail safely in these unpredictable waters we must make preparations and plans to allow us to respond when treacherous conditions face us. For if we wait until that time before we act, it is unlikely that we will survive.

> "When you are drowning, it's too late to learn to swim."

While the seas are calm, an unprepared ship and crew is generally indistinguishable from a well prepared ship and crew. In fact the unprepared ship will often seem preferable to many, setting sail before other more well prepared ships - not having to waste time gathering and studying the correct charts, loading extra emergency rations, checking the presence and quality of the life-rafts nor performing preventative maintenance on the engine. Often the unprepared ship will set sail and return with a hold full of fish while the prepared ship is still making good their preparations.

The unprepared ship will often catch more fish than other more well prepared ships - not having to comply with safety regulations they are able to cast and wind in the nets much faster and therefore fill their holds faster. Holds also have more space due to the absence of emergency equipment which means more fish can be stored before having to return to port to offload them.

It is not a case of "if" the ship will meet the storm. It is a case of "when".

What preparations has your Enterprise made for its own "Perfect Storm"?

Kevin Lee Smith
The Pragmatic Mariner

The SEP

If you have a goal (reduce costs for example) the way to achieve it tends not to be to directly address that goal. The best way is to do something that will lead to that goal - aka understand what is related to that goal and then manipulate those things. (Increase quality for example which leads ultimately to reducing costs - See Deming's work).

Truly effective and holistic Enterprise Transformation aims to get people to do "what is right" not by telling them what is right but by creating the environment that allows them to "do what is right" almost naturally. There is no path to Enterprise Transformation. Enterprise Transformation is the path.

Holistic Enterprise Transformation is like something caught in the corner of your eye that when you try to look directly at it, it disappears as if by magic and you are left with an uneasy feeling that you are going mad and the best way to proceed is to ignore it in the hope it doesn't happen again.

The problem for most people and for most Enterprises is that this environment of holistic transformation is everyone's responsibility and therefore no one's responsibility.

It is effectively a SEP - Somebody Else's Problem.

Whilst this condition has been known of and documented for many years (generally from a psychological and philosophical point of view) it is most aptly described by Douglas Adams in his third fictional book (described by Douglas as "a trilogy in four parts" - the double joke being that it actually consists of five books!) of the "The Hitchhikers Guide to the Galaxy" series) entitled "Life, the Universe and Everything".

Two of the characters, Ford Prefect and Arthur Dent, are watching a cricket match.

Ford Prefect seems to be distracted by something.

He keeps jumping up and down, shaking his head and blinking…

"Something's on your mind isn't it?" said Arthur.

"I think," said Ford in a tone of voice which Arthur by now recognized as one which presaged something utterly unintelligible, "that there's an SEP over there."

He pointed. Curiously enough, the direction he pointed in was not the one in which he was looking. Arthur looked in the one direction, which was towards the sight-screens, and in the other which was at the field of play. He nodded, he shrugged. He shrugged again.

"A what?" he said.

"An SEP."

"An S ...?"

"... EP."

"And what's that?"

"Somebody Else's Problem."

"Ah, good," said Arthur and relaxed. He had no idea what all that was about, but at least it seemed to be over. It wasn't.

"Over there," said Ford, again pointing at the sight-screens and looking at the pitch.

"Where?" said Arthur.

"There!" said Ford.

"I see," said Arthur, who didn't.

"You do?" said Ford.

"What?" said Arthur.

"Can you see," said Ford patiently, "the SEP?"

"I thought you said that was somebody else's problem."

"That's right."

Arthur nodded slowly, carefully and with an air of immense stupidity.

"And I want to know," said Ford, "if you can see it."

"You do?"

"Yes."

"What," said Arthur, "does it look like?"

"Well, how should I know, you fool?" shouted Ford. "If you can see it, you tell me."

Arthur experienced that dull throbbing sensation just behind the temples which was a hallmark of so many of his conversations with Ford. His brain lurked like a frightened puppy in its kennel. Ford took him by the arm.

"An SEP," he said, "is something that we can't see, or don't see, or our brain doesn't let us see, because we think that it's somebody else's problem. That's what SEP means. Somebody Else's Problem. The brain just edits it out, it's like a blind spot. If you look at it directly you won't see it unless you know precisely what it is. Your only hope is to catch it by surprise out of the corner of your eye."

"Ah," said Arthur, "then that's why ..."

"Yes," said Ford, who knew what Arthur was going to say.

"... you've been jumping up and ..."

"Yes."

"... down, and blinking ..."

"Yes."

"... and ..."

"I think you've got the message."

"I can see it," said Arthur, "it's a spaceship."

- Douglas Adams (Life, the Universe and Everything)

This book is not a spaceship.

This book is your opportunity.

To catch something...

.eye ruoy fo renroc eht fo tuo...

Who Should Read This Book?

Anyone and everyone that is involved (in whole or in part) in the Transformation of Enterprises, from CxO's and Directors to Database Support technicians. From Project Managers to Business Analysts. From Management Consultants to Programmers, and any one of a thousand other job titles that are (in whole or in part) concerned with the Transformation of Enterprises.

More specifically, POET is of most use to the CEO, COO, CIO and CTO and the wider executive team for it is they who have the Accountability and Responsibility for the Efficient and Effective design of the Enterprise Transformation Processes. Ultimately the person who would get most benefit would be the Chief Transformation Officer (CXO) - a role that does not currently exist in 99.9% of all Enterprises. One of POET's main tenets is not only that every Enterprise should have a Chief Transformation Officer but those that do not will be massively overtaken by those that do. The person currently working in an Enterprise that is probably most suitable to taken on this role is likely to be the CIO or IT Director. Not because the role is an IT focussed role but because he/she is probably already the most senior person related to the whole Transformation domain.

In addition, since PEAF inherits from POET, anyone who will read and/or utilise PEAF should also read POET.

What Does This Book Tell Me?

POET does not tell you how to be a CxO, Executive, Strategic Planner, Enterprise Architect, Business Architect, Solution Architect, Portfolio Planner, Portfolio Manager, Change Planner or a Technology Executive or a Business Architect or an IT Director or a Change Architect or a Business Consultant or an Application Technician or an Enterprise Planner or an Enterprise Administrator or an IT Coordinator or a Solution Architect, etc.

What POET does do is expose a holistic environment and context of Methods, Artefacts, Culture and Environment that all of those people exist within. The glue that brings all the parts together into a choreographed whole which makes the whole so much more than just the summation of its parts.

POET takes you on a journey. A journey of discovery. A Journey of understanding. From Strategy to Deployment. From the highest level of strategy within an Enterprise that is conceived and worked on by board members right down to the low level deployment of physical changes made to the Enterprise's Methods, Artefacts, Culture and Environment in support of that strategy.

At each part of this journey, there are different players, with different roles, different backgrounds, aspirations, with differing skeletons in the closet, doing different things at different times with different things to different things for different reasons, and yet, the whole must operate together.

Pragmatic Ontology

Enterprise Transformation

Pragmatic 365
CONNECTING THE DOTS

"The only constant is change!" has been the battle cry for many years but just being able to deal with change is no longer enough. The new battle cry is "The only constant is the acceleration of change!"

How an Enterprise effects the whole of Transformation is becoming a Strategic Strength or a Strategic Weakness, where massive business opportunities can be gained or massive business problems will result.

POET (by providing a framework) allows those involved in the Transformation of Enterprises (from the "Chief Transformation Officer" to those physically deploying the changes, and all those in between) to take a coherent and holistic view of the MAGIC of the Transformation part of an Enterprise (from Strategy to Deployment) to allow Executive Management (by enabling informed decisions) to improve it

Not the Transformation of Operations, but the Transformation of Transformation, to better enable the Transformation of Operations.

> # KEYPOINT:
>
> The only constant is the ACCELERATION of change. POET helps you cope with the punishing G-Force, by driving the Transformation of Transformation™.

> # ADOPTION:
>
> Management: Instigate a project to ensure everyone related to Transformation is trained in POET/XOET.

Questions to Ponder

- What do you use, for the Operating model for your Enterprise's Transformation capability?

Adoption

The Adoption section of POET begins at Step 4. Steps 1 to 3 are contained in PEFF and are the same regardless of what part of the Transformation domain is being matured, as steps 1 to 3 define which part requires attention.

> # KEYPOINT:
>
> The Adoption section of POET defines 'HOW' it should be adopted and used.

Questions to Ponder

- ◆ Do you think Enterprise Transformation frameworks should explain HOW they should be adopted?
- ◆ Which Enterprise Transformation frameworks does your Enterprise currently use?
- ◆ Did they explain how you should adopt them, or leave you to figure it out for yourself?

Elaborating

Logical

Step 4

Design Changes

Physical

> # KEYPOINT:
>
> Designing Changes allows you to decide what to change from POET to your own XOET.

Questions to Ponder

- ◆ Has your Enterprise executed this step yet?
- ◆ If not, would it be beneficial to do so?
- ◆ Who in your Enterprise is the person that can decide to execute this step and provide the mandate and resources to do so?
- ◆ Who in your Enterprise is the person that can execute this step?

Adoption > Step 4 > Actions

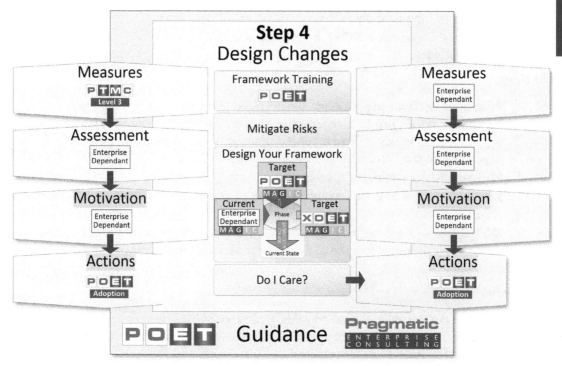

© Pragmatic 365 (2008-2021)

Here we see the basic structure for the information and process for an Adoption step.

Inputs

On the left is the input. Measures, which drove the Assessment (against those measures), which created the Motivation, to perform the Actions of this step. For all steps (Except Step 1) the input on the left comes from the previous step. For Step 1, the input on the left comes from outside the Enterprise (the Enterprise's Context).

For all steps (Except Step 0) the input on the left comes from the previous step. For Step 0, the input on the left comes from outside the Enterprise (the Enterprise's Context).

Outputs

The Actions of this step generate the outputs on the right. More detailed Measures are created, which drive the Assessment (against those measures), which drives the Motivation (or not), to perform the Actions of the next step. For all steps (except Step 6) the output on the right is passed to the next step.

Guidance

Guidance is provided by POET and optionally by engaging a Consultant from

Pragmatic EC.

14 - Adoption

Purpose

- Understand how to apply POET.
- Design the Enterprise's XOET by starting with POET and modifying and augmenting it as required.

Actions

- **Framework Training** – Obtain the required understanding in the chosen framework (POET) to be able to use it. This can include reading books, attending workshops, self-study or instructor led training, or any combination thereof depending on the Enterprise and the individuals involved.
- **Mitigate Risks** – Mitigate risks as they occur.
- **Design Framework** – Using the POET as a base, design your Enterprise Dependant XOET.
- **Do I Care?** – Based on the Assessment, what is the Motivation to proceed, and does the Motivation allow the C-Suite to care enough to warrant proceeding to the next step.

Resources

- It could take less than 4 weeks do this, given appropriate training and resources, however, in practice this work may be spread over many weeks due to the availability of the individuals required.
- Mandatory
    - POET Knowledge.
    - C-Suite:
        - An appetite to execute it.
    - Transformation Project Members:
        - Time to expose their knowledge and views.
    - Transformation Managers (PMs, Heads of, xxx Managers, etc)
        - Time to expose their knowledge and views.

- Advisable

    - **Pragmatic EC**.
    - **P3** – The **Pragmatic** Publishing Platform.

Risks

- A reluctance by Management to allow this work to proceed (Important/Non-Urgent work aka Quality Time), due to the resources required already being maxed out on day to day work (Important/Urgent work aka Firefighting).
- Using POET without the sufficient understanding.

KEYPOINT:

Use POET to design your own

XOET.

ADOPTION:

EA Project Team: Follow the 4th step

in POET for maturing your

Transformation capability.

Constructing

Physical

Step 5

Develop Changes

Operational

KEYPOINT:

Developing Changes allows you to

create your own XOET.

Questions to Ponder

◆ Has your Enterprise executed this step yet?

◆ If not, would it be beneficial to do so?

◆ Who in your Enterprise is the person that can decide to execute this step and provide the mandate and resources to do so?

◆ Who in your Enterprise is the person that can execute this step?

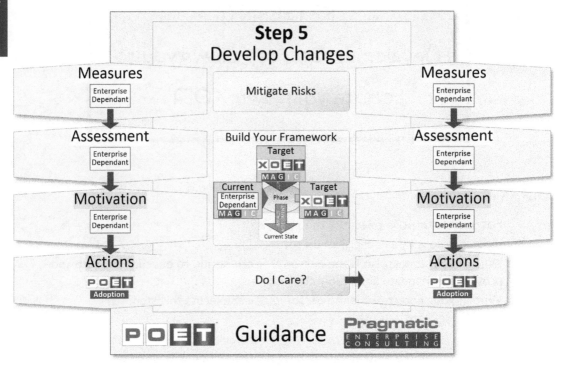

© Pragmatic 365 (2008-2021)

Here we see the basic structure for the information and process for an Adoption step.

Inputs

On the left is the input. Measures, which drove the Assessment (against those measures), which created the Motivation, to perform the Actions of this step.

For all steps (Except Step 0) the input on the left comes from the previous step. For Step 0, the input on the left comes from outside the Enterprise (the Enterprise's Context).

Outputs

The Actions of this step generate the outputs on the right. More detailed Measures are created, which drive the Assessment (against those measures), which drives the Motivation (or not), to perform the Actions of the next step. For all steps (except Step 6) the output on the right is passed to the next step.

Guidance

Guidance is provided by POET and optionally by engaging a Consultant from

Pragmatic EC.

Purpose

- Create the Enterprise's XOET based on the Enterprise's XOET design.

Actions

- **Mitigate Risks** – Mitigate risks as they occur.
- **Develop Framework** – Using the POET as a base, create your Enterprise Dependant XOET.
- **Do I Care?** – Based on the Assessment, what is the Motivation to proceed, and does the Motivation allow the C-Suite to care enough to warrant proceeding to the next step.

Resources

- It could take less than 2 weeks do this using P3, however, in practice this work may be spread over many weeks due to the availability of the individuals required and not using P3.
- Mandatory
    - POET Knowledge.
    - C-Suite:
        - An appetite to execute it.
    - Transformation Project Members:
        - Time to expose their knowledge and views.
    - Transformation Managers (PMs, Heads of, xxx Managers, etc)
        - Time to expose their knowledge and views.

- Advisable

    - **Pragmatic EC**.
    - **P3** – The **Pragmatic** Publishing Platform.

Risks

- A reluctance by Management to allow this work to proceed (Important/Non-Urgent work aka Quality Time), due to the resources required already being maxed out on day to day work (Important/Urgent work aka Firefighting).
- Using POET without the sufficient understanding.
- Not using P3 – The Pragmatic Publishing Platform.

KEYPOINT:

Use P3 to develop your own XOET.

ADOPTION:

EA Project Team: Follow the 5th step

in POET for maturing your

Transformation capability.

Transitioning

Operational

Step 6

Rollout Changes

Physical World

> # KEYPOINT:
>
> Rollout Changes allows you to rollout your own XOET for people to use.

Questions to Ponder

- ♦ Has your Enterprise executed this step yet?
- ♦ If not, would it be beneficial to do so?
- ♦ Who in your Enterprise is the person that can decide to execute this step and provide the mandate and resources to do so?
- ♦ Who in your Enterprise is the person that can execute this step?

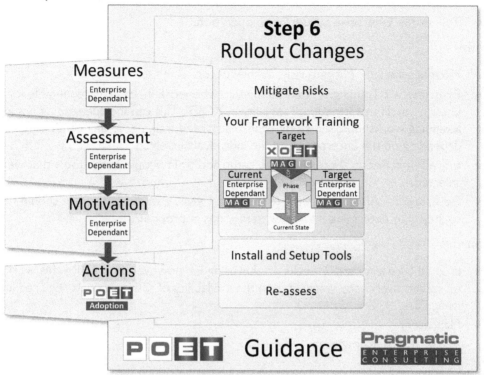

© Pragmatic 365 (2008-2021)

Here we see the basic structure for the information and process for an Adoption step.

Inputs

On the left is the input. Measures, which drove the Assessment (against those measures), which created the Motivation, to perform the Actions of this step.

For all steps (Except Step 0) the input on the left comes from the previous step. For Step 0, the input on the left comes from outside the Enterprise (the Enterprise's Context).

Outputs

The outputs are the deployed changes to the MAGIC of the Enterprise's Transformation Capability.

Guidance

Guidance is provided by POET and optionally by engaging a Consultant from

Pragmatic **EC**.

24 - Adoption

Purpose

♦ Rollout the Enterprise's XOET into operation.

Actions

♦ **Mitigate Risks** – Mitigate risks as they occur.

♦ **Framework** Training – Train the people who work in, or are accountable for, the Enterprises Transformation Capability in XOET. This can include reading books, attending workshops, self-study or instructor led training, or any combination thereof depending on the Enterprise and the individuals involved.

♦ **Install and Setup Tools** – Install, setup and train people in the tools that were selected.

♦ **Re-assess?** – After some time (6 months, 1 year, etc) the Enterprise should return to Step 1 to determine if another iteration is appropriate.

Resources

♦ It could take less than 2 weeks do this using P3, however, in practice this work may be spread over many weeks due to the availability of the individuals required and not using P3.

♦ Mandatory

  ♦ POET Knowledge.
  ♦ C-Suite:
    ▪ An appetite to execute it.
  ♦ Transformation Project Members:
    ▪ Time to learn and understand XOET.
  ♦ Transformation Managers (PMs, Heads of, xxx Managers, etc)
    ▪ Time to learn and understand XOET.
  ♦ Tool Vendor
    ▪ Contract to buy, install and train people.

♦ Advisable

  ♦ **Pragmatic EC**
  ♦ **P3** – The **Pragmatic** Publishing Platform.

Risks

♦ A reluctance by Management to allow this work to proceed (Important/Non-Urgent work aka Quality Time), due to the resources required already being maxed out on day to day work (Important/Urgent work aka Firefighting).

♦ Using XOET without the sufficient understanding.

♦ Not using P3 – The Pragmatic Publishing Platform.

> ## KEYPOINT:
>
> Use P3 to train your staff in your
>
> own XOET

> ## ADOPTION:
>
> EA Project Team: Follow the 6th step
>
> in POET for maturing your
>
> Transformation capability.

Methods

Methods

KEYPOINT:

The Methods section of POET

defines 'WHAT' should be done,

'HOW' and 'WHEN'.

ADOPTION:

C-Suite: Instigate a review of the

Methods used in the Enterprise's

Transformation Capability, to

determine if their maturity is

appropriate.

Questions to Ponder

- ◆ With respect to your Enterprises Transformation capability, what Methods are employed?
- ◆ Are those Methods documented? Understood?
- ◆ Are they fit for purpose?
- ◆ Are they followed? All the time? Only when it suits?
- ◆ Which of them are Good? Why? Bad? Why?

Methods > Phases

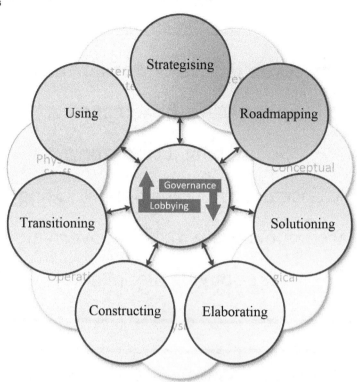

© Pragmatic 365 (2008-2021)

These are the fundamental phases of Transformation which sit between the fundamental levels of Transformation.

Starting at Strategising,, the transformation at each phase takes us closer to the physical world.

- ♦ **Strategising** - Why Should I Care?
- ♦ **Roadmapping** - Plan of action.
- ♦ **Solutioning** – High Level design and detailed planning.
- ♦ **Elaborating** – Detailed design.
- ♦ **Constructing** - Building the changes.
- ♦ **Transitioning** - Deploying the changes.
- ♦ **Using** - Using the changes.

The critical piece here, that connects and keeps all these phases synchronised and working together coherently, is Governance and Lobbying.

Methods

KEYPOINT:

The seven phases of transformation (Strategising, Roadmapping, Solutioning, Elaborating, Constructing, Transitioning, Using) are connected with the Governance & Lobbying discipline.

ADOPTION:

Management: Adopt the seven phases of Transformation - Strategising, Roadmapping, Solutioning, Elaborating, Constructing, Transitioning, Using and the Governance & Lobbying discipline that connects them.

Questions to Ponder

- ◆ Do you agree with these fundamental phases?
- ◆ If not, what would you change and why?
- ◆ What fundamental phases does your Enterprise define?
- ◆ If it does not, does that cause any problems or issues?

◆   If so, how will you solve them?

Methods

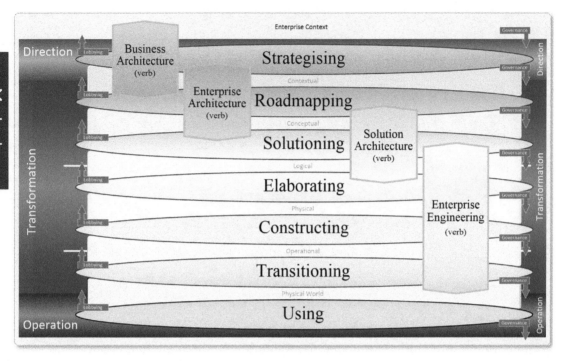

© Pragmatic 365 (2008-2021)

Here we see the fundamental Phases of Enterprise Transformation, laid out over the domains of the Enterprise.

The Direction part of the Enterprise feeds requirements for transformation into the Transformation part of the Enterprise which delivers change into the Operations part of the Enterprise.

It should be noted that the Transformation part of the Enterprise may also deliver change into the Direction, Support or even Transformation (the whole point of POET) part of the Enterprise but we just show Operations here as that is the most common occurrence.

These Phases of Transformation are not strict and rigid waterfall type "processes", but every journey has to be split up into parts, and these high level Phases form the high level parts of the journey, by which to consider holistically, how Transformation is effected from the formulation of Strategy to the Deployment of change into the Enterprise.

For each Phase, the **How** that is effected is done by the next Phase down, and the **Why** comes from the Phase above.

The key to the Transformation cascade working together holistically and coherently is the Governance and Lobbying disciplines which use the concept of Transformation Debt™.

The white horizontal line at the top of the Transformation domain delineates the transition planning work from the project execution work. Everything below that white line is effectively "projectland" The white horizontal line at the bottom of the transformation domain delineates project execution work from the deployment work.

Our remit is not only what is happening in one of these areas. Our remit is what is happening in all of these areas. In general people work within these areas and in most Enterprises these people try to improve what they do (if they are allowed) and how they do it. This is a laudable thing to do, however, no one is looking at the whole cascade and ensuring that the whole cascade is effective and efficient. The parts are being optimised at the expense of the whole. POET provides the basis for Senior Management to address optimising the whole of Transformation, for it is the output of the whole that most important rather than the output of each Phase - this in fact, may mean the de-optimisation of some or all of the parts. For this reason, everything in POET applies equally to all Phases of the Transformation cascade and is the unifying holistic and coherent context in which all Transformation work is performed.

In terms of naming these phases there are four fundamentals.

- ◆ **BA - Business Architecture (verb)** consists of "doing":
    - ◆ Enterprise Context modelling.
    - ◆ Business Model modelling.
    - ◆ Business Capability Model modelling.
    - ◆ Business Motivation Model modelling.
- ◆ **EA - Enterprise Architecture (verb)** consists "doing":
    - ◆ Operating Model modelling.
    - ◆ Roadmap Model modelling.
- ◆ **SA - Solution Architecture (verb)** consists of "doing":
    - ◆ Modelling Logical Solutions to business problems defined in the Roadmap.
- ◆ **EE - Enterprise Engineering (verb)** consists of "doing" all project level work:
    - ◆ Elaborating (primarily detailed physical design).
    - ◆ Constructing (primarily building and testing).
    - ◆ Transitioning (primarily rolling change out into live operation).

Please see **Methods > Overview > Levels > Basics** for a description of the information being used in each phase.

Methods

Methods

KEYPOINT:

Business Architecture feeds

Enterprise Architecture feeds

Solution Architecture feeds

Enterprise Engineering.

ADOPTION:

Management: Ensure everyone in the

Enterprise understands which phases

are part of BA, EA, SA and Enterprise

Engineering.

Questions to Ponder

- ◆ Do you agree with these Phase boundaries?
- ◆ How does your Enterprise map onto them?
- ◆ Does everyone working within the Transformation domain understand how where they work, fits into the whole?
- ◆ If not, would there be a benefit if they did?
- ◆ What will you do to allow people to understand how they fit into the whole, and what will you use?

Methods > Phases > Resource Utilisation

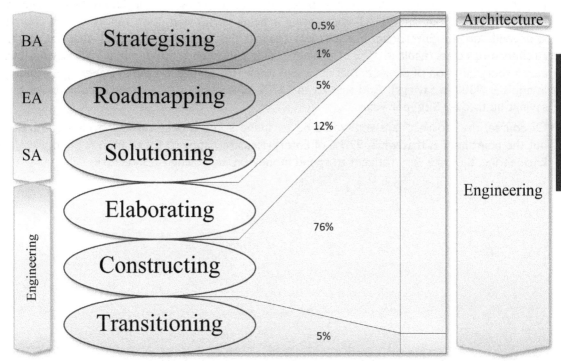

© Pragmatic 365 (2008-2021)

Here we see an illustration of how much resource (time, money, people, etc) is expended in each phase, expressed as a percentage of the annual spend on Transformation. These are not scientifically researched figures, but an approximation based on my experience of 40 years working in the Transformation capability of multiple companies and performing multiple roles.

It can easily be seen that the majority of the resource (some 93%) is spent on Engineering phases; Elaborating (detailed designs and capability sourcing), Constructing (building, installing and testing capabilities), and Transitioning (capability rollout), while the minority (7%) is spent on Business, Enterprise and Solution Architecture.

It is obvious therefore, that if we want to improve the effectiveness and efficiency of our Transformation capability (from Strategising to Transitioning) we should concentrate on improving Engineering, since that is where the majority of the work is done. Right?

Well, let's see...

If we consider a scenario where we are spending $10M per year on Transformation efforts, and we have decided to invest $10k to improve the way we perform Transformation, where will we get the most bang for our buck? In this scenario, we are therefore spending $9.3M on Engineering, and $700k on Architecture.

If we elect to spend our $10k to improve Engineering and let's say we can get a 10% reduction in cost (on $9.3M) this means we will save $930k per year thereafter.

If we elect to spend our $10k to improve Architecture and let's say that we also can get a 10% reduction in cost (on $700k) this means we will save $70k per year thereafter.

So, the right choice is clearly to spend our 10k on improving Engineering and reap a $930k saving year on year. Right?

Not quite. What we are not taking into account, is the fact that an improvement to Architecture, also brings about an improvement in Engineering. Not in HOW Engineering is being performed, but on WHAT Engineering is being performed upon and WHY. Of course it depends on the Enterprise, but it is not beyond the realms of possibility that improving Architecture could result in 10% of projects being cancelled (resulting in a 930k saving) but also a reorganisation of projects that brings another 10% savings on the Engineering (resulting in another 930k in savings). Add that to the $70k of savings in Architecture, could bring the savings up to over $2M per year.

Of course, the "correct" answer would be to spend some money on improving both areas, but the point here is that while 99.9% of Enterprises are happy to spend money on improving Engineering, they are very reticent to spend money on improving Architecture.

KEYPOINT:

99.9% of Enterprises are happy to spend money on improving Engineering, but are very reticent to spend money on improving Architecture.

ADOPTION:

Management: Assign more resources to improving Architecture.

Questions to Ponder

- ◆ Do you agree with this percentage split?
- ◆ If not, what percentages would you apply?
- ◆ Do those percentages prove or disprove the assertion that Architecture has a massive impactr despite its size?

Strategising
(aka Business Architecture)

Sometimes called Business or Enterprise Strategy

e.g. Value Propositions, Cost Structure, Revenue Streams, Partners, Channels, etc, Mission, Vision, Strategies, Tactics, Goals and Objectives

Methods

KEYPOINT:

Strategising is what the C-Suite does.

ADOPTION:

Management: Ensure everyone in the Enterprise understands what the term Strategising refers to.

Questions to Ponder

- Does your Enterprise recognise Strategising as a phase?
- Does your Enterprise recognise how this work it fits into the whole Transformation domain?
- If not, how does it make sure that it works coherently with the phases around it?
- What does your Enterprise call this phase?
- Who in your Enterprise is accountable for this work being performed?
- Who do they hand the output of their work over to?

Roadmapping
(aka Enterprise Architecture)

Sometimes called Annual Business Planning or Transition Planning

Creates a portfolio of projects and roadmaps to be initiated over the coming year(s)

KEYPOINT:

Roadmapping is "doing" Enterprise Architecture.

ADOPTION:

Management: Ensure everyone in the Enterprise understands what the term Roadmapping refers to.

Questions to Ponder

- Does your Enterprise recognise Roadmapping as a phase?
- Does your Enterprise recognise how this work it fits into the whole Transformation domain?
- If not, how does it make sure that it works coherently with the phases around it?
- What does your Enterprise call this phase?
- Who in your Enterprise is accountable for this work being performed?
- Who do they hand the output of their work over to?

Methods > Phases > Solutioning

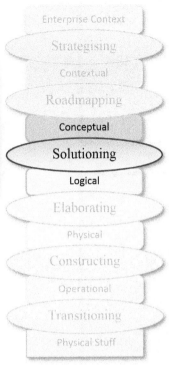

Enterprise Context
Strategising
Contextual
Roadmapping
Conceptual
Solutioning
Logical
Elaborating
Physical
Constructing
Operational
Transitioning
Physical Stuff

Methods

Solutioning
(aka Solution Architecture)

Sometimes called Initiating

e.g. Logical Designs for particular parts of the Enterprise focussed on particular Business Objectives

© Pragmatic 365 (2008-2021)

Methods

> ## KEYPOINT:
>
> Solutioning is "doing" Solution Architecture.

> ## ADOPTION:
>
> Management: Ensure everyone in the Enterprise understands what the term Solutioning refers to.

Questions to Ponder

- ◆ Does your Enterprise recognise Solutioning as a phase?
- ◆ Does your Enterprise recognise how this work it fits into the whole Transformation domain?
- ◆ If not, how does it make sure that it works coherently with the phases around it?
- ◆ What does your Enterprise call this phase?
- ◆ Who in your Enterprise is accountable for this work being performed?
- ◆ Who do they hand the output of their work over to?

Methods > Phases > Solutioning > A Pragmatic Approach

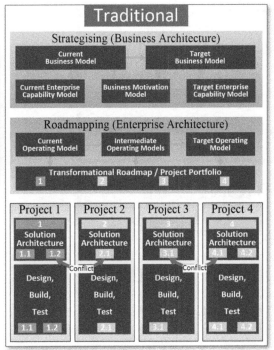
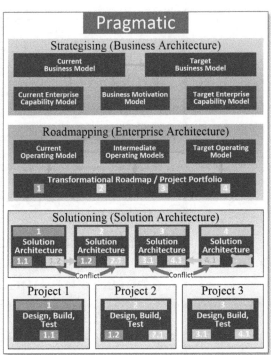

© Pragmatic 365 (2008-2021)

Here we talk about how and why **Pragmatic** suggests moving Solution Architecture work out of projects, and into work that happens before projects begin to execute.

In both models the Business Architecture and Enterprise Architecture work is executed which results in a portfolio of projects to move the Enterprise from its Current Operating Model, through Intermediate Operating Models, towards an aspirational Target Operating Model. It should be noted however, that while the Traditional and **Pragmatic** approaches are diagrammed the same, it is more than likely that many enterprises may not follow the traditional/**Pragmatic** approach as the approach of many Enterprises is normally very haphazard.

These structures are modelled at the conceptual level and all efforts to reduce errors are of course made. However, as we all know (but largely ignore) the devil is in the detail…

This means that no matter how careful the Roadmapping (EA) work is done, it is inevitable that as the Solution Architecture works proceeds:

- ♦ **Problems** (things that could decrease the Effectiveness, Efficiency, Agility or Durability or the Enterprise or increase the Cost, Time or Risk of the work) will come to light that the EAs did not envisage.

- ♦ **Opportunities** (things that could increase the Effectiveness, Efficiency, Agility or Durability or the Enterprise or decrease the Cost, Time or Risk of the work) will also come to light that the EAs did not envisage.

Please note that the description that follows, is based on what I personally witnessed on 90% of the projects I worked on over a 25 year period.

In the traditional model (used by probably 95% or more of Enterprises) the four projects identified in the project portfolio begin to execute. As they execute people on the project (usually but not always the Solution Architect) talk to people on other projects and realise that there are conflicts between part of project 1's work and part of project 2's work, and part of project 3's work and part of project 4's work.

The (usually) SA raises these conflicts with the Project Managers of he respective projects and advise on what changes should be mode to resolve these conflicts. However, the way Project Managers are driven (correctly) is largely to put blinkers on and protect the integrity of their project as much as possible, which often means not wanting the change anything about the project, especially scope. This is resisted even more if the change of scope, also makes their project dependent upon another project. Perhaps the SA gives up or perhaps the conflict (and resolution) is raised to the Project Board, but again, the blinkers and focus of the project always tends to resist anything changing it.

And so, the conflicts are not resolved with predictable results.

Failures occur that could have been avoided.

Opportunities for benefit are lost.

So, let's see what is going on the **Pragmatic** world...

In the **Pragmatic** world, the same conflicts occur, but now that the SA work is not shackled by the tactical focus of a large project, the conflicts have an excellent chance of being resolved. In this example, we solve the first conflict by moving the 1.2 work from project 1 to project 2. The second conflict is solved by moving the 4.1 work into project 3, but as a result of doing that, it is discovered that the 4.2 work is no longer required at all.

The resulting projects are structured in a much better way before they start executing the very expensive and time consuming Engineering phases and Elaboration, Construction and Transitioning. We end up with 3 well focussed projects with the fourth removed completely.

Methods

> # KEYPOINT:
>
> Do not constrain Solution
>
> Architecture in executing projects.

> # ADOPTION:
>
> Management: Move Solution
>
> Architecure work out of individual
>
> projects and execute SA as a
>
> program.

Questions to Ponder

- ♦ Does your Enterprise recognise Roadmapping as a phase?
- ♦ Does your Enterprise recognise how this work it fits into the whole Transformation domain?
- ♦ If not, how does it make sure that it works coherently with the phases around it?
- ♦ What does your Enterprise call this phase?
- ♦ Who in your Enterprise is accountable for this work being performed?
- ♦ Who do they hand the output of their work over to?

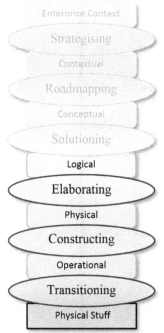

Project Execution
(aka Design, Build/Test, Deploy)

Sometimes called Engineering

All the work that happens when the project portfolio executes which finally results in the deployment of changes to the MAGIC™ of the Enterprise.

© Pragmatic 365 (2008-2021)

- **Solutioning** - where a project starts up, requirements are understood and developed, various possible solutions are identified and considered, and a high level solution is chosen. (Please note that the word Solution is being used in its widest sense, not meaning an IT solution - although a solution may include IT.
- **Elaborating** - where this high level solution is developed into the designs required to "build" the solution.
- **Constructing** - where the designs are used to "build" the solution.
- **Transitioning** - where the solution (comprising changes to the MAGIC) is deployed into Operations.
- **Using** (from the Operation Domain) - where the changed environment is utilised.

> # KEYPOINT:
>
> Elaborating, Constructing and Transitioning is "doing" Projects.

> # ADOPTION:
>
> Management: Ensure everyone in the Enterprise understands what the term Project Execution refers to.

Questions to Ponder

- ♦ Does your Enterprise recognise Project Execution phases?
- ♦ Does your Enterprise recognise how this work it fits into the whole Transformation domain?
- ♦ If not, how does it make sure that it works coherently with the phases around it?
- ♦ What does your Enterprise call this phase?
- ♦ Who in your Enterprise is accountable for this work being performed?
- ♦ Who do they hand the output of their work over to?

Methods > Phases > Pattern

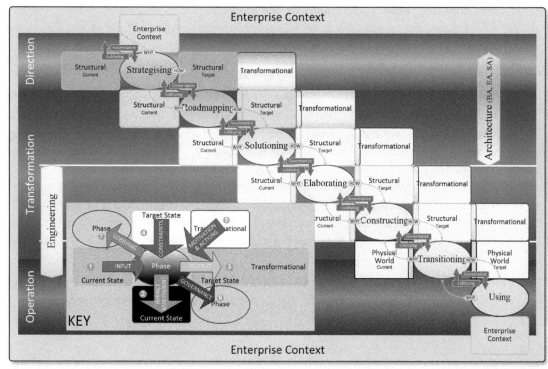

© Pragmatic 365 (2008-2021)

Here we see how the Phases of Transformation exist in a holistic and coherent cascade from Strategic intent at the top, down to deployed change at the bottom. For each phase, we can say that the information regarding **WHY** we are doing what we are doing (Transformational) and **WHY** we are doing it this way (Structural), flows from the phase above, and the information regarding **HOW** what we are doing will be made real (or operationalised) is accomplished by the phase below.

For each phase (or ellipse) the same basic pattern of work is being carried out.

1. The structural starting point (as defined by MAGIC) for each phase is what currently exists, and is shown on the left of each ellipse.
2. This structural starting point for one phase, also acts as the information to perform impact analysis on, and is shown below each phase.
3. The structural and transformational output for each phase is shown on the right of each ellipse.
4. This structural output for one phase, also acts as the information that provides constraints, and is show above each phase.

You will notice in the main diagram, that the some of the boxes are only showing slivers. This illustrates the fact that scope of work of each project at these levels, and therefore only deals with part of the Enterprise's Architecture and Engineering Models at a time rather than the whole.

5. We also see how the Transformational Artefacts (as defined by MAGMA) exist in this holistic and coherent cascade, by providing the Motivation and Actions that drive each phase.

6. Finally we see that each phase performs Governance on the phase below, to ensure that Principles, Polices and Standards are followed...

7. And Lobby's the phase above, to raise Transformation Debt™ when the Principles, Polices and Standards cannot be adhered to, and the reasons why.

So, for each phase (or ellipse) the same basic pattern of work is being carried out:

♦ The inputs of **Why are we doing it** and **Why are we doing it this way** flow from the phase above.

♦ The outputs to the right consist of the transformation needed to effect the change within the constraints of the **Why are we doing it this way**. This transformational information consists of detailed information to perform the next phase and high level information to perform all subsequent phases.

♦ These outputs are produced in the context of what currently exists at that level - to the left, and in the context of what currently exists - at the level below.

♦ Governance is performed down to the phase below. Lobbying is performed up to the phase above.

This simple pattern is the key to enable the whole Transformation domain to work together in a coherent and connected manner, allowing us the absolute best chance of success.

KEYPOINT:

Use the Transformation cascade to link the phases together.

ADOPTION:

Management: Ensure everyone in the Enterprise understands how the phases and levels of Transformation link together.

Questions to Ponder

- Do you think that this basic pattern can help to keep the whole aligned and connected and why?
- Does your Enterprise consider how the structural information at each level is used and reused by other levels?
- Do you think that this basic pattern can help to keep the whole aligned and connected and why?
- Does your Enterprise consider how the transformation information at each level is used and reused by other levels?

Methods > Phases > Models

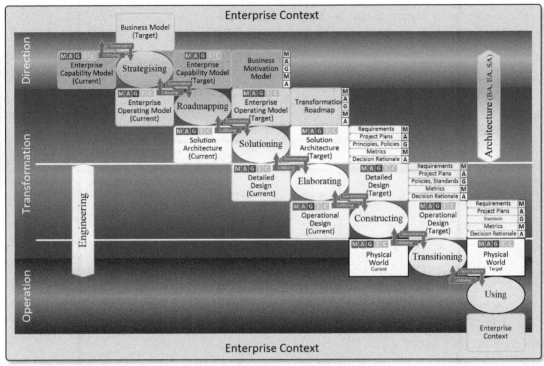

© Pragmatic 365 (2008-2021)

To aid understanding, here we see the Transformation Cascade of Phases, but with common names in place of the base structural/transformational names.

It is therefore obvious of the dependencies between each of the artefacts used by each phase. With these dependencies clearly shown, the error of creating an artefact without the proper dependent artefacts can hopefully be avoided.

> # KEYPOINT:
>
> Understand how common artefacts
>
> relate to the Phase cascade.

> # ADOPTION:
>
> Management: Ensure everyone in the
>
> Enterprise understands the
>
> dependencies between common
>
> Artefacts.

Questions to Ponder

- ◆ Do you recognise any of these common Artefacts?
- ◆ Does your Enterprise utilise any of them?
- ◆ If so, which ones does it use, and for each one, are the required pre-requisites in place to be able to produce them?
- ◆ If not, which artefacts does it use and where would you place them on the Phase cascade?

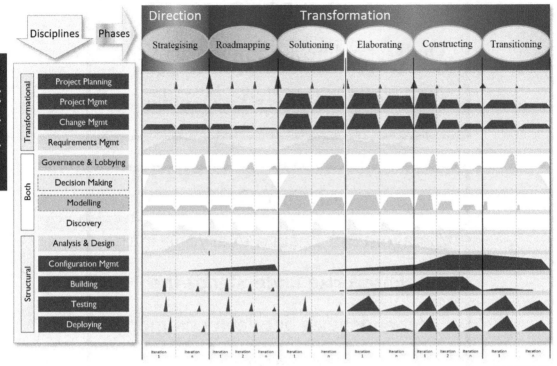

© Pragmatic 365 (2008-2021)

Here the phases are across the top and the disciplines are down the side. The coloured humps give an indication of when each discipline is used and to what degree. Some of you will notice the similarity with RUP (Rational Unified Process). **POET does not use RUP and does not mandate anyone that uses POET should adopt RUP.** However, POET does recognise some important fundamentals that are present in RUP, which POET has also adopted:

♦ Firstly, POET (like RUP) recognises Phases vs Disciplines and that the mapping of disciplines to phases is complex and not a simple one-to-one mapping. In addition POET also adds the disciplines of Modelling, Discovery, and Governing & Lobbying.

♦ Secondly, POET (like RUP) is iterative and recognises that within each of the phases, the work carried out may not be of a simple waterfall nature but is more naturally of an iterative nature.

We also need to point out that while RUP is IT Project Centric, POET is Enterprise Transformation centric, recognising that Transformation has an Enterprise scope (not just IT) and encompasses Strategising and Roadmapping as well as Project Execution.

Note the background colours:

♦ Light blue for disciplines that predominately work on Structural Information (MAGIC).

♦ Light red for disciplines that predominately work on Transformational information (MAGMA).

♦ White for disciplines that work on both Structural and Transformational information.

The disciplines that are not grey (which form the backbone of **Pragmatic** Transformation) are defined in more detail later.

So, starting to look at the disciplines and phases contained in RUP, the question was, "What work is going on in the Strategising and Roadmapping phases?". It turns out the it's the same!

So, I extended the use of the basic disciplines to the left. Essentially, the only difference between the use of Analysis and Design in the project phases, and the use of Analysis and Design in the Strategising and Roadmapping phases, is the information that is being Analysed and Designed. The same is true for all the other disciplines also, to a greater or lesser extent.

To complete the work going on in the Strategising and Roadmapping phases I added more key disciplines that are sadly very immature in many Enterprises. Having done so, I then realised that these disciplines are also used (and mostly immature) in the Project level phases also (Solutioning, Elaboration, Constructing and Transitioning)

And so they we added there too, which provides us with a complete overview of the key disciplines used throughout the Transformation domain.

At this point, it is also worth point out, that Frameworks aimed at maturing parts of the Transformation domain, could be focussed around Phases or around Disciplines. For example, PRINCE2 is organised around the **Project Planning** and **Management** disciplines (horizontally), whereas EA frameworks such as PEAF are organised around the **Strategising** and **Roadmapping** phases (vertically). In general, this distinction is largely hidden and exists because without POET there is no context to position them within.

Methods

Methods

> # KEYPOINT:
>
> The Disciplines are used to a greater or lesser extent in each phase.

> # ADOPTION:
>
> Management: Ensure everyone in Transformation is provided appropriate training in the disciplines they use to perform their tasks.

Questions to Ponder

- Does your Enterprise recognise the complicated mapping of Disciplines to the Phases of Transformation?
- If yes, how is this evidenced?
- If not, do you think it would be a good idea?
- Does your Enterprise recognise Modelling, Discovery, Decision Making and Governance & Lobbying as disciplines that require an appropriate amount of time and resources to execute?
- If not, does that create any problems or issues?
- What needs to be done to alleviate them?

Methods > Disciplines > Capability Model

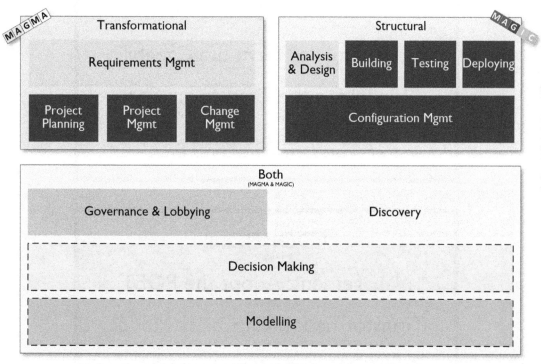

© Pragmatic 365 (2008-2021)

Here we present the Capability Model for the Transformation Capability of the Enterprise.

When talking about Capability Models, most Enterprises only consider the O part of DOTS, that is, they only consider the Capabilities required for the Operation part of the Enterprise.

While the Capabilities required for the Operation part of the Enterprise are of paramount importance (for it is those Capabilities which perform the actions that the Enterprise was created to perform, e.g. banking, drilling oil wells, providing healthcare services, etc) we must not forget the other strategically important parts of the Enterprise such as the domain we are concerned with here, aka the Transformation Capability of the Enterprise.

Hang on….. This is a capability model right? Isn't a capability mode an Artefact of Transformation? So shouldn't this be in the Artefact section of POET not the Methods???

Good question!

The answer is no. Whilst a capability model is an Artefact, it is a Methodological Artefact!

Methods

> # KEYPOINT:
>
> The Disciplines form the Capability
> Model for the Transformation
> Capability of the Enterprise.

> # ADOPTION:
>
> Management: Adopt the POET
> Transformation Capability Model.

Questions to Ponder

- ◆ Does your Enterprise have a Capability Model for the Trasnsformation Capability of the Enterprise?
- ◆ If not, do you think it would be a good idea?
- ◆ Do you agree with Pragmatic's Transformation Capability Model?
- ◆ If not, what would you change, and why?

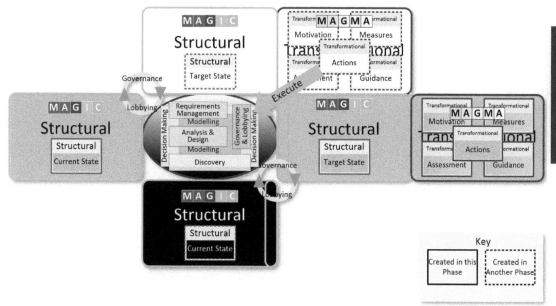

© Pragmatic 365 (2008-2021)

Here we have highlighted one phase of the transformation cascade to look at, but please keep in mind that although we are using one phase as an example, everything you will now see can be equally applied to any other phase.

Over this graphic we have added the important disciplines to the Phase ellipse, and boxes indicating the models in use to the levels.

- ◆ Solid lines indicate models that are created in this phase. In other words, outputs. For example, the Orange Current and Target state Structural boxes.
- ◆ Dotted lines indicate models that are created in another phase (either below or above). In other words, inputs. For example, the Pink Target Structural State from the phase above, and the Yellow Current Structural State from the phase below.
- ◆ Models indicated with blue lines are Structural models (defined by MAGIC). Models indicated with red lines, are Transformational models (defined by MAGMA).

There are five fundamental disciplines defined:

- ◆ **Requirements Management** - Where requirements are understood and refined to the level required to drive the phase.
- ◆ **Discovery** - Where information about the current structural state is obtained.
- ◆ **Analysis & Design** - Where the information about the Target state and the means to achieve it is created.
- ◆ **Governance & Lobbying** - Where the information is reviewed and any Transformation Debt™ is exposed and managed.
- ◆ **Modelling & Decision Making** - Overall pseudo-disciplines which are used by all other disciplines.

Methods

KEYPOINT:

MAGIC relates to the Structural information and MAGMA relates to the Transformational information that each phase consumes and produces.

ADOPTION:

Management: Ensure any work going on in Transformation, identifies whether it is working on Transformational and/or Structural information.

Questions to Ponder

♦ Are there other fundamental disciplines that you think should be included?

♦ What are they and Why do you think they are missing?

Methods > Disciplines > Overview > Artefacts

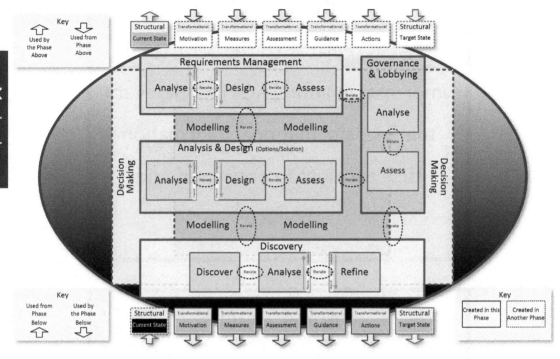

© Pragmatic 365 (2008-2021)

Here we have expanded the disciplines and moved the various models to the top and bottom of the diagram.

- ♦ Solid lines indicate models that are created in this phase. Outputs.
- ♦ Dotted lines indicate models that are created in another phase (either below or above). Inputs.
- ♦ An arrow at the top pointing up, indicates that information from this phase is used by the phase above.
- ♦ An arrow at the top pointing down, indicates that information from the phase above is used by this phase.
- ♦ An arrow at the bottom pointing up, indicates that information is used from the phase below.
- ♦ An arrow at the bottom pointing down, indicates that information from this phase is used by the phase below.

All disciplines are of an iterative nature.

The interaction between these disciplines is also of an iterative nature.

Methods

KEYPOINT:

The 6 main disciplines are: Discovery, Requirements Management, Analysis & Design, Governance & Lobbying, Modelling and Decision Making.

ADOPTION:

Management: Review the maturity of the 6 main disciplines (Requirements Management, Analysis & Design, Discovery, Governance & Lobbying, Modelling and Decision Making.

Questions to Ponder

- Does your Enterprise allow for iteration in and between these disciplines?
- If not, does that create any problems?
- If so, what needs to be done to alleviate them?

Methods > Disciplines > Overview > Orchestration

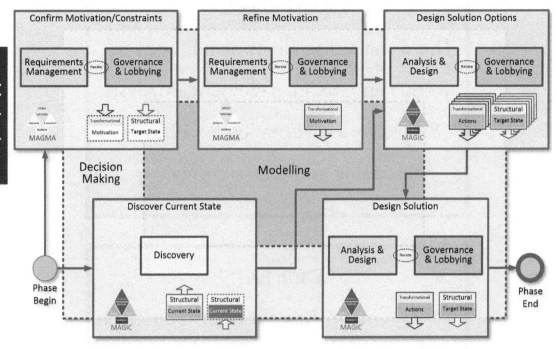

© Pragmatic 365 (2008-2021)

Here we see how these disciplines are orchestrated together to form the work carried out within any phase. Note that Governance & Lobbying is not carried out once at the end but instead is continuously occurring.

We begin by **Confirming the Motivation and Constraints** we have been given and then go on to **Refine the Motivation** to the level required for this phase. At the same time we can begin to **Discover the Current State** that exists which is our starting point for what needs to be transformed. Having understood the requirements and the current state to a sufficient level we then go on to **Design Solution Options** and to choose an option. Finally we can do the "Real Work" which is to **Design the Solution**.

It is funny (or maybe that should be depressing) that many Enterprises operate Transformation processes that force people to work solely on the Design Solution work, without having done the necessary other work. The problems and issues associated with that kind of approach is obvious to understand - and yet it still happens in many Enterprises.

One particular project I once worked on (this is just one example of many) only had the Design Solution work in it and no Discovery. Being Mr Picky, insisted on doing the Discovery work (because it is impossible to change what you cannot see) before I did the Design Solution work. Instead of being thanked, my contract was not renewed.

Methods

KEYPOINT:

Use discipline Orchestration to guide the overall work going on in a Phase.

ADOPTION:

Management: Ensure the basic discipline orchestration is followed in each phase.

Questions to Ponder

♦ How does your Enterprise orchestrate the Transformation disciplines?

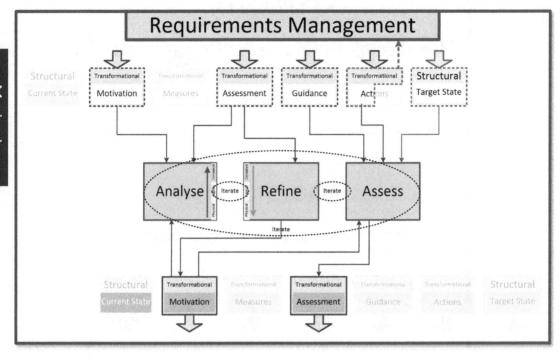

© Pragmatic 365 (2008-2021)

Here we see the main sub-disciplines involved in Requirements Management.

Note that these disciplines are highly iterative and that iterations could take milliseconds inside someone's head or could take weeks or even months.

The specific plan/process that will be followed is passed from the phase above.

Analyse

♦ Here the Requirements we are passed from the phase above, are understood and the reasons for them (in the context of the Assessment we are passed from the phase above).

♦ This is accomplished in many ways, but one way is to use different types of abstraction (Omission, Composition, Generalisation, Idealisation) in effect, moving up the abstraction hierarchy.

Refine

♦ Here the Requirements we are passed from the phase above, are refined to the level that this phase requires (in the context of the Assessment we are passed from the phase above).

♦ This is accomplished in many ways, but one way is to use different types of elaboration (Inclusion, Decomposition, Specialisation, Realisation) in effect, moving down the elaboration hierarchy.

Assess

♦ Here the Requirements are assessed and the reasons for the refinements are recorded.

Following this discipline, the Governance & Lobbying discipline is utilised to ensure that the work done is fit for purpose and that any problems or opportunities that have been discovered by performing it are documented and raised for resolution.

Methods

> # KEYPOINT:
>
> Requirements provided to a phase,
>
> will never by sufficient for that phase.

> # ADOPTION:
>
> Management: Ensure that
>
> requirements are refined at the
>
> beginning of a phase not the end.

Questions to Ponder

- ◆ Does your Enterprise even recognise this as a discipline?
- ◆ How does this discipline map to your Enterprise?
- ◆ Are there any problems with how your Enterprise executes this discipline?
- ◆ Does the discipline your Enterprise uses include all of these required inputs and outputs?
- ◆ If not, what do you need to change? Who is Responsible for making them? And who is Accountable for making sure the changes are made?
- ◆ Does your Enterpise train people in this discipline?
- ◆ If not, do you think it would be beneficial to do so? If so, who will you talk to, to make it happen?

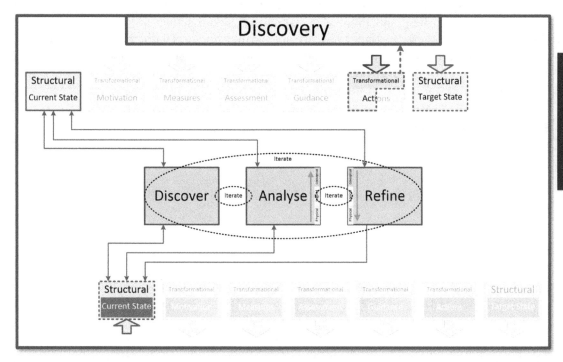

© Pragmatic 365 (2008-2021)

Here we see the main sub-disciplines involved in Discovery.

Note that these disciplines are highly iterative and that iterations could take milliseconds inside someone's head or could take weeks or even months.

The specific plan/process that will be followed is passed from the phase above.

Discover

♦ Here information about the current state at the current level and about the current state at the level below is obtained.

♦ Some information may already exist in the Current models, but a lot of the information (especially initially) will be scattered throughout the Enterprise - in Documents, Diagrams, Spreadsheets, Mind maps, Checklists, the Intranet and last but not least People's Heads.

Analyse

♦ Here information about the current state at the current level and about the current state at the level below is analysed and understood.

♦ This is accomplished in many ways, but one way is to use different types of abstraction (by Omission, by Composition, by Generalisation or by Idealisation) in effect, moving up the Abstraction hierarchy.

Refine.

♦ Here information about the current state at the current level and about the current state at the level below is refined.

♦ This is accomplished in many ways, but one way is to use different types of abstraction (by Inclusion, by Decomposition, by Specialisation or by Realisation) in effect, moving down the Abstraction hierarchy.

The process of discovery is akin to walking into a dark room. Initially you do not know what is in the room, or even the shape of the room. As you discover more and more information, lights are turned on here and there illuminating the darkness. The things near the light are illuminated clearly, things further away are illuminated but not with the same clarity. This causes us to be attracted to none, some, or all of these things we see further away which allows our journey of discovery to continue. As we walk through this land of discovery, walls and doors also appear. Some of the walls are high, some low. Some are made of paper, some of glass, some of concrete. Some areas entice us, others seem intimidating and dark in nature.

There are known knowns, and there are unknown knowns....

Methods

> ## KEYPOINT:
>
> Finding information to perform a job is just as important as performing the job.

> ## ADOPTION:
>
> Management: Ensure that Discovery work is identified and estimated properly.

Questions to Ponder

- ♦ Does your Enterprise even recognise this as a discipline?
- ♦ How does this discipline map to your Enterprise?
- ♦ Are there any problems with how your Enterprise executes this discipline?
- ♦ Does the discipline your Enterprise uses include all of these required inputs and outputs?
- ♦ If not, what do you need to change? Who is Responsible for making them? And who is Accountable for making sure the changes are made?
- ♦ Does your Enterpise train people in this discipline?
- ♦ If not, do you think it would be beneficial to do so? If so, who will you talk to, to make it happen?

Methods

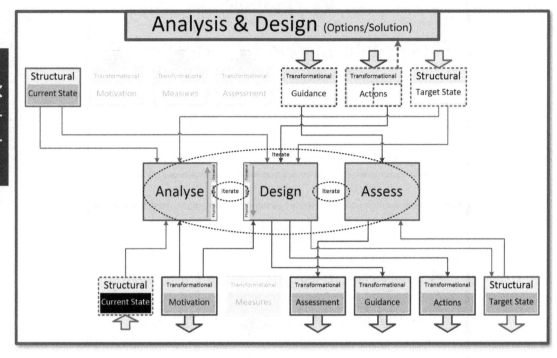

© Pragmatic 365 (2008-2021)

Here we see the main sub-disciplines involved in Analysis & Design. Note that these disciplines are highly iterative and that iterations could take milliseconds inside someone's head or could take weeks or even months.

The specific plan/process that will be followed is passed from the phase above.

Analyse

Here we take…

- ◆ the Target State (from the phase above). Because this is what drives us (and constrains us) structurally - Why are we doing it this way?
- ◆ the Current State (from this phase). Because this is our starting point as to what currently exists - Where are we starting from?
- ◆ the Current State from the phase below. Because this is our starting point as to what currently exists at the next level of abstraction - How "implementable" are our decisions
- ◆ the Refined Requirements from this Phase. Because this is the reason for us doing this. Why are we doing it?

This is accomplished in many ways, but one way is to use different types of abstraction (by Omission, by Composition, by Generalisation or by Idealisation) in effect, moving up the Abstraction hierarchy.

Design

Here we take…

- ◆ the Target State (from the phase above). Because this is what drives us (and constrains us) structurally - Why are we doing it this way?

- ♦ the Current State (from this phase). Because this is our starting point as to what currently exists - Where are we starting from?
- ♦ the Guidance, High Level Plan for Subsequent Phases, and the Target State (from the phase above).
- ♦ the Refined Requirements from this Phase.

and use them to create

- ♦ the Target State for this phase.
- ♦ a detailed plan for the next phase and high level plan for subsequent phases.
- ♦ guidance to be used by the next phase.

This is accomplished in many ways, but one way is to use different types of abstraction (by Inclusion, by Decomposition, by Specialisation or by Realisation) in effect, moving down the Abstraction hierarchy.

Assess...

- ♦ Here the Design is assessed and the reasons for it are recorded.

Following this discipline, the Governance & Lobbying discipline is utilised to ensure that the work done is fit for purpose and that any problems or opportunities that have been discovered by performing it are documented and raised for resolution.

Methods

Methods

> # KEYPOINT:
>
> Architecture and Engineering lie at the heart of Analysis and Design.

> # ADOPTION:
>
> Management: Ensure that Architecture and Engineering Paradigms are used appropriately for Analysis and Design in all Phases.

Questions to Ponder

♦ Does your Enterprise even recognise this as a discipline?

♦ How does this discipline map to your Enterprise?

♦ Are there any problems with how your Enterprise executes this discipline?

♦ Does the discipline your Enterprise uses include all of these required inputs and outputs?

♦ If not, what do you need to change? Who is Responsible for making them? And who is Accountable for making sure the changes are made?

♦ Does your Enterpise train people in this discipline?

♦ If not, do you think it would be beneficial to do so? If so, who will you talk to, to make it happen?

Methods > Disciplines > Modelling

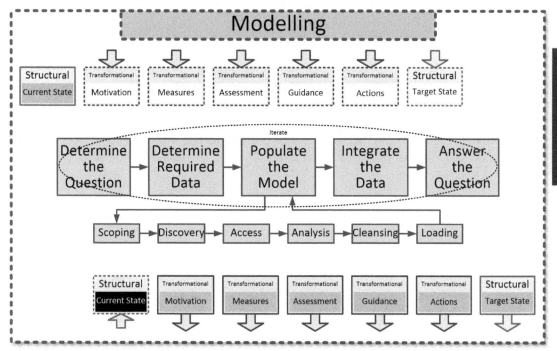

© Pragmatic 365 (2008-2021)

NOTE: The Modelling Discipline is special. It could be called a Meta-Discipline. It is special because it is never done on its own, It's only every used by the other disciplines.

Here we see the five main sub-disciplines of Modelling:

Determine the Question

♦ Here we identify a question that needs to be answered. There is no reason to model anything unless it will be used to answer a question. Either the question cannot currently be answered or the quality and confidence in an existing answer is too low to be useful.

Determine Required Data

♦ Having understood what the question is, here we identify what information will be required in order to answer it.

Populate the Model

● Here we find the information identified and populate the model with it. This should be thought of as effectively a data migration exercise - as illustrated by the sub process shown.

Integrate the Data

♦ Here we ensure that information that has been loaded into the model is sustainable and will be maintained.

♦ For each source of the information loaded, there are two alternatives (which were identified in the Analysis Phase of the **Populate the Model** sub process).

Either...

♦ The source is removed - The people and/or processes and/or technology using the original source will stop using it and will use the information in the model in the future.

or...

♦ The source is preserved - The necessary MAGIC is put in place to enable the synchronisation and management of the data going forward with the people using it.

Answer the question

♦ Having populated the model, it is now possible to use the model in concert with the tools and analyses provided by the modelling tool to answer the question.

KEYPOINT:

1. Only model things to answer a question. 2. Treat model population as a Data Migration exercise. 3. Integrate/remove source data.

ADOPTION:

Management: Ensure that Modelling exists and is treated as a data migration exercise.

Questions to Ponder

- ◆ Does your Enterprise even recognise this as a discipline?
- ◆ How does this discipline map to your Enterprise?
- ◆ Are there any problems with how your Enterprise executes this discipline?
- ◆ Does the discipline your Enterprise uses include all of these required inputs and outputs?
- ◆ If not, what do you need to change? Who is Responsible for making them? And who is Accountable for making sure the changes are made?
- ◆ Does your Enterpise train people in this discipline?
- ◆ If not, do you think it would be beneficial to do so? If so, who will you talk to, to make it happen?

Methods

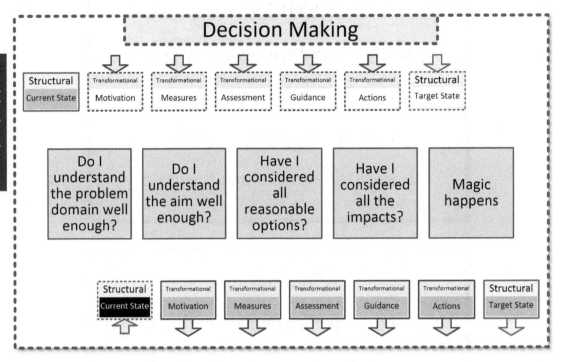

© Pragmatic 365 (2008-2021)

Decision making is the bedrock of everything that happens within the Transformation Capability of all Enterprises. Hundreds of decisions are made every day, thousands a month and probably millions per year. Each decision has the power to have a positive impact, but also has the power to make a negative impact. Decisions made in the higher up Phases (Strategising, Roadmapping, Solutioning) are likely to have more impact (positive or negative) than decisions made in the lower phases (Elaboration, Constructing, Transitioning).

Decision making, is not so much trying to understand how to make good decisions, its more about how to avoid making bad ones. This does not mean that bad decisions will not be made because politics can destroy anything, but it will at least alleviate us from some of the more common and mundane reasons why bad decisions get made.

It's also not so much about making good or bad decisions, because that can be very subjective. A decision by a customer to not buy a bottle of Champagne may well be a good decision from their point of view if their aim is to save money, but a very bad decision from the point of view of the bar owner. So, it's not really about the end result of the decision that is important, but more about how we go about it. Is it a reasonable method?

Do I understand the problem domain well enough?

I have a saying

> "If you don't know what the solution is, you don't understand the problem
> well enough."
>
> *- Kevin Lee Smith*

When making any decision, it is usually quite easy if you understand the problem that is requiring a decision to be made. If you understand the problem very well, solutions tend to appear in your mind as if by magic. So, don't rush to making a decision,

Do I understand the aim well enough?

This is similar to above but instead of considering the "input", we consider the "output" i.e. what are we trying to achieve why making this decision. For the same reasons as above, if we are not 100% clear on what we are trying to achieve, there is not much chance of us achieving it.

Have I considered all reasonable options?

Many times, people rush to judgment on making decisions. Often making a decision is finished as soon as a decision can be arrived at, but the "best" decisions tend to come when all options are on the table to be compared.

Have I considered all the impacts?

Many decisions turn out to be extremely sub-optimal purely because of unintended consequences. In my book, you only get unexpected consequences if you did not spend enough time, considering impacts in the first place. You should consider the Impact of a decision on you, other people, the thing the decision is being made about and other things. Another dimension to keep in mind is time, so for all the things you are considering the impact on, you should also consider the impact in the near term, mid term and long term impact.

KEYPOINT:

1. Only model things to answer a question. 2. Treat model population as a Data Migration exercise. 3. Integrate/remove source data.

ADOPTION:

Management: Ensure that Modelling exists and is treated as a data migration exercise.

Questions to Ponder

♦ Does your Enterprise even recognise this as a discipline?
♦ How does this discipline map to your Enterprise?
♦ Are there any problems with how your Enterprise executes this discipline?
♦ Does the discipline your Enterprise uses include all of these required inputs and outputs?
♦ If not, what do you need to change? Who is Responsible for making them? And who is Accountable for making sure the changes are made?
♦ Does your Enterpise train people in this discipline?
♦ If not, do you think it would be beneficial to do so? If so, who will you talk to, to make it happen?

Methods > Disciplines > Decision Making > Culture

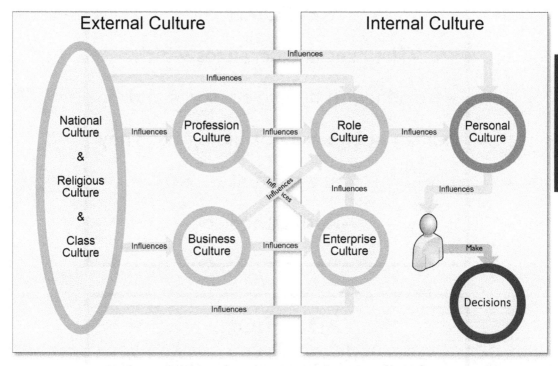

The culture that operates within all Enterprises is an intricate web and weave of culture from different places. National cultures can differ wildly for example from Brazil to Germany to Japan. Religion plays a part, more so in some places than others. Class structures can exist which produce their own culture. All these things influence Professional and Business culture. Professional Culture relates to the culture associated with particular professions, like Engineering or Accounting or Nursing or IT which go on to influence the people that exist within those professions. Business culture relates to the culture associated with particular Business sectors like Banking or Pharmaceuticals or Retail or Academia which go on to influence the overall culture of a particular Enterprise.

Culture also includes how the Enterprise motivates a person (carrots and sticks) by using things such as money, job security and career progression.

All these things come together to produce a personal culture that influences each person in the daily decisions they make. The more decision making responsibility a person has, they more culture is important.

KEYPOINT:

"The crucial differences which distinguish human societies and human beings are not biological. They are cultural."

-Ruth Benedict

ADOPTION:

C-Suite: Initiate an investigation into the different Cultures at play in the Enterprise.

Questions to Ponder

- ◆ Do you understand the Culture in your Enterprise?
- ◆ Have you modelled it?
- ◆ If you haven't modelled it, how can you see it?
- ◆ If you can't see it, how can you understand it?
- ◆ If you don't understand it, how can you change it?

Methods > Disciplines > Decision Making > Making Them

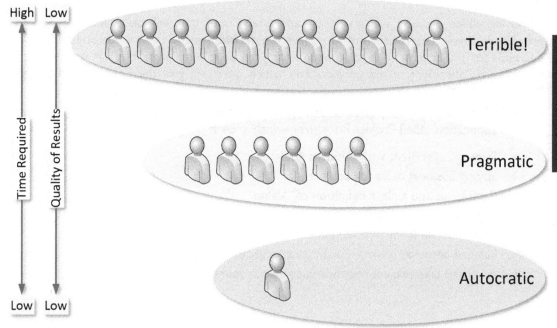

© Pragmatic 365 (2008-2021)

How many decisions do you think 1 person makes in a day? Some sources estimate that, on average, an adult makes approximately 35,000 conscious decisions, every day. You could categorise these decisions into various types, for instance:

At one end of the scale there are **Mundane** decisions (for you or someone else) such as, what to eat for lunch, or should I go for a walk. However, it should be noted that, when a **Mundane** decision is made, it may, in the fullness of time, turn out to be a **Life Changing** decision.)

At the other end there are **Life Changing** decisions (for you or someone else) such as, should I change jobs or not, or should I send my child to school a or school b. It should be noted that, when a Life Changing decision is made, it may, in the fullness of time, turn out to not to be a **Life Changing** decision, and instead was actually a **Mundane** decision.)

You could also categorise decisions in terms of the things they are made about, for instance:

Yourself, your family, your car, your house, other people, or the company you work for.

This is our area of interest – decisions being made in relation to the company you work for. Specifically in our case, the decisions being made in relation to the Planning, Execution and Governance of change (aka Transformation).

Since we are **Pragmatic** (we concentrate on the fundamental 20% that causes 80% of the benefits) we should not only concern ourselves with Life Changing decisions (i.e. those that are known to be life changing when they are made) but also those decisions that look like mundane decisions but actually turn out to be life changing. For us, other people in the Enterprise, customers of the Enterprise, or the Enterprise itself.

There are various methods/processes/techniques/ways/frameworks for making decisions, but one that is of specific interest is the Analytic Hierarchy Process (AHP). AHP is of specific interest, firstly, because it is a structured technique for organizing and analyzing complex decisions, and secondly, because it is well suited where they are more than one decision maker and a consensus needs to be reached. AHP (based on mathematics and psychology) was developed by Thomas L. Saaty in the 1970s and has been extensively studied and refined since then.

Choosing which projects will go ahead, and which ones that will be culled is a perennial problem for every Enterprise, and very often the decisions made turn out to be Life Changing decisions for the Enterprise (and sometimes for the people making them!). A major factor is the strategic alignment of the projects and which ones will give the Enterprise the biggest bang for its buck.

A vendor who is particularly good in this space is a company called Transparent Choice who have an application called Project Prioritizer which allows:

- Strategic alignment with business goals
- Strong business cases for projects
- Consensus and a clear definition of "Value"
- Impartially assess projects
- Strong buy-in from all stakeholders
- Balance between drivers, constraints, organisations and risks
- A way to take project dependencies into account

Methods

KEYPOINT:

"Too many cooks spoil the broth"

"Many hands make light work"

ADOPTION:

C-Suite: Mandate that people balance the time spent and the number of people involved in making decisions, with the quality of the decision required.

Questions to Ponder

- How are decisions made in your Enterprise?
- Are there any understood processes behind them?
- If they are not, do you think it would be a good idea to understand them?
- o you think it would be a good idea to investigate new ways of making decisions?

Methods

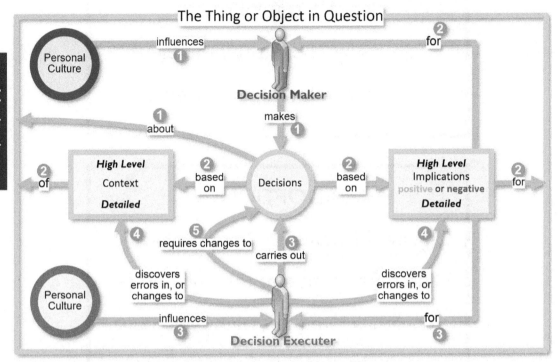

© Pragmatic 365 (2008-2021)

We all make decisions. Constantly. Every single day of our lives.

We all like to make decisions. Important people make decisions. We like to feel important. It's almost like a drug. He who decides has power. He who decides is important. But with great power comes great responsibility. And the responsibility that comes with making decisions is the responsibility to accept when you discover they are "wrong", and change them when necessary. Unfortunately, changing decisions is generally much harder than making them.

This is a big problem. This is a very very very big cultural problem. People, in general, do not like changing decisions. Especially by people that tend to make decisions, which tend to be senior people. In fact they loathe it. Despise it. Would do almost anything to avoid it. Changing a decision means you were wrong. Changing a decision means you made a mistake. For these reasons (amongst others) changing a decision tends to be seen as a really really bad thing. Changing a decision may be seen as a "climb down" or a "U-turn". Oh - how the press (and the opposition) love it when someone in government changes a decision. They are vilified, pilloried, criticised and hounded. Which is really really strange because a bad decision that was changed is definitely better than a bad decision that was not.

Of course, people want right decisions, but all decisions are made, on the basis of understanding the context the decision was based on and the implications that were known to exist at the time. Implications could be positive (something that is wanted) or negative (something that is unwanted) and the same decision could produce positive and negative implications at the same time for different things. For instance, there may be a positive implication for the Decision Maker (because a short term goal will be achieved - their bonus) but a negative implication for the Thing or Object in question (because a long term goal is compromised – an increase in costs). So, as well as a Decision Maker understanding the implications of their decision, they also have to evaluate and balance these implications in order to arrive at a decision.

There are two types of roles involved in any decision. The Decision Maker, whose job it is to make the decision, and The Decision Executer, whose whose job it is to carry out, or execute the decision.

So, let's understand the **Pragmatic** way of making decisions.

1. Decision Makers make decisions (driven in part by their own personal culture) about things or objects.

2. Those decisions are based on understanding the high level context about those things, the high level implications the decision will have for the thing in question, and the implications for the person making the decision.

3. Decision Executors (driven in part by their own personal culture) will carry out decisions, but will also consider the implication of decisions for them.

4. By attempting to carry out the decision, they will dig into more detail and will almost certainly discover more detailed Context (errors in, or changes required to), and/or more detailed Implications (errors in, or changes required to) that the Decision was based upon.

This, in turn, may require a change to the decision made.

The **Pragmatic** fundamentals to apply are:

1) Information about the context or implications that a decision is based upon is shared between the Decision Maker and Decision Executor.

2) As the decision is executed, it is highly likely that the Decision Executor will discover new information, that changes the context, and/or the implications that the decision was made upon, thereby possibly requiring a change to a decision.

3) Therefore, while the Decision Maker is responsible for making decisions, decisions, should be a collaboration between the decision maker and decision executer, and this collaboration **must continue after** the decision is made.

4) Any changes to a decision should not be viewed as mistakes, backtracking or U-turns or any other negative connotation to be avoided and hidden, but instead should be encouraged and celebrated.

This thought process is not what normally happens in Enterprises though. What normally happens is more confrontational. People tend to talk more in terms of decisions being wrong or flawed. But if we take away the instances where someone is literally incompetent, we can say that there are no bad decisions, only unknown or misunderstood context or unknown or misunderstood implications.

We have to be careful however, not to forget that a decision not only has **implications for the object** the decision is being taken about, but also **implications for the person** taking the decision. Depending on their Personal Culture (which includes how the Enterprise motivates them in terms of money, job security and career progression). If the Enterprise rewards people with bonuses for plundering the future for short term gain today, then you can hardly blame the person if they make short term decisions which plunder the future.

It is therefore critical to instil a culture that actively encourages this thought process to happen, rather than one that actively discourages it. Rather than discouraging and denigrating people who expose new **context** or **implications** (that may cause decisions to be changed) and trying to hide them, people should be encouraged and applauded for exposing new **context** or **implications**.

There are no bad people. There are no bad managers. There are no bad decisions. People make decisions based on the **context** and an understanding of the **implications** of those decisions, influenced by the culture they operate within. All decisions are made within a **context**, and within that **context** all decisions are 100% correct and valid. If they were not, the person concerned would be deemed incompetent (which is another discussion). Other people may not agree with a decision, but that is usually because they are looking at the decision through the prism of their own context and their understanding of the implications. And so disagreements about decisions are not actually disagreements about the decision itself, they are actually disagreements about the context they were made within, in addition to the Personal Culture of the person that made them, and/or the implications that are known.

When people object to a decision, sometimes it is not the decision they are objecting to, but the one or more implications of that decision. Worse than that, the person objecting can think that the decision was made specifically to create the implications they do not like.

So the way to change a decision is not to talk about the decision per se, but to change the context the decision was made within, or change the implications that were known about, or to change the culture that prevailed. But that will only work if the culture allows the context to be changed or the implications to be changed, or the culture to be changed.

In fact, it could be said that Accountability is being able to say "I made this decision because..."

"I made this decision because this was the context that was known to exist at the time the decision was made, and these are the implications that were known at the time the decision was made, and this is the culture that existed at the time.

"An error doesn't become a mistake until you refuse to correct it."

- Orlando Aloysius Battista

> ## KEYPOINT:
>
> "Unless we embrace changing decisions, we will always be stuck with bad ones."
>
> - Kevin Lee Smith

> ## ADOPTION:
>
> C-Suite: Mandate that people should be rewarded, not punished, for changing decisions.

Questions to Ponder

- ◆ Are decision makers allowed to change decisions?
- ◆ How do people react when decision makers change their decisions?
- ◆ Are decision makers open to listening to people who expose new context or implications?
- ◆ What happens to people who expose new context or implications?
- ◆ Does your Enterprise want to increase the quality of, and reduce the costs of, Transformation?
- ◆ Does your Enterprise's culture allow its culture to be changed?
- ◆ If not, what is preventing it?
- ◆ When was the last time you were "wrong"?
- ◆ When was the last time you admitted you were "wrong"?
- ◆ If those dates don't coincide, why not?

WARNING Don't Press This button!

There is a famous quote…

> "Good decisions come from experience. Experience comes from making bad decisions."
>
> *- Mark Twain*

The basic idea behind this quote is excellent, and certainly very eloquent. However, it also hides the cultural problems that tend to make its use extremely limited in practice.

Perhaps a more **Pragmatic** quote would be…

> "Good decisions come from experience. Experience comes from making bad decisions, accepting that they were bad decisions, and modifying your future decisions accordingly"
>
> **- Pragmatic**

The emphasis is not so much about making bad decisions, but about creating a culture where bad decisions can be recognised and dealt with without fear.

But it's more than that. The emphasis is not so much about creating a culture where bad decisions can be recognised and dealt with without fear, but about creating a culture where the recognition and dealing with bad decisions (as soon as possible) is a duty. A duty of all.

If you don't, you will never make good decisions.

Deming made this point many years ago…

In the manufacturing production lines of the USA in the 50's and 60's, there were red buttons placed along the line. These red buttons were emergency stop buttons that would shut down the entire line. Workers were told that if they pressed one of these buttons, they had better have a very good reason because for every second the line was stopped the company would be losing $10,000 per minute. If they could not justify pressing the button (a largely arbitrary decision by the management) they would be punished in some way, wages docked, demoted or sacked. They were actively incentivised to not press the buttons.

Deming pointed out that this narrow management view was fundamentally flawed (if you solve a problem as soon as you detect it, it will increase quality and reduce costs, whereas if you ignore a problem and are forced to deal with it later is will decrease quality and increase costs), but they did not (want to) listen. So instead Deming found someone else that would listen, namely the Toyota Motor Company in Japan.

Toyota had similar production lines with similar red buttons. However, based on Demings teachings workers were told that if they detected a problem, it was not only required of them to press the button but it was a duty as a good employee to press the button.

They were actively incentivised to press the buttons - thereby highlighting a problem as soon as it was detected so it could be solved as soon as possible.

Quality soared, costs reduced and therefore Toyota decimated the US motor industry with cars of much higher quality and much lower cost.

The only difference between the production lines of a motor company and the production lines of Enterprise Transformation is that as the line progresses the thing that people are working on is information not cars.

We need to identify as soon as possible when things are going wrong, so we can fix them as soon as possible which increases quality and reduces costs.

Methods

KEYPOINT:

Pushing the Red Button is not

recommended.

It is a necessity.

ADOPTION:

C-Suite: Mandate that people are

rewarded, not punished, for pushing

the "Red Button".

Questions to Ponder

- What happens in your Enterprise when problems occur?
- Are people applauded for exposing problems, or ignored? Lambasted?
- Would your Enterprise's Transformation capability produce more quality output if problems were identified and dealt with as and when they occur?

JUMPING TO

CONCLUSIONS

If you can't see the solution, you don't understand the problem but if you can see the solution, you may still not understand the problem! Moral of the story - Don't jump to conclusions, even if those conclusions seem to be obvious.

The problem is that, this tends to happen quite often. Many decisions that are taken are made without the required information to make them decisions as opposed to essentially arbitrary guesses.

In fact, it happens so often that in most Enterprises, there is implicit acceptance, an almost apathetic resignation that this is the way things are done with the resulting abdication of Accountability when it all goes wrong (further down the road).

"Analysis Paralysis" is a phrase often used when people who want to jump to conclusions or to repress others who may be more wary. Of course this does not mean that "analysis paralysis" cannot happen. It just means that when people use that phrase, it should set off warning bells and make people think are we really over analysing something that looks so simple or are there hidden dangers lurking below the waterline?

This missing information, when potentially exposed later, could be (or should have been) quite obvious (if only the time was spent to see them) prompting questions like "Surely you knew that at the time you made the decision?". These are "difficult" questions that cause cognitive dissonance (described earlier - or later depending on how you are reading this!) which people will tend to resolve by changing their perceptions to preserve the "correctness" of their decision. Although it wasn't the decision that was wrong it was the decision not to expose more information to inform the decision that was wrong.

> ## KEYPOINT:
>
> "Making decisions too quickly, is as bad as making them too slowly."
>
> - Kevin Lee Smith

> ## ADOPTION:
>
> C-Suite: Mandate that people don't jump to conclusions too quickly.
>
> "Measure twice, cut once."

Questions to Ponder

♦ Do people in your Enterprise jump to conclusions?
♦ Can you think of examples where this has happened in the past?
♦ Who were they? What was the impact? Why do you think they acted in this way?
♦ What needs to change to reduce the likelihood of it happening in the future?
♦ Who needs to drive that change?

Methods > Disciplines > Governance & Lobbying Discipline

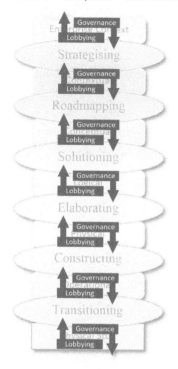

Governance & Lobbying
Aka Risk Management

The work that happens between the phases.

Governance - Ensuring compliance to structural and transformational guidance

Lobbying - Raising issues, problems and opportunities.

© Pragmatic 365 (2008-2021)

Governance & Lobbying is the glue which connects each phase together in an aligned and cooperative manner.

Governance has long been seen as either some kind of policing activity where people are either forced to comply with things or alternatively a watered down box ticking exercise. Both approaches are insidiously destructive as they appear to have solved a problem when in fact they are making things worse!

In fact the first part of governance is often overlooked - that of handover. There needs to be some handover to explain the why, to explain the constraints, to explain the reasons behind the decisions that have been taken.

The key to effective governance is balance that Lobbying provides and is built upon the simple premise that a problem or an opportunity can be discovered at any time by anyone rather than the "normal" western type management approach which tends to be the person who is right is the person who is more senior.

Things change. Always. Continually. Guaranteed. So you can either ignore that inconvenient truth or accept it and put in a method to deal with it when it does happen. In the domain of Transformation it is not only the change related to the transformation we are executing but more importantly change to the context - the why - that we must also deal with.

What we decided to do yesterday (and how and why) for many good reasons could be a massively bad thing to do today. This is a fact of life in the 21st century. So, if we are to deal with transformation in a **Pragmatic** way we need to accept this fact and deal with it rather than pretend it doesn't exist and hope for the best. The overall idea that someone creates a strategy and 24 months later it is delivered is rubbish. The plans for the project portfolio (and the reasons) could (and generally do) change as the projects execute. Therefore we need a holistic and coherent environment for transformation to happen within which allows us to backtrack as soon as possible rather than blindly following a flawed plan.

It is not only that work at any level can deviate from guidance (it will - the devil is in the detail) but also the fact that the strategic plan or roadmap changes (or should change) that causes the disconnect between each level.

> ## KEYPOINT:
>
> Recognise that Governance &
>
> Lobbying are inextricably linked.

> ## ADOPTION:
>
> Use Governance & Lobbying to
>
> connect and synchronise each phase
>
> of Transformation.

Questions to Ponder

- Does your Enterprise do Governance?
- What happens when things do not comply?
- Does your Enterprise do Lobbying?
- What happens when things do not comply?
- Does your Enterprise just issue waivers that get forgotten?
- It is a tick box exercise?
- Is it a case of might is right?
- What happens when some problem or opportunity is found in a lower phase that means it cannot comply with guidance or it would not be wise to do so?

Methods > Disciplines > Governance & Lobbying > Artefact Mapping

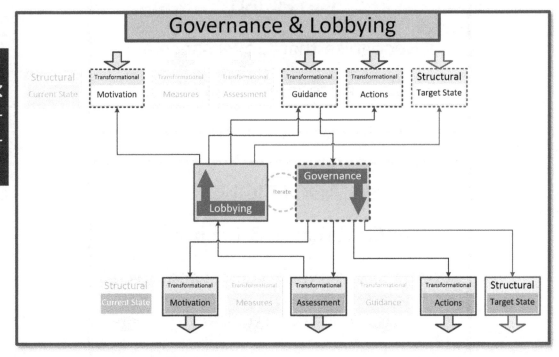

© Pragmatic 365 (2008-2021)

Governance & Lobbying occurs iteratively with Requirements Management and Analysis & Design (Options and Solution) and uses the concept of Transformation Debt™. The dotted line around Governance indicates that Governance is performed on us, by the level above. The Solid line around Lobbying indicates that Lobbying is performed by us, on the level above.

Governance

This ensures we are compliant with the intentions of the phase above.

- ◆ Guidance from the phase above is taken as an input and an assessment against it is produced.
- ◆ Either changes are made to the Motivation and/or Actions and/or the Target State to achieve compliance or Lobbying is performed.

Lobbying

This ensures that any non-compliances and/or opportunities that are identified, exposed and acted upon.

- ◆ This is accomplished using the concept of Transformation Debt™ which exposes these non-compliances as Transformation Debt™ Agreements (TDAs) which are part of the Assessment information.
- ◆ This TDA is then exposed to the phase above as input information, for consideration and decision.
- ◆ Either changes are then made to the Motivation and/or Guidance and/or Actions and/or the Target State from the phase above to remove the TDA, or the TDA being created is accepted along with its implications.

Methods

> # KEYPOINT:
>
> It is imperative that Governance is balanced by Lobbying.

> # ADOPTION:
>
> Management: Ensure that Governance is balanced by Lobbying.

Questions to Ponder

- ◆ How does this discipline map to your Enterprise?
- ◆ Does the discipline your Enterprise uses include all of these required inputs and outputs?
- ◆ If not, what do you need to change? Who is Responsible for making them? And who is Accountable for making sure the changes are made?

Methods > Disciplines > Governance & Lobbying > Transformation Synchronisation

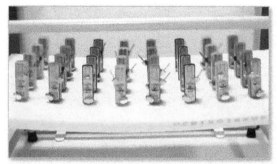

メトロノーム同期 (64個)
Synchronization of 64 metronomes

2013年9月21日，池口研究室にて撮影
Recorded by Ikeguchi Laboratory, on September 21, 2013.

www.youtube.com/watch?v=4ti3d3Is5Zg

メトロノーム同期 (32個)
Synchronization of thirty two metronomes

2012年09月14日，池口研究室前廊下にて撮影
Filmed at Ikeguchi Laboratory, on September 14, 2012.

www.youtube.com/watch?v=JWToUATLGzs

The Transformation domain is made up of many parts. These parts are in constant motion and all are trying to do the best that they can. Even if those parts start off being synchronised and working together, over time they tend to become de-synchronised and in some cases even start working against each other.

None of the parts want to work against any other part but the context they all work within does not tend to lend itself to helping the individual parts.

Here we see the results of two experiments run by the Ikeguchi Laboratory in 2012 and 2013. A number of metronomes (32 or 64) are placed on a solid platform. Since there is something that is rigidly connecting the metronomes together you might think that this will help them synchronise. When we think about this in the physical world it is immediately obvious that just placing the metronomes on a common fixed surface will not cause them to synchronise, for while they are all "connected" there is no "communication" between them.

This fixed surface can be thought of as the Governance that is performed during Transformation. Governance is the thing that we try to use to keep all parts joined up, synchronised, working toward a common goal, and connecting strategic intent to the changes that are ultimately deployed. But since governance is not a physical thing, it is not obvious that this alone will not work - although everyone expects (hopes) it will.

However, while the fixed surface (Governance) is definitely required, the key to synchronisation is Lobbying.

Lobbying is a subtle feedback loop, represented here by the fact that the fixed platform (Governance) is suspended. This suspension (Lobbying)of the platform (Governance) allows the platform itself to move slightly, and it is this (almost imperceptible) movement that causes the metronomes to synchronise. There is no outside force doing the synchronising, Synchronisation occurs because the metronomes collectively synchronise themselves.

It is this feedback loop (the suspension of the platform) that is akin to Lobbying. Lobbying allows just enough "give" in the system (and reduction of friction) to allow Governance to work effectively, keeping all the parts synchronised

KEYPOINT:

Utilise Governance and Lobbying to synchronise Transformation.

ADOPTION:

Management: Implement Governance and Lobbying.

Questions to Ponder

- ◆ Are the people working in your Enterprises Transformation domain, synchronised?
- ◆ If not, what problems does this create?
- ◆ If not, what can you do to help the synchronisation?

Methods *(vertical sidebar)*

> " **Do I write a cheap and nasty solution in order to move forward now? Or do I take more time to solve the problem properly and risk delivering less business value in the short term but possibly better business value in the long term?** "

- Ward Cunningham

© Pragmatic 365 (2008-2021)

The term "Technical Debt" (in relation to the Creation and Transformation of IT systems) was coined by Ward Cunningham March 26, 1992. He coined the debt metaphor to explain the refactoring that he was doing on the WyCash product. http://c2.com/cgi/wiki?WardExplainsDebtMetaphor

> # KEYPOINT:
>
> Technical Debt is the future problems created when we write "bad" code. (Ward Cunningham)

Questions to Ponder

- ◆ Have you heard the term "Technical Debt" before?
- ◆ How did is show itself?
- ◆ What happened when "Technical Debt" was created?

Methods > Disciplines > Governance & Lobbying > Technical Debt vs Transformation Debt™

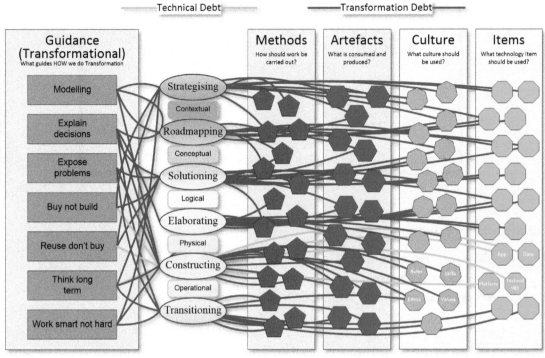

© Pragmatic 365 (2008-2021)

The concept of Transformation Debt™
(originally called Enterprise Debt™)
was created in 2008 as part of PEAF, and
was based on the concept of Technical Debt.

Pragmatic EA Ltd has since clarified
expanded and developed the concept into a
practical and easily usable methodology.

This methodology can be easily adopted to
Pragmatically mature an Enterprises
Transformation capability.

Technical Debt generally only considered one type of guidance "Think Long Term" in relation to IT Solutions (Application, Data, Platform, Technology) - illustrated on the graphic with green lines.

Transformation Debt™ takes this basic idea and expands it in 3 very important ways - illustrated on the graphic with purple lines:

- ♦ Firstly, it applies not only to IT, but also (using MAGIC) to the Methods, Artefacts, Guidance, Items (that IT is only a sub-domain of) and Culture domains.
- ♦ Secondly, it applies not only to one kind of guidance ("Think Long Term") but to all types of Guidance (Values, Principles, Policies, Standards, etc) that guide HOW we effect Transformation, and the Structural Guidance provided by the levels above.
- ♦ And thirdly, it applies not only in one phase (Constructing) but in all phases of the Transformation stack.

In this way, Transformation Debt™ sits at the heart of the Governance & Lobbying disciplines which are the glue the makes the whole Transformation cascade coherent, effective and efficient.

It provides the concept, mechanism and practical guidance that allows for problems or opportunities to be exposed (whenever and wherever they occur), and for them to then be evaluated and raised to the correct level for a decision to be made regarding their resolution in the full knowledge of the implications of doing so or not doing so.

Methods

Methods

> ## KEYPOINT:
>
> Transformation Debt™ is applying the principle of Technical Debt to all Guidance, all Phases and all Levels of Transformation.

> ## ADOPTION:
>
> Enterprise Architect: Apply the concept of Transformation Debt™. (Application of the Technical Debt concept to all guidance, all phases and all levels of Transformation.)

Questions to Ponder

- Have you heard the term "Transformation Debt™" before?
- Do you think applying "Technical Debt" to all guidance, and all parts and all phases of Transformation is useful?
- If not, why not?

Methods > Disciplines > Governance & Lobbying > Transformation Debt™ > Overview

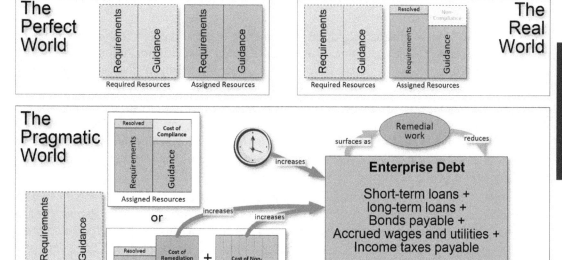

© Pragmatic 365 (2008-2021)

Let's get some definitions out of the way:

♦ **Resources** - money, time, people, etc - whatever is required to effect a transformation.

♦ **Requirements** - the resources associated with satisfying the requirement of the work.

♦ **Guidance** - the Resources associated with satisfying the things that guide and influence how we satisfy the Requirements. Things like Principles, Policies, Standards, etc, but also things like conforming to the structures and methods imposed on us.

♦ **Required Resources** - the Resources that are required to satisfy the Requirements and conform to the Guidance.

♦ **Assigned Resources** - the resources that are actually provided - which are always less than those that are required!

Don't forget that Governance & Lobbying happens at each level of the Transformation cascade and therefore each level has to conform to (or lobby against) the guidance (Structural and Transformational) from the level above.

Now, lets consider these three worlds…

The Perfect World

In the perfect world, the **Assigned Resources** (what we are given) would always equal the **Required Resources** (what we need) and there are therefore no problems. But that never happens…

The Real World

In the real world, the **Assigned Resources** very rarely (aka never) equal the **Required Resources**...

From the point of view of satisfying the Requirements, this discrepancy is usually managed as part of Requirements Management. Any requirements that cannot be met are usually identified and either resource is brought to bear to satisfy them, or they are "de-scoped". This is not where most of the problems that derail Transformation efforts lie.

From the point of view of satisfying the Guidance, this discrepancy is usually not managed, or if it is, not managed well. Often the discrepancy is ignored, or an entry placed in a risk register that is never acted upon. In fact, many Enterprises take a very dim view of exposing these problems. There may very well be valid business reasons for this, but a lot of the time this restriction is pretty arbitrary.

For example, I have personally worked on countless projects that had drop dead go live dates that, if missed, would mean the world would end - but, it never did. I have also worked on countless projects where the money required was not made available - again for some pretty arbitrary reasons - but in reality, those restrictions meant the project ended up spending far more. I am sure you have too.

Restriction of resources tends to be the very simplistic (and ultimately severely damaging) control mechanism that management uses in relation to Enterprise Transformation, as well as the simplistic management style of always asking for more for less. This leads people to produce inflated estimates (assuming they will be cut) and management to not believing them (assuming they will be inflated). Two well-known phrases come to mind:

> "There is never time to do it right, but always time to do it over."

> "A short-cut is the longest distance between two points."

For most Enterprises that's where it stops. People just have to knuckle down and muddle through somehow - put their nose to the grindstone - work as team - forge ahead - think positive thoughts - don't be negative - just-do-it etc. Perhaps some lip service is paid to this gap - some entry in a risk register that is never used for anything - but that's about it. There will be implications, but those implications are not fully known and will only be discovered later when nothing can be done about them and those that could have done something about them have moved on to far more important things.

But, let us be clear.

Not providing what is required is not the problem.

Ignoring the implications is...

The **Pragmatic** World

In the **Pragmatic** world, things start off the same as in the real world i.e. the **Assigned Resources** very rarely equal the **Required Resources**. However, in the **Pragmatic** world we accept this inconvenient truth and do something about it.

We recognise that we are creating Transformation Debt™ and there are three things we need to expose and consider:

♦ **Cost of Compliance** - What is preventing the Enterprise from complying with the guidance and what is required to allow the Enterprise to comply?

And, assuming what is required is not provided...

- ◆ **Cost of Non-Compliance** - What issues and risks going forward will this non-compliance create for the Enterprise?
- ◆ **Cost of Remediation** - What will it cost the Enterprise to become compliant in the future?

Transformation Debt™

Transformation Debt™, is what it will cost to service the debt going forward, and what it would cost to bring the work being done up to the same standard as would have been produced if the **Assigned Resources** had been provided. Note that the **Cost of Remediation** is bigger than the difference between the **Required Resources**, and the **Assigned Resources**. This is because it will always cost more to do something one way and then change it to another than it would have cost to just do it right the first time.

It should also be noted that while Transformation Debt™ can be incurred when doing Transformation, it can also be incurred when not doing Transformation, by just the passage of time. For example, by not keeping operating systems up to date or by not maintaining a building or people properly. In many ways, this type of Transformation Debt™ is more insidious as it can creep up on you unawares.

Having exposed these three key pieces of information, a Business decision can then made to either provide what is required to comply (**Cost of Compliance**) or to accept the implications of not doing so (**Cost of Non-Compliance** + **Cost of Remediation**).

If the Business decision is made to not provide what is required to comply, this Transformation Debt™ adds to the overall Enterprise Debt™.

> *Enterprise Debt*
>
> Enterprise Debt is a measure of the overall debt an Enterprise has incurred and is literally a list of the debts the Enterprise has on its books. It is a well understood accounting term meaning short and long term loans, accrued wages and utilities, income taxes payable, and other liabilities. **Pragmatic** believes that Transformation Debt™ should also be listed as a liability of an Enterprise and accounted for in the proper way.

Transformation Debt™ (like any financial debt) also has to be serviced in the form of interest payments, for example increased support costs. Like interest payments on a loan, this is a recurring cost and will continue for as long as the Transformation Debt™ it is servicing exists.

In addition, if the thing that was transformed now needs to be transformed again, there will also be an increased cost to effect that change. This change also requires resources and if the **Assigned Resources** for this change does not equal the **Required Resources** for this change we are introducing even more Transformation Debt™ into the Enterprise - a double whammy! This is akin to taking out another loan to pay the interest on a current loan!

However, it's not all doom and gloom. If it is recognised that we need to do some remedial work, (or more likely, things just get so bad the Enterprise has no choice but to do some remedial work) this reduces Transformation Debt™ and is therefore akin to paying off (some) of the overall Enterprise Debt.

Recognising and managing Transformation Debt™ provides a simple and extremely effective control mechanism for management to get back in control of their Transformation initiatives and for those working in them to produce quality work (and to be able to sleep at night!)

Managing Transformation Debt™ is not an exercise in making sure that the **Assigned Resources** always equals the **Required Resources**.

Managing Transformation Debt™ makes sure that when the **Assigned Resources** does not equal the **Required Resources** (most of the time) that the implications are exposed so that management can make informed business decisions in the light of that information.

Methods

> ## KEYPOINT:
>
> The future cost of Non-Compliance and Remediation will always be bigger than the current Cost of Compliance.

> ## ADOPTION:
>
> Management: Ensure everyone in the Enterprise understands Enterprise Debt and Transformation Debt.

Questions to Ponder

- ♦ Do you have experience of any of these scenarios?
- ♦ What happened?
- ♦ Do you think the "Pragmatic World" scenario beneficial and why?

Methods > Disciplines > Governance & Lobbying > Transformation Debt™ > Investment Profiles

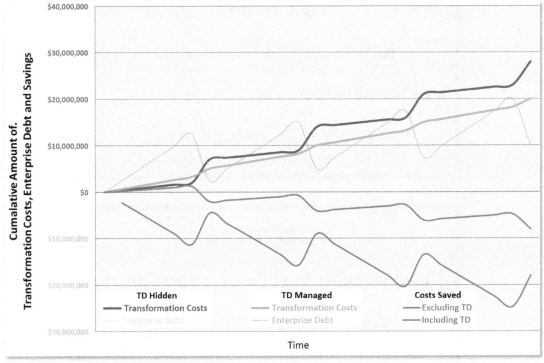

© Pragmatic 365 (2008-2021)

This diagram illustrates three main things

1) Firstly, it illustrates (in red) what happens when Transformation Debt™ is not exposed and managed. This is typical of most Enterprises.
2) Secondly, it illustrates (in green) what happens when Transformation Debt™ is exposed and managed.
3) Thirdly, it shows (in orange and blue) the savings produced when Transformation Debt™ is exposed and managed vs when it is not exposed and managed.

When Transformation Debt™ is Hidden and Not Managed

The solid red line illustrates the cumulative Transformation Costs of an Enterprise that **does not** expose and manage Transformation Debt™ and is typical of many Enterprises. The light red line shows the resulting Transformation Debt™.

Cumulative Transformation Costs rise, but very slowly, while Transformation Costs are kept low. During this time hidden Transformation Debt™ is slowly building up…

When this hidden Transformation Debt™ reaches a critical point (akin to when the pile of dirt that is swept under the carpet has become too big to ignore any longer) a very large and abrupt rise in Transformation Costs is required to deal with it. Often referred to as "getting the car out of the ditch", its focus is usually very tactical - short term and only concerned with dealing with the major issue that cannot be ignored any longer.

Having spent a large amount of money on Transformation over a very short timeframe, the focus then tends to be, once again, to keep Transformation Costs low and therefore we return to the low level of Transformation Costs we saw before and the whole process repeats itself.

Not exposing and managing Transformation Debt™ is characterised by:

♦ Low Transformation Costs while hidden Transformation Debt™ builds up…

- Followed by large, unplanned and abrupt Transformation Costs when things get too bad…
- Causing unpredictability, which leads to instability, which means management is not in Control.

These large, unplanned and abrupt rises in Transformation Costs, can often occur at the same time that an incumbent CIO is replaced by another! This is obviously not good news for the CIO, but more importantly is not good news for the entire Enterprise.

A cynical view might be this.

From the point of view of giving prospective Enterprises a feeling that someone senior is a good hire, what could be better than for a previous Enterprise to have been fantastically successful while they were there and then fall apart when they left? What could be better than to say "While I was there, they were growing well and highly profitable because I kept Transformation Costs low. When I arrived they were in the doo doo, but I turned it around! Then, after I left, without my guidance, Transformation Costs increased and profits fell. It all fell apart". Of course the reasons they managed to keep Transformation costs low was because they were raping the future.

So, what could be a perfect way to engineer this outcome? Is there one thing that could be done to achieve both of these things? Can I hit two birds with one stone?

The answer is yes you can.

All you need to do is rape the future of the Enterprise by ignoring Transformation Debt™. You will then guarantee short term benefits while you are there (for which you will be applauded and given large bonuses because everyone loves quick wins) at the same time as guaranteeing it will all fall apart when you leave.

But that's not the best part. The best part of it is, you can achieve all of this by effectively doing nothing!

(Is this the definition of Management Nirvana?)

Not exposing and not Managing Transformation Debt™ is like boom and bust in the economy, and we all know the effects of boom and bust!

When Transformation Debt™ is Exposed and Managed

The solid Green line illustrates the cumulative Transformation Costs of an Enterprise that does expose and manage Transformation Debt™. The green dotted lines shows the resulting Transformation Debt™.

Cumulative Transformation Costs rises more steeply than before, as management decisions release resources to keep Transformation Debt™ under control.

Transformation Debt™ does build up but this debt is exposed and managed and does not get as large as before, purely because we are managing it and spending money wisely.

Since we are managing Transformation Debt™, increased Transformation Costs to reduce it can be planned ahead, so that when debt reaches a critical point we can reduce it in a controlled way.

In addition, while this increased Transformation Cost solves any short term problems that may be evident it is also aligned to longer term goals.

After the increased Transformation Costs, we again return to a more moderate level of Transformation Costs and the whole process repeats its self.

Exposing and managing Transformation Debt™ is characterised by:

- An Increased level of Transformation Costs while Transformation Debt™ is exposed and managed...
- Followed by moderate Transformation Costs when planned...
- Providing predictability, which leads to stability, which means management is in Control.

Exposing and Managing Transformation Debt™ relieves this boom and bust investment cycle. The downside is that it requires an increased initial investment in the short term. The upside is that it requires lower investment over time and prevents Transformation Debt™ from spiralling out of control.

> "If you don't control your Transformation Debt™, it will control you."
>
> **- Pragmatic**

Savings Produced When Transformation Debt™ is Exposed and Managed

Looking at the two final lines - Blue and Orange. They essentially answer the question:

> "If I utilise Transformation Debt™ how much money will I save?"

The lines are shown negative as negative = savings. Positive = costs.

The Orange line shows the direct savings made by managing Transformation Debt. Essentially it is the Green line minus the Red Line. Although the Orange line does show savings over time, the important thing to note is that it costs us more initially. It is only when the first "panic" is averted later (because we managed Transformation Debt™ over time) that the savings kick in. This initial increase in costs is what needs to be "sold" to management.

The Blue line shows the savings of the Orange line added to the additional indirect savings we make by not incurring as much Transformation Debt™. Essentially it is the Orange line plus the difference between the light green dotted line and the light red dotted line.

KEYPOINT:

If you do not control Transformation Debt™ it will control you.

ADOPTION:

Management: Draw a graph of the last 20 years of transformation investment.

Questions to Ponder

- Which line most closely resembles your Enterprises Transformation cost profile?
- Do you think it is preferable to expose and manage Transformation Debt™, and if so, why?
- How much hidden Transformation Debt™ exists within your Enterprise?
- What is the interest rate you are paying?
- How long will you have to continue to pay the debt for?
- How do you intend to pay off the Debt and when?
- How close are you to maxing out your Enterprise's credit card?

Methods

	Transformation Debt™ - Hidden	Transformation Debt™ - Managed
Total Spent on Transformation	£28M	£20M
Current level of Enterprise Debt™	£20M	£10M
TOTAL	£48M	£30M
Amount Saved	**£18M** **Which equates to a 38% saving on your Enterprise Transformation Bill**	

Considering the final results the right hand side of the graph, we can see that over time the savings can be huge.

Transformation Debt™, like any debt, is not inherently a bad thing though. Used correctly it is a massively important Strategic Management tool. But like any debt, Transformation Debt™ is only bad when:

♦ It is hidden and you don't know you are incurring it
♦ You don't know how you will pay off the debt
♦ You don't know the interest rate
♦ You don't know how long you will have to pay the interest
♦ …all of the above.

When times are good, you can invest in reducing Transformation Debt™, which means when times are bad, you can lean on Transformation Debt™ by allowing a controlled increase.

However, if you do not expose and manage Transformation Debt™ your Transformation Debt™ could already be too high to allow you to ride out the bad times. If you max out your credit card, how will you be able to fix your car when the exhaust falls off?

> # KEYPOINT:
>
> Managing Transformation Debt™ can save huge amounts of money, and (probably more importantly) time.

> # ADOPTION:
>
> Management: Estimate how much money the Enterprise could save over the next 10 years, if it managed Transformation Debt.

Questions to Ponder

♦ What is your estimate (for your Enterprise) for how much money could be saved, if Transformation Debt™ is exposed and managed?

Artefacts

Artefacts

KEYPOINT:

The Artefacts section of POET defines 'WHAT' information is consumed and produced and 'WHEN'.

ADOPTION:

C-Suite: Instigate a review of the Artefacts used in the Enterprise's Transformation Capability, to determine if their maturity is appropriate.

Questions to Ponder

♦ With respect to your Enterprises Transformation capability, what Artefacts are used?
♦ Are those Artefacts documented? Understood?
♦ Are they fit for purpose?
♦ Are they used? All the time? Only when it suits?
♦ Which of them are Good? Why? Bad? Why?

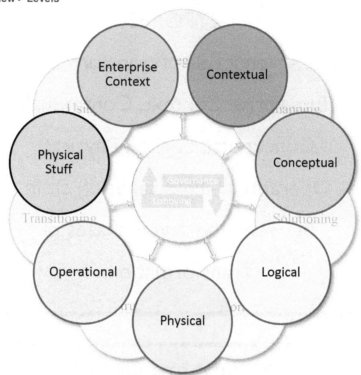

© Pragmatic 365 (2008-2021)

These are the fundamental levels that artefacts can exist at, which sit between the fundamental phases of transformation.

Starting at the Enterprise Context, the information at each level is transformed and becomes closer to the physical world.

- ◆ **Enterprise Context** - A representation of the physical world outside out Enterprise.
- ◆ **Contextual** - A representation of why we exist and how we satisfy the need for our existence?
- ◆ **Conceptual** - A representation of how we need to change.
- ◆ **Logical** - A representation of Logical Solution designs.
- ◆ **Physical** - A representation of Physical solution designs.
- ◆ **Operational** - A representation of the physical world.
- ◆ **Physical Stuff** - The physical world inside out Enterprise.

KEYPOINT:

The seven levels of transformation (Enterprise Context, Contextual, Conceptual, Logical, Physical, Operational, Physical Stuff) sit in between the seven phases of Transformation.

ADOPTION:

Management: Adopt the seven levels of transformation

Questions to Ponder

- Do you agree with these fundamental levels?
- If not, what would you change and why?
- What fundamental levels does your Enterprise define?
- If it does not, does that cause any problems or issues?
- If so, how will you solve them?

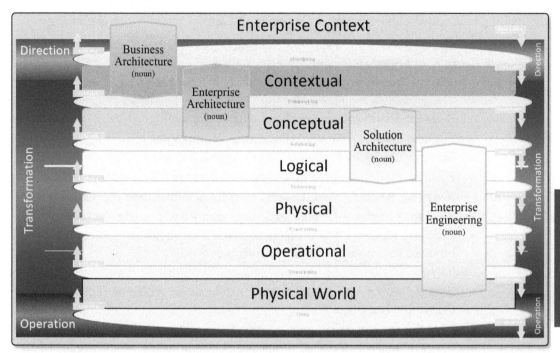

Here we see the fundamental Levels of Enterprise Transformation, laid out over the domains of the Enterprise.

The Direction part of the Enterprise feeds requirements for transformation into the Transformation part of the Enterprise which delivers change into the Operations part of the Enterprise.

It should be noted that the Transformation part of the Enterprise may also deliver change into the Direction, Support or even Transformation (the whole point of POET) part of the Enterprise but we just show Operations here as that is the most common occurrence.

These Levels of Transformation are not strict and rigid, but every journey has to be split up into parts, and these high level Levels, form the high level artefacts of the journey, by which to consider holistically, what information is required, from the formulation of Strategy to the Deployment of change into the Enterprise.

For each Level, information about the **How** that is effected, is done by the next Level down, and information about the **Why** comes from the Level above.

The white horizontal line at the top of the Transformation domain delineates the transition planning work from the project execution work. Everything below that white line is effectively "projectland" The white horizontal line at the bottom of the transformation domain delineates project execution work from the deployment work.

Our remit is not only what is happening in one of these areas. Our remit is what is happening in all of these areas. In general people work within these areas and in most Enterprises these people try to improve what they do (if they are allowed) and how they do it. This is a laudable thing to do, however, no one is looking at the whole cascade and ensuring that the whole cascade is effective and efficient. The parts are being optimised at the expense of the whole. POET provides the basis for Senior Management to address optimising the whole of Transformation, for it is the output of the whole that most important rather than the output of each Level - this in fact, may mean the de-optimisation of some or all of the parts. For this reason, everything in POET applies equally to all Levels of the Transformation cascade and is the unifying holistic and coherent context in which all Transformation work is performed.

In terms of naming these levels there are four fundamentals (note that all of this information can exist in Current, Intermediate(s) and Target(s) states:

- ◆ **BA - Business Architecture (noun)** consists of information representing:
    - ◆ Things outside the Enterprise (e.g. The Market, Legislation, Competitors, Partners, Shareholders, Suppliers, Customers, etc)
    - ◆ Business Models – How this Enterprise creates value .
    - ◆ Business Capability Models – What Capabilities are required.
    - ◆ Business Motivation Models – What motivates the Enterprise.
- ◆ **EA - Enterprise Architecture (noun)** consists of information representing:
    - ◆ Operating Models – Overall structure required to provide the Capabilities.
    - ◆ Roadmap Models – The projects and programs required to effect the change required to implement the Operating model.
- ◆ **SA - Solution Architecture (noun)** consists of information representing:
    - ◆ Logical Designs – High level solutions to business problems required to deliver the Roadmap.
- ◆ **EE - Enterprise Engineering (noun)** consists of information representing:
    - ◆ Physical Designs – Detailed designs to solve business problems required to deliver the Roadmap.
    - ◆ Constructed Systems – Built things that solve business problems required to deliver the Roadmap.
    - ◆ Live Configuration – The configuration of things that are operating in the Enterprise.

Please see **Methods > Overview > Phases > Basics** for a description of the work being done to create information on each level.

KEYPOINT:

Business Architecture, Enterprise Architecture and Solution Architecture information are closely related.

ADOPTION:

Management: Ensure everyone in the Enterprise understands which levels are part of BA, EA, SA and Enterprise Engineering.

Questions to Ponder

- Do you agree with these Level boundaries?
- How does your Enterprise map onto them?
- Does everyone working within the Transformation domain understand where their artefacts they consume and produce, fit into the whole?
- If not, would there be a benefit if they did?
- What will you do to allow people to understand how the artefacts they consume and produce, fit into the whole, and what will you use?
- If so, how will you solve them?

Artefacts > Structural (MAGIC)

Structural				
Methods	**Artefacts**	**Guidance**	**Items**	**Culture**
How should work be carried out?	What things are consumed and produced?	What will Guide us?	What things should be used?	What culture is required?
e.g. Business Functions, Practices, Processes Activities, Phases, Disciplines...	*e.g. Ontologies, Metamodels, Product Descriptions, Products...*	*e.g. Principles, Policies, Standards, Rules, Laws...*	*e.g. Locations, Technologies, Frameworks...*	*e.g. People, Values, Ethics & Trust, Language...*

MAGIC

POET uses the MAGIC ontology to allow an Enterprise to describe the Structural information of any domain and notes that this information exists at different levels of Idealisation/Realisation.

- ◆ **Methods** - How the work should be carried out.
- ◆ **Artefacts** - What things the work consumes and produces.
- ◆ **Guidance** - The things that will guide us as the Methods are executed.
- ◆ **Items** - The tools, technologies, frameworks and locations that are used to perform the work.
- ◆ **Culture** - The people and culture required.

It is important to note that Culture sits at the centre. Because - Culture trumps everything™

In fact, in addition to POET defining MAGIC, POET itself is structured using MAGIC as are all the Frameworks and Ontologies in PF².

Whilst it is very useful to have a structure like MAGIC, to map things to and to make sure that nothing has been missed, it is also important not to lose sight of the fact that these things all need to work together, cooperatively, like an organism, and the story of how that happens is as equally important.

Artefacts

KEYPOINT:

Structural information (MAGIC) needs to exist at different levels of abstraction (Idealisation/Realisation).

ADOPTION:

Management: Ensure Structural information (MAGIC) is maintained at different levels of abstraction (Idealisation/Realisation).

Questions to Ponder

♦ What ontology do you use to completely define the structural elements of your Enterprise?

♦ Are you missing anything?

Artefacts

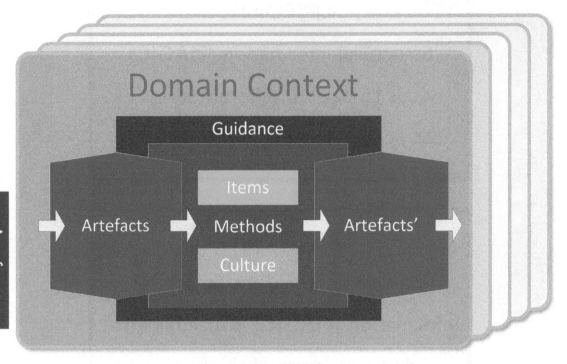

Here we illustrate how the components of MAGIC are related. Don't forget that to enable Transformation, each is represented at different levels of Idealisation/Realisation.

At the core are the Methods which execute within the Culture and Items that exists, with the whole existing within a context.

The Methods break down into Phases and Disciplines and it is these Disciplines that are utilised to varying degrees in each phase which act upon the Artefacts to varying degrees.

The Operating Model for the domain in question equates to the Contextual level information which defines an abstract representation of how the MAGIC comes together to accomplish its function.

> ## KEYPOINT:
>
> Methods act on Artefacts that are
>
> executed by Culture (people) or
>
> Items (Technologies).

> ## ADOPTION:
>
> Management: Ensure people
>
> understand the relationships between
>
> the information categorised by
>
> ## MAGIC.

Questions to Ponder

- ◆ In your Enterprise, what levels do you use for structural information?
- ◆ Do they cover all levels?

Transformational				
Motivation	**Actions**	**Guidance**	**Measures**	**Assessment**
Why are we doing the transformation?	How will we effect the transformation?	What will guide the transformation?	How will we measure the progress of transformation?	Why are we doing the transformation in this way?
e.g. Ends, Aims, Objectives, Requirements...	e.g. Means, Strategies, Tactics, Roadmaps, Portfolio's, Plans...	e.g. Principles, Policies, Standards, Rules, Laws...	e.g. CSF's, KPI's, Metrics...	e.g. Strengths, Weaknesses, Opportunities, Threats, Pro's, Cons, Issues, Risks...

MAGMA

POET uses the MAGMA ontology to allow an Enterprise to describe the Transformational information required to effect the transformation of a domain from one state to another and notes that this information can exist at different levels of Idealisation/Realisation.

- ◆ **Motivation** - The reason we are transforming, our goals, our requirements.
- ◆ **Actions** - The tasks we need to execute in order to achieve those goals and satisfy those requirements.
- ◆ **Guidance** - The things that will guide us as the Actions are executed.
- ◆ **Measures** - The metrics that will allow us to know if we have achieved our goals and satisfied our requirements.
- ◆ **Assessment** - The reasons that led to us choosing the Actions.

KEYPOINT:

Transformational information (MAGMA) needs to exists at different levels of abstraction (Idealisation/Realisation).

ADOPTION:

Management: Ensure Transformational information (MAGMA) is maintained at different levels of abstraction (Idealisation/Realisation).

Questions to Ponder

- What ontology do you use to completely define the transformational elements of your Enterprise?
- Are you missing anything?

Artefacts > Transformational (MAGMA) > Relationships

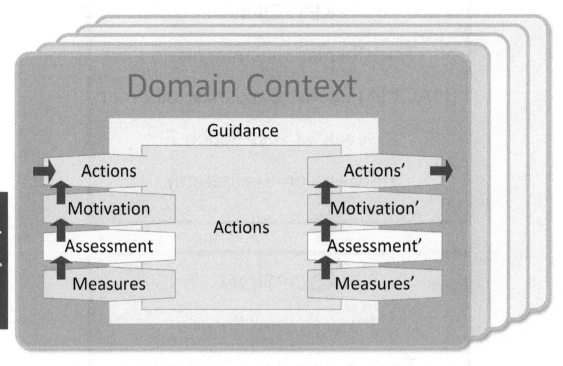

Here we illustrate how the components of MAGMA are related. Don't forget that to enable Transformation, each is represented at different levels of Idealisation/Realisation.

Motivation at the top is what drives the Transformational Information and what is produced at the bottom is primarily a set of Actions required to satisfy that Motivation.

Guidance and Measures are also produced to guide and measure those Actions, while the Assessment expresses why the Actions, Guidance, and Measures have been decided upon.

KEYPOINT:

The Motivation drives the creation of Actions and the production of Guidance (which guide those Actions), all of which are Assessed against the Measures.

ADOPTION:

Management: Ensure people understand the relationships between the information categorised by MAGMA.

Questions to Ponder

- In your Enterprise, what levels do you use for transformational information?
- Do they cover all levels?

Artefacts > MAGIC & MAGMA Derivation > Structure

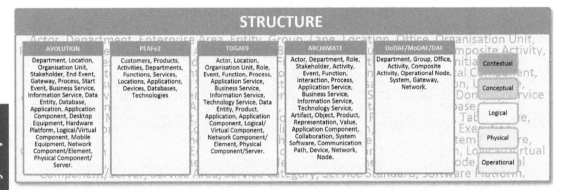

There are many meta-models out there. Some large, some small but they all tend to describe generally the same things albeit using different names a lot of the time.

Most meta-models have many entities related to the Structure of the Enterprise. The WHAT; Departments, Locations, Processes, Applications, etc, etc and most meta-models also allow for the composition and decomposition of these entities. Although not explicit, there is also the general notion that these things can exist at different levels of Idealisation/Realisation (one type of Abstraction) - from the very Ideal at the top (Contextual), to the very Real at the bottom (Operational).

Over time, many meta-model users and providers realised that while the structure of something is very important - especially in terms of being able to change it, there needs to be some other information that ties the existence of a particular structure up to some kind of requirements or notion of WHY…

KEYPOINT:

In the past, people only saw part of

the picture – they considered only

Structural information.

Questions to Ponder

♦ Since Idealisation/Realisation is the key type of abstraction related to Transformation, do you think that meta-models should explicitly define and state which entities are associated with which levels of idealisation/realisation?

♦ If not, what will you use to describe structural information in a way that enables transformation?

♦ If it is not defined, what problems do you think will result?

Artefacts > MAGIC & MAGMA Derivation > Strategy

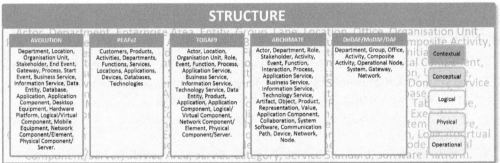

© Pragmatic 365 (2008-2021)

And so, their meta-models were extended to include information about Strategy - Mission, Vision, Goals, Objectives etc. Some meta-models were designed specifically for that purpose such as BMM - The Business Motivation Model and so were used as a basis for others. Other meta-models ignored BMM and defined their own Entities.

Again, over time, many meta-model providers (and users) realised that while the Strategy is very important, a Strategy cannot be directly executed and therefore there needs to be some other lower level information to effect the strategy or notion of HOW…

> # KEYPOINT:
>
> In the past, people only saw part of
> the picture – that Structural
> information needed Strategy
> information.

Questions to Ponder

♦ What meta-model does your Enterprise use to define the Enterprise's Strategy?
♦ If you don't, how is it defined so that others can use it and relate other information to it?
♦ If it is not defined, what problems do you think will result?

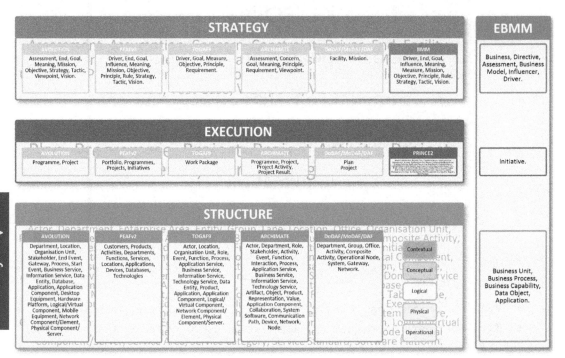

And so their meta-models were extended to include things related to the execution of change such as projects, programmes and plans etc. Some meta-model authors (recognising that a Motivation model, an Execution model and a Structural model needed to be integrated and connected) started to merge these three. One good example is the Enterprise Business Motivation Model (EBMM) by Nick Malik.

KEYPOINT:

In the past, people only saw part of the picture – that Structural information and Strategy information needed to be bridged by execution information.

Questions to Ponder

♦ What meta-model does your Enterprise use to define the information that connects the Enterprise's Strategy to the Enterprise's Structure?

♦ If you don't, how is it defined so that others can use it and relate other information to it?

♦ If it is not defined, what problems do you think will result?

Artefacts

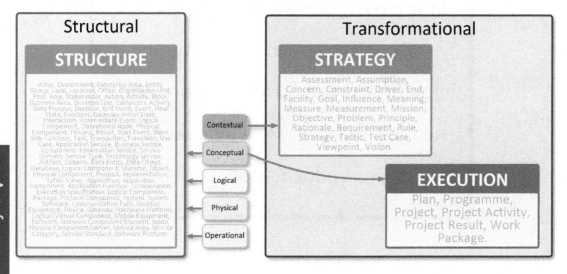

POET also recognises that all three are required, but POET also recognises that there are actually two fundamental types of information - Structural and Transformational. Many people have only thought in terms of the higher level of transformation aka Strategy and the next level of transformation of Execution. In fact the types of things within these domains exist in different forms at multiple levels. The same fundamental things but referred to using different names. For example, a plan might be called; a strategy at one level, a roadmap at another level, a project plan at another level and a work breakdown structure at another level.

> # KEYPOINT:
>
> In the past, people only saw part of the picture – that Strategy and Execution were the top two levels of abstraction and Structure was the conceptual, logical, physical and operational levels.

Questions to Ponder

- ♦ Do you agree that there are two fundamental types of information?
- ♦ Do you agree that to enable transformation, they both need to exist at different levels of Idealisation/Realisation?

Artefacts > MAGIC & MAGMA Derivation > Levels

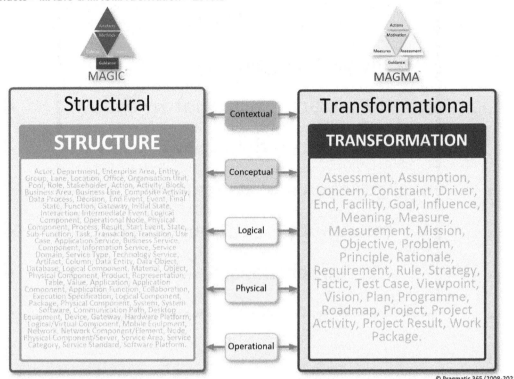

© Pragmatic 365 (2008-2021)

And so, we come to the realisation, that while it is obvious to many that Structural information exists at different levels of Idealisation/Realisation, it is now also obvious that the same should be said of the Transformational information, where the Transformational information at each level relates to the Transformation of the Structural information at the corresponding level.

While these high level groupings are useful, for real usefulness we need to define them a little more in terms of the types of information that can exist in each, hence MAGIC and MAGMA. We can then use these structures to determine how complete any meta-model is in terms of these domains.

> # KEYPOINT:
>
> There are two fundamental domains
>
> of information (Structural &
>
> Transformational) that exists at ALL
>
> levels of abstraction.

Questions to Ponder

♦ Does your Enterprise recognise and deal explicitly with Structural and Transformational information?

♦ If not, do you think there is benefit is doing so?

♦ If not, what problems are likely to result?

Artefacts > MAGIC & MAGMA Derivation > Mapping > POLDAT

POLDAT

MAGIC

MAGMA

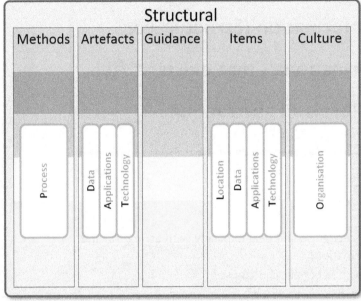

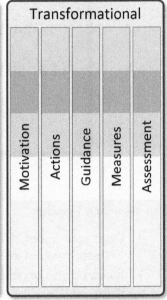

It is useful to note how other classification schemes have been used to try to fully describe the structure of something, although they tend to always concentrate around the Logical and Physical levels (yellow and green).

POLDAT (Process, Organisation, Location, Data, Applications, Technology) is a common one:

- ♦ **Process** comes under the **Methods** domain of MAGIC - which is a higher level category including other things such as Functions and Practices.
- ♦ **Organisation** comes under the **Culture** domain of MAGIC- which is a higher level category including other things like culture, relationships and people.
- ♦ **Location** comes under the **Items** domain of MAGIC - which is a higher level category including other things such as Frameworks and Technology (not just IT).
- ♦ If the **Data**, **Applications** and **Technology** are being used to perform the Methods, then they would come under **Items**.
- ♦ If the **Data**, **Applications** and **Technology** are being produced by the Methods, then they would come under **Artefacts**.

People, Process and Technology is another:

- ♦ **People** come under the **Culture** domain of MAGIC - which is a higher level category including other things like culture, relationships and organisational structure.
- ♦ **Process** comes under the **Methods** domain of MAGIC - which is a higher level category including other things such as Functions and Practices.
- ♦ **Technology** (generally interpreted as IT) comes under the **Items** domain of MAGIC - which is a higher level category including other things such as Frameworks, Locations and other Technologies.

> ## KEYPOINT:
>
> POLDAT provides for Structural information at mostly conceptual, logical and physical levels, and no Transformational information.

> ## ADOPTION:
>
> Enterprise Architect: Think in terms of MAGIC and MAGMA, not POLDAT.

Questions to Ponder

- ♦ Do you use People Process, Technology, and if so, what are you missing?
- ♦ Do you use POLDAT, and if so, what are you missing?
- ♦ What are you using and are you missing anything?

BMM

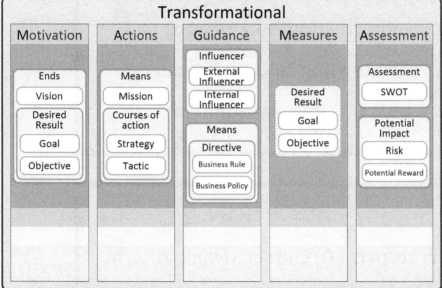

© Pragmatic 365 (2008-2021)

It is useful to note how other classification schemes have been used to try to describe the transformation of something. The Business Motivation Model (BMM) is a common scheme although it only covers the contextual (pink) level.

- **Ends** (including the Vision and the Desired Result comprising Goals and Objectives) come under the Motivation domain in MAGMA - which is a higher level category including other things like Requirements.

- **Means** (including the Mission and the Course of action comprising Strategy and Tactics) come under the Actions domain in MAGMA - which is a higher level category including other things like Roadmaps, Portfolios and Project Plans. Although Directives (comprising Business Rules and Policy) is also part of the Means domain in BMM, it more correctly comes under the guidance domain in MAGMA.

- **Assessment** (including SWOT and Potential Impact comprising Risk and Potential Reward) come under the Assessment domain in MAGMA - which is a higher level category including other things like Transformation Debt™ and Pros and Cons.

- **Influencer** (comprising external and internal) comes under the Guidance domain of MAGMA - which is a higher level category including other things such as Values, Principles, Policies and Standards.

> ## KEYPOINT:
>
> BMM provides for Transformational information only relating to Strategising, and no Structural information.

> ## ADOPTION:
>
> Enterprise Architect: Think in terms of MAGIC and MAGMA, not BMM.

Questions to Ponder

- Do you use BMM and if not what do you use in its place?
- Is there a well-defined structure used for documenting Enterprise Strategy, and if not, what problems is that likely to cause?

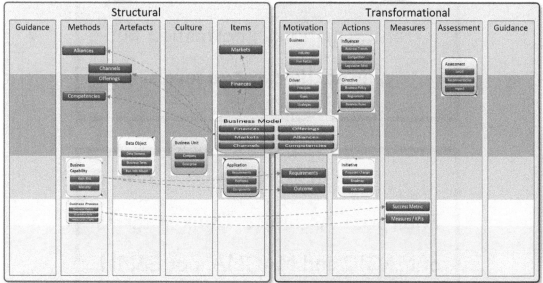

© Pragmatic 365 (2008-2021)

The Enterprise Business Motivation Model (EBMM v3.5 - Nick Malik) is interesting because it attempts to define entities in both the Structural and Transformational areas, although again it only covers the higher levels. It was formed from OMG's BMM by Microsoft's Internal EA team and is influenced by the writings of well-known authors like Geary Rummler, Alan Brache, and Alexander Osterwalder.

With respect to Structure:

- ◆ Business Capability and Business Process come under the Methods domain of MAGIC.
- ◆ Data Object comes under the Artefacts domain of MAGIC (unless Data Objects are being used to perform the Methods, in which case they could come under Items)
- ◆ Business Unit comes under the Culture domain of MAGIC.
- ◆ Application comes under the Items domain of MAGIC (unless Applications are being produced by the Methods, in which case they could come under Artefacts)

With respect to Transformation:

- ◆ Business, Business Model and Driver come under the Motivation domain in MAGMA (although the Principles sub area really sits under Guidance).
- ◆ Initiative comes under the Actions domain in MAGMA.
- ◆ Assessment comes under the Assessment domain in MAGMA.
- ◆ Influencer and Directive come under the Guidance domain of MAGMA (which as previously stated should also include Principles).

> # KEYPOINT:
>
> EBMM covers most Structural and Transformational information but only at the top two levels.

> # ADOPTION:
>
> Enterprise Architect: Think in terms of MAGIC and MAGMA, not EBMM.

Questions to Ponder

- Do you know of any other meta-models which define both Structural and Transformational information in an integrated way?
- Are the meta-models you use integrated, if not what problems are likely to result?
- How do you integrate Structural and Transformational artefacts?
- If you don't, does it cause problems that your Structural and Transformational artefacts are not related?

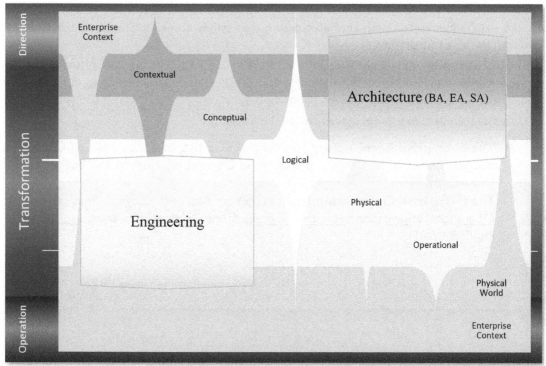

© Pragmatic 365 (2008-2021)

Here we see the fundamental levels of Enterprise Transformation based on the fundamental levels of Idealisation/Realisation.

The Direction part of the Enterprise feeds **Contextual** information into the Transformation part of the Enterprise which delivers **Physical Things** into the Operations part of the Enterprise.

It should be noted that the Transformation part of the Enterprise may also deliver **Physical Things** into the Direction, Support or even Transformation (the whole point of POET) part of the Enterprise but we just show Operations here as that is the most common occurrence.

The fundamental levels are:

♦ The **Enterprise Context** consists of all the things that are not part of the Enterprise (i.e. not directly under its control) but affect or is affected in some way by it. Things like Customers, Suppliers, Partners, Regulators, etc.

♦ The **Contextual** level consists of the Enterprises Strategy (Mission, Vision, Goals, Objectives, Strategies, Tactics, etc).

♦ The **Conceptual** level consists of Transformational Roadmaps (Business and Technical), Conceptual Structural Models (Current, Target and Intermediate), and definitions of a series of programs projects and initiatives that effect the transformation.

♦ The **Logical** level consists largely of Logical structural designs.

♦ The **Physical** level consists largely of Physical structural designs.

♦ The **Operational** level consists largely of the CMDB - Configuration Management Database.

While these levels are often portrayed as separate it should be noted that the information at each level is not insular. The information at each level is fundamentally related to the information in the other levels and it is these relationships which are of paramount importance as they provide the glue that makes the whole coherent.

Most relationships occur with the information that exists above and below each level and diminish for levels further away.

This also illustrates that while people may be working with information primarily at one particular level, they need access to information at other levels to understand context (from above) and to understand implications (from below).

In terms of naming these levels there are two fundamentals:

◆ The **Enterprise Architecture Model (EA)** consists of Contextual and Conceptual information set in the Context of Enterprise Context information and Logical information.

◆ The **Enterprise Engineering Model (EE)** consists of the Logical, Physical and Operational information set in the Context of the Conceptual information and the Physical World.

> # KEYPOINT:
>
> All levels of the Enterprise Transformation model are used in all phases.

> # ADOPTION:
>
> Management: Ensure that all levels of information are readily available to people working in all Phases.

Questions to Ponder

- Does your Enterprise have the concept of an EA Model and an EE Model?
- If not, should it?
- Where does your Enterprise draw the boundaries?
- Do the boundaries exist?
- How are they managed?

Artefacts > Ontology > Basics > Mapping to Phases

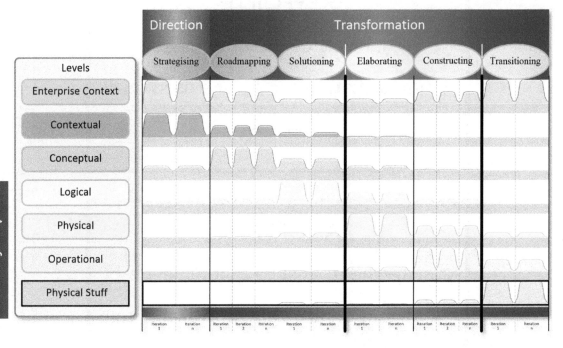

© Pragmatic 365 (2008-2021)

Here the phases of Transformation are across the top and the levels of information down the side. The coloured humps give an indication of when the information at each level is used and to what degree. Some of you will notice the similarity with RUP (Rational Unified Process). **POET does not use RUP and does not mandate anyone that uses POET should adopt RUP.**

As can be seen, while each phase is centred around using all of the information from a particular level, each phase also utilises information in levels above (For Requirements, Governance and Lobbying), and in levels below (for Impact Assessment, Governance and Lobbying).

KEYPOINT:

Information from all levels are used in
each phase.

ADOPTION:

Management: Ensure that all
information from each level can be
used in each phase

Questions to Ponder

- Does your Enterprise recognise the complicated mapping of levels of information required to the Phases of Transformation?
- If yes, how is this evidenced?
- If not, do you think it would be a good idea?
- If not, does that create any problems or issues?
- What needs to be done to alleviate them?

Artefacts > Ontology > Basics > Volatility, Volume, Impact & Population

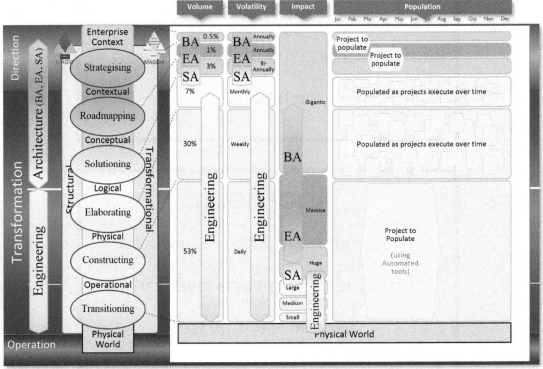

© Pragmatic 365 (2008-2021)

Volume

This view gives an indication of the volume of information (as a percentage of the whole) that exists at each level. It can be seen that volumes increase the further down the phases we go. This seems pretty obvious but this fact tends to be ignored in most Enterprises. This therefore illustrates that an Enterprise Architecture Model is actually quite small in terms of the volume of information where a common misconception is that it is very large and therefore cannot be populated easily.

Volatility

Here we see the approximate rate of change for each of the levels of the structural and transformational Models.

- ♦ The **Contextual** level (consisting of the Enterprise's Strategy - some call Business Strategy) tends to change annually. In general an Enterprise's overall strategy changes very slowly.
- ♦ The **Conceptual** level (consisting of the Business, Technical and Transformational roadmaps and portfolio of programmes and projects) tend to change annually or bi-annually. In general Enterprises tend to largely create/update these once per year as part of the annual business planning cycle.
- ♦ The **Logical** level (consisting largely of the Logical designs of the Enterprise) changes more often, perhaps monthly as transformation projects execute.
- ♦ The **Physical** level (consisting largely of the Physical designs of the Enterprise) changes more often again, perhaps weekly as transformation projects execute.
- ♦ The **Operational** level (consisting largely of the CMDB - Configuration Management Database) changes more often still, perhaps on a daily basis.

Both the **Contextual** and **Conceptual** levels could also be changed at any time due to pressures in the Enterprise context such as Mergers & Acquisitions, etc.

Impact

Here we see the potential impact of decisions made at each level. The impact could be positive or negative. Good decisions will have positive effects, bad decisions will have negative effects. In general, the impact will be felt in terms of the effectiveness and efficiency of subsequent phases and in terms of the effectiveness and efficiency of what is ultimately deployed.

If good decisions are made, the impact will be felt in terms of reduced costs, reduced timescales, reduced risks and increased agility and durability of the transformation. If bad decisions are made, the impact will be felt in terms of increased costs, increased timescales, increased risks and decreased agility and durability of the transformation.

The impact (positive or negative) is greater the higher up the Transformation Phases we go. For example, bad decisions made in the Roadmapping phase that are not picked up until we get to Construction can be severe and difficult and costly to correct (from a resource point of view but also from a cultural point of view), whereas bad decisions made in the Transitioning phase are mild by comparison and generally tend to be of low cost to correct (from a resource point of view but also from a cultural point of view). Conversely, good decisions made in the Roadmapping phase can have massive benefits for the Construction phase whereas good decisions made in the Transitioning phase will not have as much impact.

Since the Enterprise Architecture Model is concerned with the Contextual and Conceptual information set in the context of the Enterprise Context and the Logical Information, it is obvious what impact (positive or negative) this can have if done well or done badly. This is why Enterprise Architecture is so important for many Enterprises.

NOTE An interesting point to note here is that, the time to see the effects of decisions made at the higher levels (good - if good decisions are made, bad - if bad decisions are made), takes longer to be found/realised than at the lower levels. This is a perfect storm/environment for people to make bad decisions!

Good decisions that have positive benefit cannot be proved and can be easily rejected, with any naysayers being accused of having their head in the clouds with no proof to back them up.

Bad decisions that have bad effects cannot be proved and can be easily be accepted, with any naysayers being accused of being negative with no proof to back them up.

It is for these reasons (and probably others) that it is easier for bad decisions to be made rather than good decisions, especially when the culture of the Enterprise supports it.

Population

Here we propose how each level of information should be populated and some ball-park timescales.

♦ Information at the **Enterprise Context, Contextual** and **Conceptual** levels can be and should be populated by a concerted effort to so - a project, which is generally the annual Strategy and Business Planning work that many Enterprises undertake on an annual basis.

♦ Information at the **Operational** level could also be populated by a project, despite the volume of information involved. This is because automated tools can be deployed to break the back of this work although interpretation and massing by humans is still required.

♦ Information at the **Logical** and **Physical** levels is normally far too large to be populated by a single project and also tends to be very difficult to obtain. While a project could be created to populate this information wholesale, the time and money involved is usually very high with the benefits of doing so only realised over a long timeframe as subsequent projects utilise the information collected. A more **Pragmatic** approach is to populate this information as and when individual projects from the project portfolio require it. Every project will need to create some of this information for the purposes of being able to execute the project anyway, and so capturing this over time in an ordered and well managed way, will mean that the information builds up gradually on an as-needed basis. Some may say, **Pragmatically**!

KEYPOINT:

Ensure that the Logical and Physical levels are populated over time as a deliverable of executing projects.

ADOPTION:

Management: Instigate Projects to populate the Enterprise Context, Contextual, Conceptual and Operational levels of the Transformation information.

Management: Ensure all executing Projects populate the Logical and Physical levels of Transformation information, as they execute.

Questions to Ponder

- ◆ Does your Enterprise understand the low volume of information required for a complete EA Model?
- ◆ Does your Enterprise understand the large volume of information required for a complete EE Model?
- ◆ Does your Enterprise populate this information in a Pragmatic way?
- ◆ Can you improve the way your Enterprise populates and maintains this information?

Artefacts > Ontology > Basics > Two Why's

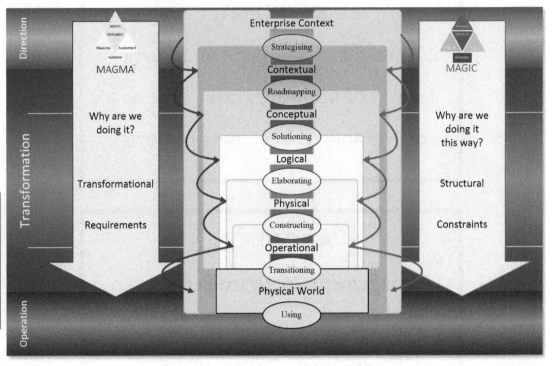

© Pragmatic 365 (2008-2021)

The artefacts at each level should not really be considered as separate boxes but more as a Russian doll of artefacts where the levels above provide an encompassing context for the levels below. In this way, these levels of artefacts are not separate and disconnected are much more cohesive and provide the context and environment for the levels below them.

Who, What, Why, When, How, Where - the Six interrogatives made famous by Rudyard Kipling (and John A. Zachman of course!) What could be simpler? But those six words are much more complicated that the simple categorisations they intimate. Why is probably the most important but there are (at least) two important Whys. Why are we doing something in the first place, and why are we doing what we are doing, in the way we are doing it.

The **Why are we doing it** generally relates to MAGMA and could be simply stated as **Motivation** (or requirements) that are refined the further down we go.

The **Why are we doing this way** general relates to MAGIC and are effectively constraints that become more strict the further down we go (although the **Assessment** domain of MAGMA also constitutes a **Why are we doing this way**).

KEYPOINT:

Be aware that there are two main Whys: 1. Why are we doing it. 2. Why are we doing it this way.

ADOPTION:

Management: Ensure that all parts of the Enterprise understand the difference between why a Transformation is happening, and why the Transformation is being executed in the way it is.

Questions to Ponder

- ♦ Does your Enterprise think of the two Whys?
- ♦ When people in your Enterprise talk about why they are doing something, do they always talk about the same why or do they talk at cross purposes?
- ♦ Does one group think more in terms of Why are we doing it and other groups think more in terms of Why are we doing it this way? (Remember the difference between a Strategic project being executed in a Tactical way)

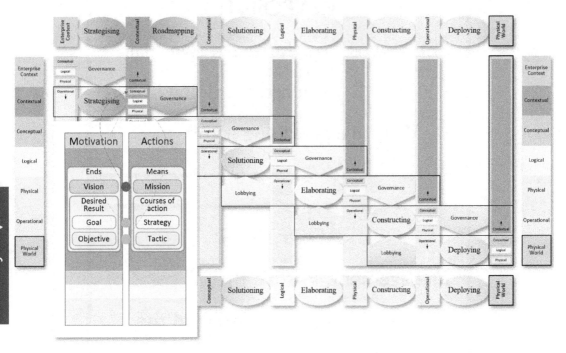

This view shows the recursive nature of idealisation/realisation levels in the Structural and Transformational models used.

What this means is that, while there is an overall flow (Contextual, Conceptual, Logical, Physical and Operational) from the top of the transformation stack to the bottom, we also recognise that within each level, information could be Conceptual, Logical or Physical. The Physical sub-level of each level being the required output, but recognising that in order to produce it, work at the Logical and Conceptual sub-levels may be required.

The Contextual sub-level effectively comprises the information from all levels above, and the Operational sub-level effectively comprises the information from all levels below.

At each level (Contextual, Conceptual, Logical, Physical) the information we need to produce at that level is Physical (wrt to that level) but in order to produce it we may need to first build more abstract information (Logical and/or Conceptual).

A good example is where OMG's Business Motivation Model (BMM) fits, which is at the Contextual level with respect to the whole Transformation domain.

What we need to produce at this level are Objectives and Tactics because this is what is required to feed into the next level. But we can't just write down our Objectives and Tactics, we need to define more abstract things like Vision and Goals (for Objectives) and Mission and Strategies (for Tactics)

Although, the relationships are a little more complicated than that:

◆ An Objective is not **part-of** a Goal (decomposition), or a **type-of** Goal (specialisation). An Objective is a **transformation-of** a Goal (realisation).

◆ A Goal is not **part-of** a Vision (decomposition), or a **type-of** Vision (specialisation). A Goal is a **transformation-of** a Vision (realisation).

- ♦ A Tactic is not **part-of** a Strategy (decomposition), or a **type-of** Strategy (specialisation). A Tactic is a **transformation-of** a Strategy (realisation).
- ♦ A Strategy is not **part-of** a Mission (decomposition), or a **type-of** Mission (specialisation). A Strategy is a **transformation-of** a Mission (realisation).

So we can say...

From the pov of the whole Transformation Domain...	From the pov of the Contextual Level...	
Enterprise Context	Contextual	
Contextual	Conceptual	Vision, Mission
	Logical	Goals, Strategies
	Physical	**Objectives, Tactics**
Conceptual		
Logical	Operational	
Physical		
Operational		

Artefacts

> # KEYPOINT:
>
> For each phase, be aware that Context comes from above, and levels below Operationalise it.

> # ADOPTION:
>
> Management: Provide Workers the Context they need to do their job, and the mandate they need to ensure their work is operationalised.

Questions to Ponder

- ◆ Does your Enterprise represent the information at each of the main levels in terms of Conceptual, Logical and Physical (BMM does)?
- ◆ If not, would it be beneficial to think in this way?

Artefacts > Ontology > Basics > Transitions

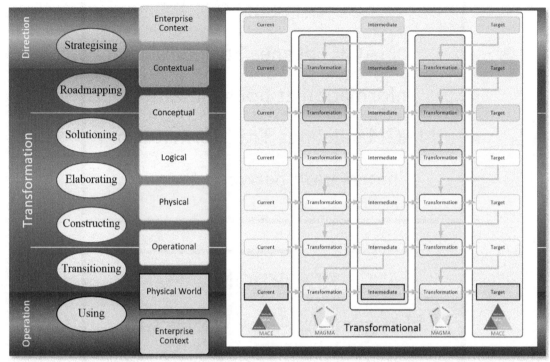

© Pragmatic 365 (2008-2021)

The interaction between the Structural and Transformational artefacts are shown here. All of the boxes with rounded lines relate to models (based on their associated meta-models).

The Structural Models relate to the information about the structure of the Enterprise at various levels of Transformation abstraction and can exist in two main states:

◆ **Current** - What currently exists.

◆ **Target** - What is required to exist. There may also be zero or more **intermediate** states and there may also be more than one target state representing different scenarios.

The Transformational models relate to the reasons for the Transformation along with information required to effect the transformation from one state to the next.

As you can see these models do not and should not exist in a vacuum. They are all connected and related to one another.

> ## KEYPOINT:
> MAGIC defines Structural information at points in time, MAGMA defines Transformational information between them.

> ## ADOPTION:
> Management: Allow workers to create the information necessary to do their job.

Questions to Ponder

- Is the information you use to execute Transformation connected and related to the information it needs to be?
- If it isn't, what problems is that likely to create?
- Are you experiencing any of those problems?

Artefacts > Ontology > Detail > Structural & Transformational

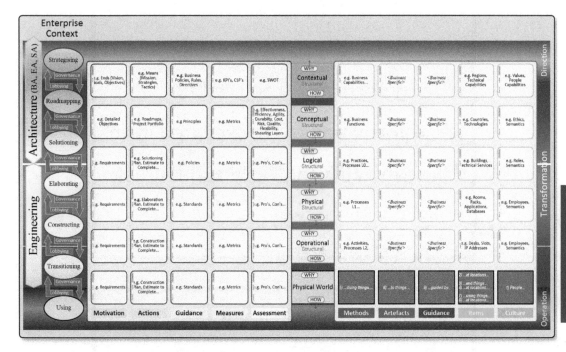

Here we see how the three fundamental ontologies from POET are woven together.

On the right we show the Structural ontology - MAGIC. On the left the Transformational ontology - MAGMA. Down the middle the Ontology for the fundamental parts of all Enterprises - DOTS.

Looking at the centre, it is the transformation domain we are interested in but we set that domain in the context of the Direction Domain above which drives it and the Operations domain below which it "delivers" into. (It should be noted however, that the transformation domain could also "deliver" into the Direction, Support or Transformation domains, but only the Operation domain is shown for clarity)

The words in the boxes give some examples of the Structural and Transformational information you would expect to see at each level.

KEYPOINT:

This is the complete map of information required for Transformation to be executed in an Effective, Efficient, Agile and Durable way.

ADOPTION:

Management: Map the Artefacts of Transformation to MAGIC and MAGMA over the seven layers of Transformation, to determine where the gaps and overlaps are.

Questions to Ponder

- In what way does your Enterprise consider Transformational as well as Structural models at all levels?
- What ontologies and meta-models are you using?
- How do they map to, and fit into, the POET Ontology?
- Are they any gaps or overlaps?
- If there are gaps and or overlaps, is it useful to know that?
- What will you do to fill the gaps and remove the overlaps?

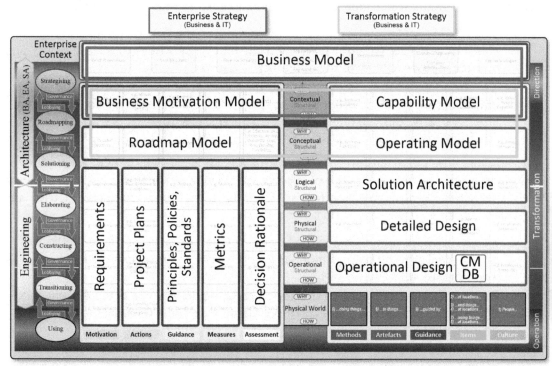

© Pragmatic 365 (2008-2021)

In order for people to understand POETs fundamental structural and transformational ontology, here we map the names of common documents/models/artefacts etc, that many people are familiar with (although perhaps, not everyone defines them in the same way!)

Looking at the top of the diagram, this information corresponds to what many people refer to as the Business Model. It corresponds to the Enterprise Context level. Since this information is part of the Direction domain, the specific ontologies used are defined in POED. Any metamodels actually used, can be very business dependant (and dependent upon the C-Suite's experience) but typically utilise things like the Business Model Canvas (BMC) as illustrated here.

On the right we can see the Structural information represented at different levels of Idealisation/Realisation, with names that are commonly used to refer to parts of it.

- ♦ **The Capability Model** corresponds to the Contextual level of MAGIC. It defines the fundamental capabilities required to support and enable/operationalise the Business Model.
- ♦ **The Operating Model** corresponds to the Conceptual level of MAGIC. It defines the highest level structural view of the Enterprise, required to deliver the Capability Model.
- ♦ **The Solution Architecture** corresponds to the Logical level of MAGIC. It defines (for each solution/project) the logical designs.
- ♦ **The Detailed Design** corresponds to the Physical level of MAGIC. It defines (for each solution/project) the physical designs.
- ♦ **The Operational Design** corresponds to the Operational level of MAGIC. It defines the actual things being rolled out, including the CMDB which represents a model of all the IT that is being rolled out.

On the left we can see the Transformational information represented at different levels of Idealisation/Realisation, with names that are commonly used to refer to parts of it.

- ◆ **The Business Motivation Model** corresponds to the Contextual level of MAGMA. It defines (at a high level) what the Enterprise wishes to achieve (Ends), and how it proposes to achieve them (Means).
- ◆ **The Roadmap Model** corresponds to the Conceptual level of MAGMA. It defines the actions that must be taken to structurally change the Enterprise from the current Structural state, through Intermediate Structural states, towards the Target Structural state.

The remaining levels of Transformational information (as defined by MAGMA) tend to be considered more in terms of the type of information existing rather than centred around the levels themselves. People generally talk of Requirements, Plans, Principles, Metrics and (hopefully, but not generally) the Rationale for decisions.

- ◆ **Requirements** correspond to the Logical to Operational levels of the Motivation part of MAGMA, and provide more and more clarity about what is driving the Transformation.
- ◆ **Project Plans** correspond to the Logical to Operational levels of the Actions part of MAGMA, and provide more and more clarity about how the transformation will be executed.
- ◆ **Principles, Policies & Standards** correspond to the Logical to Operational levels of the Guidance part of MAGMA, and provide more and more clarity about what guides how the transformation.
- ◆ **Metrics** correspond to the Logical to Operational levels of the Measures part of MAGMA, and provide more and more clarity about how we are measuring progress and success.
- ◆ **Decision Rationale** correspond to the Logical to Operational levels of the Assessment part of MAGMA, and provides more and more clarity about the decisions that have been made and why.

There are another two common used names that are composed of parts of this information. Namely:

- ◆ **The Enterprise Strategy** (shown with a blue line), which consists of the Business Motivation Model and Capability Model set in the context of the Business Model.
- ◆ **The Transformation Strategy** (shown with a green line), which consists of the Roadmap Model and Operating Model, set in the context of the Business Motivation Model and the Capability Model.

KEYPOINT:

Enterprise Strategy is the Business Motivation and Capability models, set in the context of the Business Model. Transformation Strategy is the Roadmap and Operating models, set in the context of the Capability and Business Motivation models'

> ## ADOPTION:
>
> Management: Ensure that all parts of the Enterprise understand the dependencies between the Business model, the Business Motivation model, Capability models, Operating models and Roadmap models. Management: Ensure that all parts of the Enterprise understand the dependencies between the Enterprise Strategy and Transformation Strategy.

Questions to Ponder

♦ Where does your Enterprise's Business Model, Business Motivation Model, Capability Model, Roadmap and Operating Model fit into your Enterprises Transformation domain?

♦ Do you have the required basic information, in a usable format, to allow your Enterprise to produce the Business Motivation Model and Operating Model?

♦ Do you have the required basic information, in a usable format, to allow your Enterprise to produce the Roadmap and Operating models?

Artefacts > Ontology > Detail > Meta-models

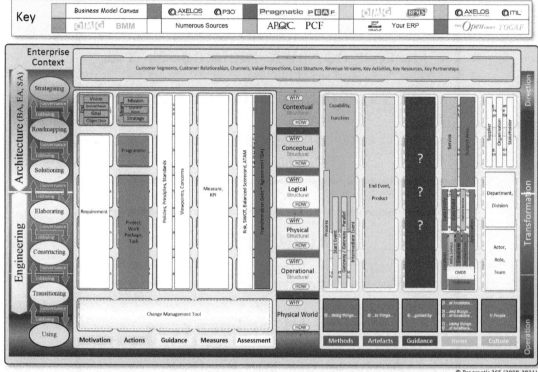

© Pragmatic 365 (2008-2021)

If we intend to model all the information we have identified, we will need a Metamodel, aka a list of Entities and their Relationships of the things that we will model. It would be nice to choose one, however in reality, one Metamodel to cover the entire Transformation domain does not exist and so a hybrid approach is needed.

Here we see an example of a full hybrid meta-model, constructed by taking the most appropriate things from various meta-models from various frameworks, and producing a meta-model with 100% coverage. We say 100% coverage because it covers both Structural and Transformational information, from a Strategy to Deployment perspective.

You may be surprised that the part that **Pragmatic** contributes (in red) is so small. This is perfectly understandable as **Pragmatic** have always asserted that lack of meta-models has rarely been the reason for EA's failure and since there are already a multitude of Metamodels already in existence it would be churlish to re-invent the wheel so to speak. **Pragmatic** has, however, made a massive contribution by the introduction of Transformation Debt™ Agreements (TDAs) that allow the exposing and management of Transformation Debt™.

In addition **Pragmatic**'s contribution is by the definition of the Ontology that all these other frameworks co-exist within, aka DOTS, MAGIC and MAGMA.

Having said that, it has become obvious over time, that the lack of a single coherent metamodel, coupled with the difficulty most tools have in using hybrid metamodels, creates a massive problem for Enterprise and therefore a full **Pragmatic** Metamodel is in production, which will cover all domains and all levels.

> # KEYPOINT:
>
> There is no single metamodel, that covers all the information required for Transformation.

> # ADOPTION:
>
> EA Project Team: Develop a Hybrid Metamodel for Enterprise Architecture and Engineering modelling.

Questions to Ponder

- What Hybrid Meta-model are you currently using?
- Is this a good starting point for a complete and Pragmatic meta-model?
- Who could create such a hybrid meta-model?
- How would you implement such a hybrid meta-model?
- How long would it take to create?
- Are there any tools that can implement and utilise Hybrid Meta-models?

Guidance

Guidance

KEYPOINT:

The Guidance section of POET defines what information is used to guide people in their decision making.

ADOPTION:

C-Suite: Instigate a review of the Guidance used in the Enterprise's Transformation Capability, to determine if their maturity is appropriate.

Questions to Ponder

♦ With respect to your Enterprises Transformation capability, what Guidance is used?
♦ Is the Guidance documented? Understood?
♦ Is it fit for purpose?
♦ Is it used? All the time? Only when it suits?
♦ Which part of the Guidance is Good? Why? Bad? Why?

Context is King™

© Pragmatic 365 (2008-2021)

Context is King™. It really is!

However, as mind-bogglingly important as context is, it is equally mind-bogglingly difficult to talk about. The reason is that when you talk about the context of a "thing" you stop talking about the "thing" itself. This is extremely disconcerting and possibly upsetting for many people. People (including me) like to talk about a "thing" and if someone wants to talk about something else which is not "the thing" then, well, it's not the "thing" is it?

- ◆ "It's off topic."
- ◆ "We're going off at a tangent."
- ◆ "Let's take that offline."
- ◆ "Let's put that in the parking lot."

You will find things like that in many books about "How to run an effective meeting" etc but who is to say something is off-topic? Clearly the person saying it does not think it is "off-topic" or he would not have said it!

Context is extremely important for the correct understanding of anything, so in this section, we look at the Context of PEAF by understanding what problem it exists to solve, how in general it achieves that and how it relates to other Frameworks and Ontologies with respect to Enterprise Architecture.

Every "thing" exists within a context. You, me, this room, a car, a smile, a thought, an Enterprise, a molecule, a planet. What you understand the context of anything to be can massively change your understanding of it and therefore the validity of any decisions you make about it. Sometimes the context can change massively but the implications are small, sometimes the context can change very subtly but the implications can be massive. It is this fact that makes context and our understanding of it far too important to ignore. It is for this reason that all the Frameworks and Ontologies in PF² start with a section called Context.

Context comes into play whenever decisions are made. And decisions are made by everyone, day in day out, week after week, month after month, year after year. It could be said that decisions are the lifeblood of every enterprise. But without context, the blood is very sick, and decisions could be fatal.

KEYPOINT:

Context is King™ because context can fundamentally change how something is viewed and therefore the basis of the decisions that are made about it.

ADOPTION:

Management: Ensure that Context is always considered in relation to any decisions.

Questions to Ponder

♦ What's does "Context is King™" mean to you?
♦ Does your Enterprise make sure that Context is always known and understood?

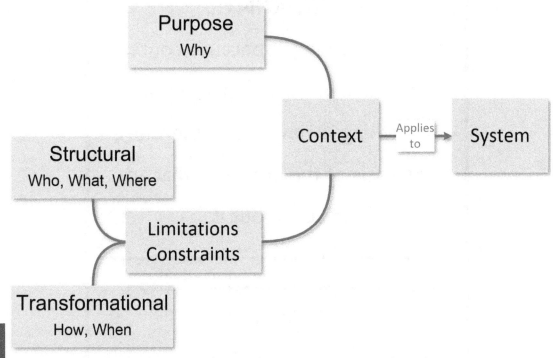

© Pragmatic 365 (2008-2021)

Context is made of different types:

◆ Requirements define why a System exists. It's raison d'être. For example, the purpose of a plant is to reproduce, nothing more. But Requirements can also be complex with multiple purposes that interact in complex ways. For example, the purpose of a concert is to provide entertainment to a group of humans but it is also to make money for the promoters and performers and increase awareness of the performers "brand" while at the same time providing gainful employment to various other people and giving the performers a massive ego boost!

◆ Constraints define things which limit or constrain the System in some way. These constraints can be Structural in nature or Transformational. For example, a plant is constrained structurally by the ground it exists within and transformationally by the limitations of photosynthesis.

It should also be noted that the context of a System can also be deemed to be a System and therefore that every Context has a Context!

Context is comforting; context is good - Have you ever been in a traffic jam - feeling irritated and frustrated. A lot of that comes from not knowing the context for the jam - the WHY. Like queuing at the doctors, it's not the wait that's the problem, it's not knowing how long the wait will be or why you are waiting that is frustrating.

Losing sight of context, or not paying attention to it, is akin to losing spatial awareness in the cockpit of an aircraft. Many have crashed because the pilots have become disconnected from their environment. Similarly many have also crashed because the pilots spent so much time concentrating on solving problems with the aircraft they lost sight of the bigger picture.

Eastern Air Lines Flight 401 crashed into the Florida Everglades in December 1972 killing 101 people because the entire flight crew (4 people with over 50,000 hours of flying experience and a combined age of 192) became so preoccupied with a burned out landing gear indicator light they didn't notice that the autopilot had become disconnected, prompting the incredible phrase "Who's flying the plane?". There are many other examples.

You could also view Context is an inalienable human right and to deny people context is a form of abuse.

But can lack of Context be a good thing? Yes!

Our context (knowledge, experiences, etc) is very small when we are young, but our capacity to see and create new things is vast. The reason is precisely because we ARE NOT constrained by our context.

The older we get, the more context (knowledge, experiences, etc) we accumulate and take on board, and our capacity to see and create new things reduces, precisely because we ARE constrained by that context.

Some people, as they get older, are still able to put aside their context (as vast as it may be) and therefore still possess a great capacity to see and create new things.

As we shall see later, in the Culture section of POET, this is the battle between chaos and order, the child and the adult. Neither is good or bad per se, it's just a question of balance.

> # KEYPOINT:
>
> The Context of something is comprised of Requirements, and Structural and Transformational constraints.

Questions to Ponder

- ◆ Are you aware of the things in your context?
- ◆ What are they?
- ◆ How do you interact with things in your context?
- ◆ How do you the things in your context interact with you?
- ◆ Who is "flying" the aircraft of Enterprise Transformation in your Enterprise?
- ◆ Are they spatially aware?
- ◆ If not, what would help them to concentrate on the bigger picture?

Items

> # KEYPOINT:
>
> The Items section of POET defines 'WHAT' tools and frameworks are required, 'WHERE' and 'WHEN'.

> # ADOPTION:
>
> C-Suite: Instigate a review of the Tools and Frameworks used in the Enterprise's Transformation Capability, to determine if their maturity is appropriate.

Questions to Ponder

- With respect to your Enterprises Transformation capability, what Items (Frameworks/Tools) is used?
- Are those Frameworks/Tools documented? Understood?
- Are they fit for purpose?
- Are they used? All the time? Only when it suits?
- Which of them are Good? Why? Bad? Why?

The Architecture Paradigm™

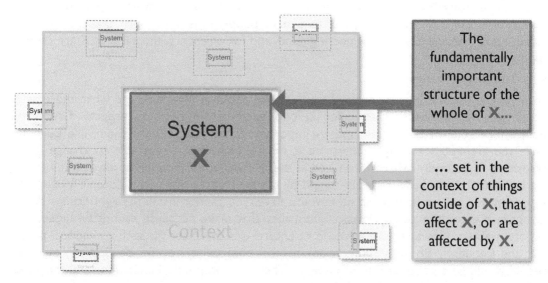

© Pragmatic 365 (2008-2021)

The Architecture Paradigm™ exists to help people deal with the Structural Complexity and Transformational Volatility of things. When things get too volatile or too complex, The Architecture Paradigm™ can help. But what do we really mean by "Architecture"?

Here we see an illustration of what we define to be a system. A system can represent anything; a boat, a car, an application, a business process an Enterprise. We can also see that any system exists within a context. A context that is made up of other systems, in whole or in part.

So what do we define architecture to be?

The architecture of anything (X) is…

> "The fundamentally important structure of the whole of X…"

The first import term here is "fundamentally important". What does that mean? It means things of "Architectural significance". What does that mean? That's a bit more difficult to pin down, because what is architecturally significant changes depending on many factors, most of which come from the context.

The second important term here is "the whole of". This means we do not look at only one part of X, we look at the whole of X. In its entirety.

So, that sounds like a good definition.

> "The fundamentally important structure of the whole of X…"

And that is where many definitions and peoples understanding of Architecture ends. But it is missing the most crucial and important aspect…

"… set in the context of things outside of X that affect X, or are affected by X."

So, when you consider the architecture of something (X in this case) we do not only look at X. We also look at what is outside of X. It's context. And as we have learned before, since "Context is King™", one might say that the context is the most important part of architecture, but also, the component that many people miss. Many miss this crucial aspect because most people have an engineering mind, and for engineers, the parts of X are of most importance.

The Building Analogy

Many people use the building analogy when talking about architecture and while there are a lot of generic similarities they differ in two extremely important respects. Firstly, the architecture of a lot of things is mostly important to be able to build them, like Buildings, while the architecture of the Enterprise is mostly important to be able to change it. To Transform it. Secondly, what is produced in the Building world is tangible, physical things that can be seen and touched - they are bound by the laws of physics, and it doesn't matter how important you are or how much money you have, you cannot install the light fittings before you have erected the ceiling. Physical anomalies that make no sense cannot be hidden and forgotten about. However, in the world of Enterprises there are no such limitations, people can, and frequently do install "the lights" before "the ceiling", or decide that an "effluence outlet" would be a good idea in a "kitchen". There are no physical limitations and the scope for hiding or ignoring things that are bad is immense.

> ## KEYPOINT:
>
> X Architecture, is the fundamentally important structure of the whole of X, set in the context of things outside of X, that affect X, or are affected by X.

> ## ADOPTION:
>
> Management: Ensure people understand what Architecture is, and is not.

Questions to Ponder

- What do you think "The Architecture Paradigm™" is?
- Does it agree with Pragmatics Definition?
- What do others in your Enterprise think?

© Pragmatic 365 (2008-2021)

Many times when explaining what Architecture is, people use the building analogy. Imagine you built a house without a master plan, by continuously adding and changing it over a long period of time without a broad plan of what you were doing. You might end up with something like this:

- 160 rooms, 40 bedrooms and 2 ballrooms.
- 47 fireplaces, 10,000 window panes, 17 chimneys
- 2 basements, three elevators.
- Doors and stairways that lead nowhere
- Steam and forced-air heating
- Push-button gas lights

The Winchester Mystery House is a well-known California mansion that was under construction continuously for 38 years. It once was the personal residence of Sarah Winchester, the widow of gun magnate William Wirt Winchester, but is now a tourist attraction. Under Sarah Winchester's day-to-day guidance, its "from-the-ground-up" construction proceeded around-the-clock, without interruption, from 1884 until her death on September 5, 1922.

The mansion is renowned for its size and utter lack of any master building plan and is often used as a perfect example of bad Architecture. In fact, it is a perfect example of good Architecture! How come I hear you cry?

The story goes that after her husband's death, Sarah Winchester became obsessed by the all the ghosts from the people her husbands guns had killed. Having consulted a (very wily) clairvoyant (with good connections to building companies!), she was told that the ghosts needed to be "deflected" if they came through windows and doors and the only way to stop them was to confuse them by putting doors on walls the led nowhere, etc. Unfortunately that meant the ghost were deflected so another false door or internal window was needed…. Etc, etc, etc. Think of it as Feng Shui on Acid!

The point is this.

Any "good" architecture ONLY EXISTS to fulfil a customer's needs.

It does not exist to "look" nice (unless that's what the customer wants of course!).

In general, "good" architecture tends to "look" nice, but the key thing for people to understand is to concentrate on satisfying the client, not making perfect pretty architectures.

This building, although totally "crazy" and "wrong" to some peoples eyes, is actually "perfect" in the clients eyes, hence, by definition, its "good" architecture.

A little piece of trivia - A film "Winchester" (released in 2018) staring Helen Mirren, tells a dramatized story of Sarah Winchester and the house. Although the film shows a lot of the houses interior, very little filming took place at the actual mansion.

https://www.imdb.com/title/tt1072748/

> # KEYPOINT:
>
> Any "good" Architecture ONLY
> EXISTS to fulfil a customer's needs.

> # ADOPTION:
>
> Enterprise Architect: Realise that
> good Architecture is defined by the
> client, not the Architect.

Questions to Ponder

- Can you think of other architectures that are actually good but look terrible?
- What is a better architecture for roads? The USA system of perpendicular roads with many crossroads and single roads between places or the British system that is more akin to a redundant network?

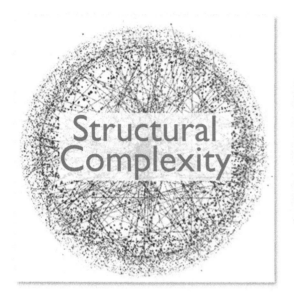

Structural Complexity
=

Number of different Systems
+
Number of Relationships between
those Systems.

All things have a level of Structural Complexity

Structural Complexity is not the same as size or quantity but can be related. Structural Complexity is more a function of the number of different things and the number of relationships between them.

For example, a typical car park might contain 500 parts (cars) but the car park has low complexity because a) they are all cars - things of the same type and b) the only relationships that exist between them are from each car to its immediate neighbour or from each car to a map.

On the other hand a typical car contains around 10,000 parts (components) but most of those parts are different and the relationships between them are many and varied, from obvious/direct relationships like the accelerator is related to the throttle body to subtle/indirect relationships such as the cooling output of the air conditioning unit is related to the number of people in the car.

From these two examples, it can be seen that Complexity is also a function of how deep we look into the "thing" in question. If we take the example of the car park and say that the thing in question is not only the cars but also the "things" that make up the cars, then the car park changes from having a low complexity to a high complexity.

Transformational Volatility merely refers to how often the "thing" changes - its rate of change.

In fact, increasing Structural Complexity can be very beneficial, for example the structural complexity of most back seats in cars today is very high compared to their structural complexity 40 years ago. But this increased complexity exists for a purpose - to allow an end user of the car to convert the car to a van easily without having to go back to the factory to have them do it. So there is a notion of good and bad complexity.

Good or helpful complexity is defined as:

Items

- ◆ Complexity which exists for an identifiable benefit.
- ◆ Tends to be created on purpose - by explicitly architecting or designing it into things when they are created or changed, although can also be created by accident (e.g. implicitly by the good working practices of individuals).
- ◆ Created with the knowledge of, and acceptance of, its implications.
- ◆ Tends to increase the effectiveness, efficiency, agility and durability of the thing in question and its transformation.

Bad or unhelpful complexity is defined as:

- ◆ Complexity which exists for no identifiable benefit.
- ◆ Tends to be created by accident - by the passage of time, although can also be created on purpose (e.g. explicitly by the self-interests of individuals - in which case it would be viewed as good complexity by that individual).
- ◆ Created without little or any knowledge of, or acceptance of, its implications.
- ◆ Tends to decrease the effectiveness, efficiency, agility and durability of the thing in question and its transformation.

KEYPOINT:

Structural Complexity is a function of the number of things something is composed of, and the number of relationships between them.

Questions to Ponder

♦ Are you aware of your Enterprise's Structural Complexity?
♦ How would you define it?
♦ How would you measure it?
♦ Do you care?

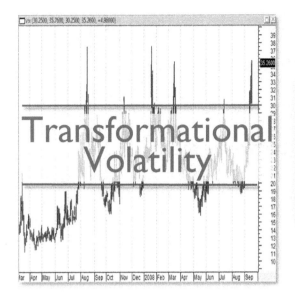

Transformational Volatility

=

Rate of change of Systems

All things have a level of Transformational Volatility.

Transformational Volatility merely refers to how often the "thing" changes - its rate of change.

Enterprises exist in a never ending turbulent sea of change, caused by internal forces and the volatility of the ever changing external context of customers, competitors, legislation, the global economy etc, and of course technology.

> # KEYPOINT:
>
> ## Transformational Volatility is the rate
>
> ## of change of something.

Questions to Ponder

♦ Are you aware of your Enterprise's Transformational Volatility?
♦ How would you define it?
♦ How would you measure it?
♦ Do you care?

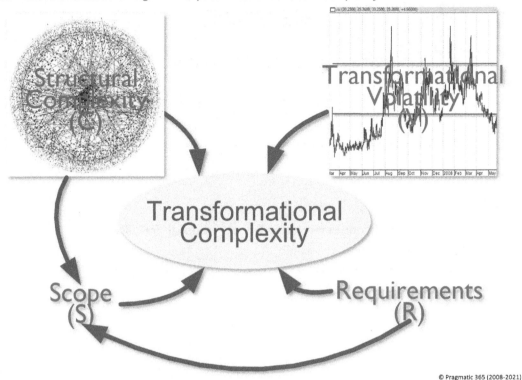

© Pragmatic 365 (2008-2021)

Transformational Complexity is a function of:

- The Structural Complexity of the system being transformed (C).
- The Transformational Volatility of changing the system (V).
- How much of the system needs to be changed - its Scope (S).
- The reason for the changing the system - the Requirements (R).

To complicate matters, Scope is also a function of the Structural Complexity of the "thing" being transformed and the Requirements. For example, a small requirement may cause a large change to the "thing" in question purely because of that "thing's" structural complexity. Conversely a large requirement may cause a small change to the "thing" in question again purely because of that "thing's" structural complexity.

While Transformational Complexity is low, people can deal with it easily, but as Transformational Complexity rises tools and techniques are required to cope. One tool/technique specifically designed to address this is The Architecture Paradigm™.

> "Seven thousand years of known history of humankind establishes that the only known strategy for accommodating extreme complexity and extreme change is… **ARCHITECTURE!!!**"
>
> *- John A. Zachman*

> # KEYPOINT:
>
> Transformational Complexity is a function of the Structural Complexity and Transformational Volatility of something.

Questions to Ponder

- ♦ Are you aware of your Enterprise's Transformational Complexity?
- ♦ How would you define it?
- ♦ How would you measure it?
- ♦ Do you care?

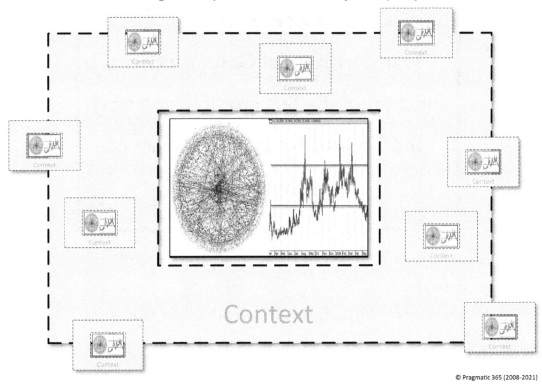

Since, as we have seen before, all things exist with a context, it is also important to remember that it is not only the Structural Complexity and Transformational Volatility of the "thing" in question but also the Structural Complexity and Transformational Volatility of all the "things" that make up its context.

> # KEYPOINT:
>
> Contextual Volatility & Complexity is defined as the Structural Volatility & Transformational Volatility of the context of something.

Questions to Ponder

- Are you aware of the Structural Complexity of your Enterprises Context?
- How would you define it?
- How would you measure it?
- Are you aware of the Transformational Volatility of your Enterprises Context?
- How would you define it?
- How would you measure it?
- Are you aware of the Transformation Complexity of your Enterprise Context?
- How would you define it?
- How would you measure it?

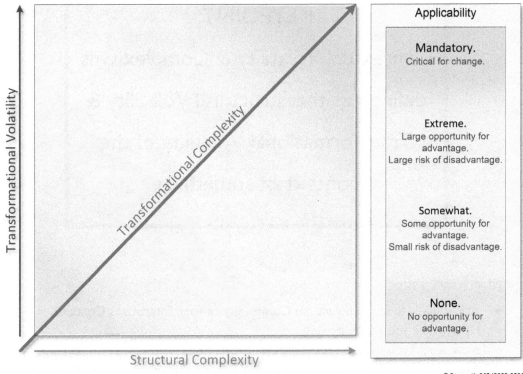

Justification for the investment required to make the changes necessary to utilise The Architecture Paradigm™ cannot be based on numbers or normal simple cost/benefit justification. Any attempt to do so will end in disaster. Any potential benefits tend to be hard to understand, quantify and express (especially in terms of impact on the bottom line) and the realisation of the benefits after the Transformation of Transformation tend to be slow and cannot be as immediately felt. This is because the benefits of improving Transformation only materialise after subsequent projects (which Transform other things like Operations), execute within that improved Transformation environment.

> "You Can't 'Cost-Justify' Architecture"
>
> *- John A. Zachman.*

Justification MUST therefore be based on understanding when it's applicable and when it's not. Just as there are times when use is critically important, there are also times when it is of no use whatsoever. The trick is to understand where you are on that continuum and more importantly where you are likely to be in the short, medium and long term.

How applicable and beneficial it is, is a function of the Structural Complexity and Transformational Volatility of the "thing" in question which come together to form Transformational Complexity. Therefore the applicability of utilising The Architecture Paradigm™ rises as a function of rising Structural Complexity Transformational Volatility aka Transformational Complexity. If Transformational Complexity is low then use of The Architecture Paradigm™ is of little use but as Transformational Complexity rises, use of The Architecture Paradigm™ becomes mandatory.

> # KEYPOINT:
>
> The Architecture Paradigm™ is only applicable when Structural Complexity and Transformational Volatility are high enough.

Questions to Ponder

- Where is your Enterprise on this graph?
- Where will it be in the next one, three, five years?
- What will you do then?
- What will you do now to prepare for then?

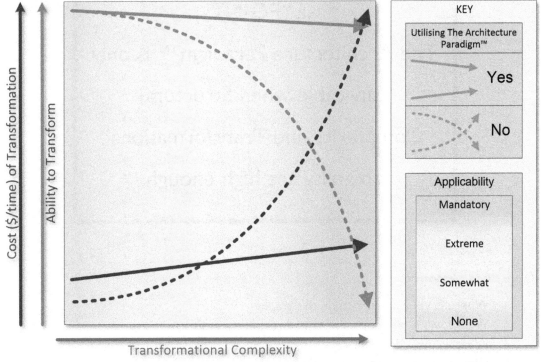

© Pragmatic 365 (2008-2021)

Here we see how the Cost of Transforming some "thing" and the Ability to Transform some "thing" changes as Transformational Complexity increases.

The dotted lines indicate the result if we DO NOT USE The Architecture Paradigm™

- **The Cost of Transformation** (the red dotted line) - starts very low but rises exponentially as Transformational Complexity rises. Ultimately it rises to a point where the cost of Transforming becomes prohibitive.
- **The Ability to Transform** (the green dotted line) - starts very high but falls exponentially as Transformational Complexity rises. Ultimately it falls to a point where the Ability to Transform becomes impossible.

The solid lines indicate the result if we DO USE The Architecture Paradigm™

- **The Cost of Transformation** (the red solid line) - starts very low, and while it does rise as Transformational Complexity rises, this rise tends to be more linear and manageable.
- **The Ability to Effect Transformation** (the green solid line) - also starts very high, and while it does fall as Transformational Complexity rises, this fall tends to be more linear and manageable.

Deciding to adopt The Architecture Paradigm™ (increasing the maturity in its use) in one or more domains, requires that an Enterprise make adjustments to the MAGIC used in those domains.

> # KEYPOINT:
>
> As Transformational Complexity rises, use of the Architecture Paradigm™ becomes mandatory, to preserve your ability to transform, and manage the cost of transformation.

> # ADOPTION:
>
> C-Suite: Accept that while Architecture may sometimes be not applicable, at others times, it is mandatory.

Questions to Ponder

- Where is your Enterprise on this graph?
- Where will it be in the next one, three, five years?
- What will you do then?
- What will you do now to prepare for then?

Items

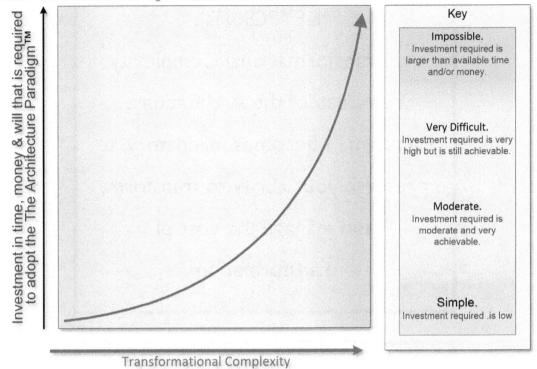

Key

Impossible.
Investment required is larger than available time and/or money.

Very Difficult.
Investment required is very high but is still achievable.

Moderate.
Investment required is moderate and very achievable.

Simple.
Investment required .is low

Investment in time, money & will that is required to adopt the The Architecture Paradigm™

Transformational Complexity

These adjustments to the MAGIC used for Transformation take an investment of time, money and most importantly commitment. How much time, money and commitment is required, is a function of the current Transformational Complexity that exists.

The higher the current level of Transformational Complexity it is being adopted to deal with, the higher the initial investment of time and money and will, will be. This is due to a negative feedback effect. When The Architecture Paradigm™ is not used, any changes made tend to increase the Structural Complexity of the thing being changed, not because it needs to be that complex, but because of a lack of knowledge about the thing being changed. This negative feedback loop is cumulative and can run out of control as the rule of compound interest takes over. The cost of understanding and sorting out the Structural Complexity rises each time another change is made meaning each time there is an opportunity to make the changes necessary to be able to use The Architecture Paradigm™, the appetite for doing so, the will, reduces. This is a downward spiral into oblivion.

So as the need to make the adjustments increase, the appetite (and therefore commitment) to make them, decreases. If left too late, there comes a time when the amount of time and money and will required is just not available, and the "thing" in question will cease to be able to transform at all. When you are drowning, it's too late to learn how to swim.

> # KEYPOINT:
>
> As the need to utilise Architecture increases, the appetite to do so will decrease.

> # ADOPTION:
>
> C-Suite: Recognise that as the need to adopt The Architecture Paradigm™ increases, the appetite (and therefore commitment) to do so, decreases.

Questions to Ponder

- Where is your Enterprise on this graph?
- Where will it be in the next one, three, five years?
- What will you do then? What will you do now to prepare for then?

Items

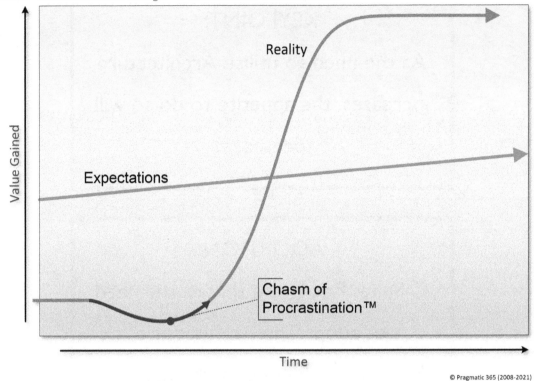

© Pragmatic 365 (2008-2021)

They say that time is a great healer. But time is also a great destroyer. Time is the main problem when trying to justify the changes (and therefore the investment) required to adopt and utilise The Architecture Paradigm™.

As with anything, there is a time lapse between making the investment in utilising The Architecture Paradigm™ and reaping its benefits. This is because just making the changes required to utilise The Architecture Paradigm™ creates no benefit in and of itself. The benefits of spending the money making those changes only come from the use of those changes as time progresses.

The worst mistake people make when thinking about and justifying the use of The Architecture Paradigm™ is that their expectations of short term value are too high and their expectations of long term value are too low. In reality, short term value is much less than expected but long term value is much higher than expected. In fact the curve is more of an S shape where initially there is a slight decrease in value (when adopting anything new) then a slow increase in value, followed by an abrupt increase in value, followed by a return to a more linear increase in value over time as maximum value is achieved.

Justification for The Architecture Paradigm™ cannot be based on the benefit of the next project or even the next two, three or four projects. In fact, the next project (and possibly the second and third projects) may well run slower and cost more money. This is the Chasm of Procrastination.

Many people think (incorrectly) that justifying use of The Architecture Paradigm™ is as easy (and should be as easy) as justifying whether to buy a kettle or not - buy a kettle today, get the benefit tomorrow. In actuality, justifying an investment in adopting or becoming more mature in your use of The Architecture Paradigm™ is more akin to justifying spending 30K on going to university for four years where you gain zero benefit for four years and at the end of the four years there is still no immediate benefit and no guarantee that you will a) get a job or b) that even if you do get a job, you will earn more than what you would be earning if you had not saved 30K and gained four years of experience instead. Another example might be buying insurance, having to pay and pay and pay for something that you many never actually use or get any benefit from whatsoever.

> # KEYPOINT:
>
> The short term value of Architecture
>
> is overestimated.
>
> The long term value of Architecture
>
> is underestimated.

> # ADOPTION:
>
> C-Suite: Do not overestimate the
>
> short term value, or underestimate
>
> the long term value, that use of The
>
> Architecture Paradigm™ can provide.

Questions to Ponder

- ◆ Do people in your Enterprise expect Architecture to have immediate benefit?
- ◆ What will you do to explain it doesn't?
- ◆ What will you do to explain that benefits come down the line?
- ◆ Do you want to accept the risk of not using The Architecture Paradigm™?
- ◆ Is the Management of your Enterprise in the Chasm of Procrastination™?

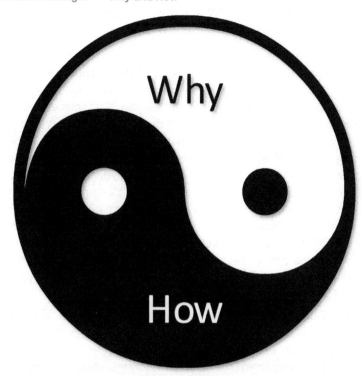

© Pragmatic 365 (2008-2021)

I remember being a small boy growing up in 1970's England - Pele, Rivelino and Zico dancing in colour on my black and white TV - the long hot summer of '76 - David Bowie telling us that "*We could be Heroes*" - Adidas SL76 trainers - accidentally shooting my friend in the head with an airgun - Space Hoppers - my first kiss! Everything seemed new. Everything seemed exciting. I had the feeling of limitless possibilities that always come with youth and the belief that I could achieve anything. I also remember that I had an innate desire to understand things. That burning desire took me in two different directions and both of those directions were driven by questions… HOW and WHY.

Asking How - Looking Down - Structural

The first direction was asking the question HOW or more correctly "How do things work". This desire drove me to take things apart (much to the annoyance of my mother as I rarely approached putting things back together again with the same vigour that I had exhibited when taking them apart) to see what they were made of and how those parts worked and were connected together. Initially starting on small battery powered things like torches, telephones, and radios, etc but gravitating to larger items that also had the power to kill me such as electric irons, lighting, electric door bells (yes they used to be 240v in those days!) and record players. On more than one occasion my inquisitiveness caused me to accidentally electrocute myself. Firstly when still almost a baby I thought "I wonder what will happen if I push this knitting needle into the socket thing on the wall" (For those who are interested in what happened, my mother reports that there was a bright flash of blue light and a loud bang. This loud bang was shortly followed by a more muted bang as my head hit the wall opposite that I had been thrown against) and later when holding a light socket in my hand and plugging the other end into a wall socket. I am sure there were other times but the unintended electroshock therapy I had been subjecting myself to, appears to have had the unintended side-effect of clouding my memory! Regardless of this, I was very much interested in HOW things worked.

Asking HOW is the fundamental question The Engineering Paradigm™ forces us to contemplate. For without knowing HOW something is constructed we cannot know HOW to change it or what the unintended implications of any change will be.

Asking Why - Looking Up - Contextual

I very quickly learned that although answering the HOW question was interesting, the HOW question seemed to have a logical end point and therefore my interested waned. It then occurred to me to ask WHY things existed in the first place and WHY they were constructed as they were. I also soon discovered that answering the WHY question appeared to have no end at all and whatever was provided as a response could lead onto another WHY. Many people just got plain angry (especially teachers - although it applied to anyone in authority - which when you're ten years young - is everyone!) as it made them think that I was just trying to annoy them. This was not the case at all - I really did want to know WHY. Many years later it occurred to me that the reason that people tended to get angry was because people either a) had not actually considered that question themselves at all and had no idea WHY or b) could answer the first or maybe even the second WHY but then reached a limit of their knowledge and instead of saying I don't know would proffer "interesting" reasons which did not make sense which only made me ask WHY even more, which got them more annoyed, etc, etc, etc.

For, me there has to be a point. To achieve something. A WHY. For without a point or reason for something it is literally - well - pointless! Even things that I enjoy doing have to have a purpose higher than just enjoying them. A purpose that achieves something. For example, I love driving. Driving anything; cars, vans, lorries, taxis, dumper trucks, anything. So you might expect that when I bought the best car I have ever owned (A Porsche Boxster S) that I would go for long drives around the countryside to enjoy driving it. I loved to drive that car, the smell of the leather, the weight of the steering, the sweet sound of the flat-six Boxer engine, but I could not "just go for a drive". There had to be a purpose, there had to be a reason there had to be a WHY. It didn't matter what it was (going to the shops to buy a loaf of bread, going to work, giving my daughter or son a lift) but there did need to be a goal. I needed a WHY.

Asking WHY is the fundamental question The Architecture Paradigm™ forces us to contemplate. For without knowing WHY we need to change something we cannot know HOW to change it. To use an example of Deming's:

> "If you ask me to clean that table I cannot. You may want to use it to store surgical implements. You may want to eat off it, you may want to put a plant pot on it. Without knowing WHY I cannot clean the table. Don't tell me HOW to clean the table - tell me WHY you want the table cleaned."
>
> *- W.E. Deming*

> ## KEYPOINT:
>
> Why is the most important question.

> ## ADOPTION:
>
> Enterprise Architect: Always ask
>
> WHY? (At least 5 times.)

Questions to Ponder

- What is your burning desire?
- Do you annoy people by asking questions?
- Do people tell you how to do things or do they tell you why?

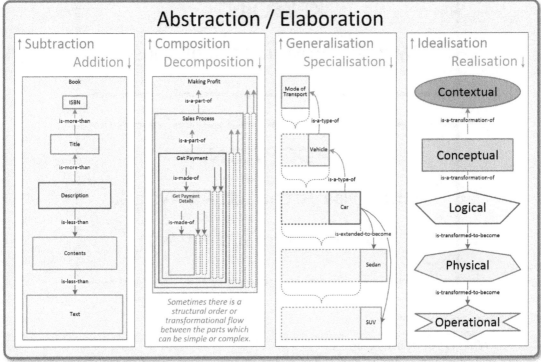

© Pragmatic 365 (2008-2021)

There is no reason to Abstract or Elaborate anything unless the abstracted or elaborated information is to be used for something. Abstraction is a process used to remove or suppress information that is less relevant to the user of the information at the abstracted level. Elaboration is a process used to create or add information that is more relevant to the user of the information at the elaborated level.

Abstraction and Elaboration, therefore, are mechanisms which allows the same fundamental thing to be viewed by different stakeholders with potentially very different viewpoints and there is no theoretical limit to how many times information can be abstracted or elaborated. Whether you view something as being an abstraction or an elaboration is defined by the direction you are looking. If you are looking up to a more abstract level, the information is said to be an elaboration of the information above. If you are looking down to a more elaborated level, the information is said to be an abstraction of the information below.

POET uses, and advocates the use of the four primitives of Abstraction and Elaboration:

♦ **Subtraction/Addition** - These are the simplest types of Abstraction and Elaboration.
  ♦ Moving up, we abstract things by removing information. We subtract from them to make smaller things.
  ♦ Moving down, we elaborate things by adding information. We add to them to make bigger things.
♦ **Composition/Decomposition** - The second most complex types of Abstraction and Elaboration.
  ♦ Moving up, we abstract things by grouping them together into larger things. We Compose them into larger parts.
  ♦ Moving down, we elaborate things by breaking them apart into smaller things. We Decompose them into smaller parts.

- **Generalisation/Specialisation** - The third most complex types of Abstraction and Elaboration.
    - Moving up, we abstract things by creating more generic things. We Generalise them into more general things.
    - Moving down, we elaborate things by creating more specific things. We Specialise them into more specific things.
- **Idealisation/Realisation** - The most complex, and most important, of all types of Abstraction and Elaboration
    - Moving up, abstracts things by transforming them into more idealised things. Akin to Analysis and Architecture.
    - Moving down, we elaborate things by transformation them into more real things. Akin to Design and Engineering.

> # KEYPOINT:
>
> There are 4 types of Abstraction / Elaboration.

> # ADOPTION:
>
> Enterprise Architect: Apply the four types of Abstraction/Elaboration appropriately.

Questions to Ponder

- Do all people involved in Transformation understand the differences between these types of abstraction?
- Do all people involved in Transformation know how to "move up" and "move down" effectively?
- If not, what impact is that likely to have?

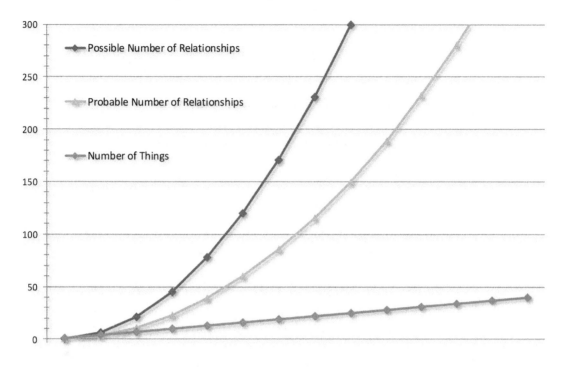

Whilst identifying things is very important, what is an order of magnitude more important is how those things are related. Understanding how things relate allows us to ask questions of the information more than just simple "give me a list of..." type questions. The negative aspect of this is that the lines are much much harder to create and maintain than the boxes, which probably goes a long way to explain why in general they are not.

The value that can be obtained and the difficulty in maintaining the information increases because the number relationships (lines) between things tends to increase in a polynomial fashion (using the formula $n*(n-1)/2$) which is a fancy way of saying that while the number of things rises linearly, the number of possible relationships (combinations – not permutations) between them rises faster and faster.

In fact this also illustrates one of the problems with the adoption of The Architecture Paradigm™. The red line could be thought of the value that is created over time, which can be seen to be very low initially and a good increase in value only happens later as the volume of information builds up. In this world where management insatiably calls for the picking of low hanging fruit and quick wins, anything that takes time to provide value tends to be seen as worthless.

Items

KEYPOINT:

The relationships between things rises in a polynomial fashion.

ADOPTION:

Management: Provide people the tools and time to deal with the fact that the relationships between things, rise in a polynomial fashion.

Questions to Ponder

- How much time is spent in your Enterprise understanding and maintaining relationships?
- What problems exist with documenting and maintaining relationships?
- Who should be responsible for maintaining relationships?
- Are people in your Enterprise given the appropriate time and resources to find, model and maintain relationships?

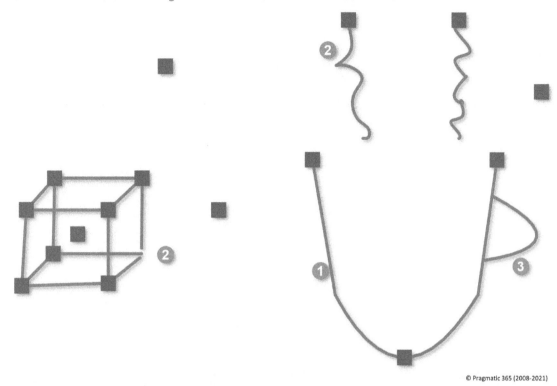

© Pragmatic 365 (2008-2021)

What are these boxes telling you?

The Value is in the Lines not the Boxes™. This phrase expresses one of the key aspects of The Architecture Paradigm™. In fact, it could be said that Architecture IS the relationships - the lines and not the boxes, the space between the boxes, the relationship of the lines to the spaces.

Another way to think of it is how the brain thinks (no pun intended). The brain is composed of "things" - neurons, and "relationships" - synapses. At birth your brain has about 86 billion neurons. It has been estimated that the brain of a three year old child as about thousand, thousand billion (1 quadrillion or 10^{15}) synapses. By adulthood, although the brain increases in size by about five times, the number of neurons do not increase. Most of the growth is done by the growth of the synaptic connections - learning. Interestingly, in adulthood the number of synaptic connections falls through the process of Synaptic Pruning, stabilizing by adulthood from 1,000 thousand billion to around 100 to 500 thousand billion (trillion 10^{12}) If anyone ever told you that Architecture was not brain surgery, maybe they should think again! So while the neurons (boxes) are important, it is the synapses (lines) that are much more important.

It is only when we add the lines, that the boxes make sense to us. Indeed, we could remove the boxes altogether, and the important information will still be visible.

It is also important to note that lines:

♦ Don't necessarily have to be straight, as shown by #1.
♦ Don't necessarily have to connect to a box at both ends, as shown by #2.
♦ Don't necessarily have to connect to boxes at all, but may instead connect to other lines, as shown by #3.

KEYPOINT:

Lines (relationships) are an order of magnitude more important than the boxes.

ADOPTION:

C-Suite: Understand and utilise the power of relationships.

Questions to Ponder

♦ Do you agree that there is massive value in "the lines" vs "the boxes"?
♦ What "lines" will you draw to allow you to see the value?

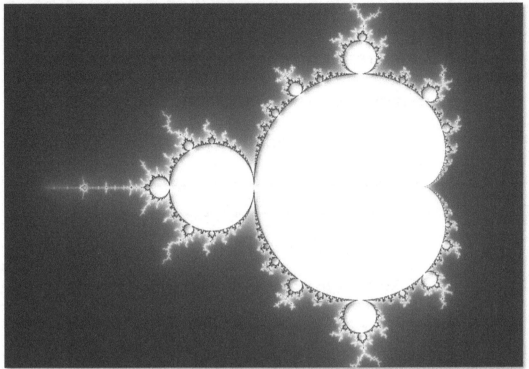

© Pragmatic 365 (2008-2021)

Here we see the Mandelbrot Set. An illustration of one of the most important and powerful patterns known to man (and nature) - Recursion.

There are two types of patterns:

♦ Firstly we recognise that patterns exist everywhere in just about everything and especially in nature - a self-optimising system for the sustainability of living organisms that are Effective (reproduction), Efficient, Agile and Durable. Hmmm - sounds la bit like an Enterprise! Patterns promote efficiency and elegance in the structure (Architecture) of things and how they work. Things that have discernible patterns tend to be much better than those that do not.

♦ Secondly we recognise that patterns can be used as high level general solutions to commonly occurring problems. A (design) pattern allows us to reuse these solutions with a high degree of certainty that they are effective and efficient. Someone (and probably many people) have already done "the hard work" and this allows us to "stand on the shoulders of giants". They can be small or large and their size does not necessarily imply importance.

Design patterns can be structural (aka how something is organised) or transformational (aka how something is changed). Some patterns can be a mixture of the two - for example Software Design patterns tend to consist of structure as well as algorithms, whereas other patterns can be purely structural such as technical reference models.

Architects see patterns everywhere. Their brains are hard wired that way. Why do we look for patterns? Because patterns reduce complexity. Where they cannot see a pattern they tend to create one! This tends to be an iterative process where a pattern is initially chosen, mostly on gut feel, and then that pattern is used to map things to it. In the process of doing that it may be seen that the pattern was not correct and so the pattern is changed and we repeat the loop.

Architecture is essentially patterns/styles. For buildings, many people look at a building and say "wow - look at the architecture" which implies the physical building itself. Actually the architecture is not the building itself. The architecture is the patterns/styles behind the physical building such as Art Deco, Georgian, Regency, Modernist, Gothic, etc. There are hundreds of Architectures (Architectural styles) in the Building domain.

However, there is also a downside to patterns. Patterns promote conformity and sameness (within limits) and so careful consideration should be given to when patterns should be considered to be a friend or an enemy.

Items

> # KEYPOINT:
>
> Look for patterns in everything.

> # ADOPTION:
>
> Enterprise Architect: Look for
>
> patterns in everything.

Questions to Ponder

- Do you agree that there is massive value in patterns?
- How much time is spent in your Enterprise understanding and maintaining patterns?
- What problems exist with documenting and maintaining patterns?
- Who should be responsible for maintaining patterns?
- Are people in your Enterprise given the appropriate time and resources to find, model and maintain patterns?

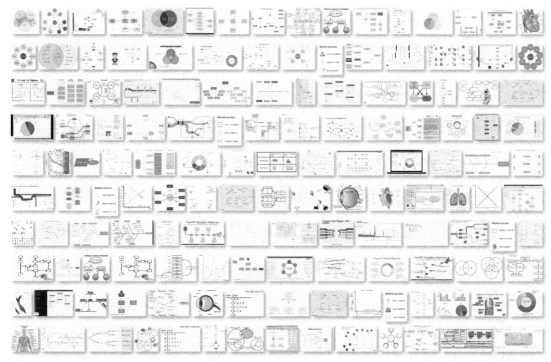

Models

At a fundamental level, a model is merely a collection of structured information with zero or more relationships that represent something of interest. These days models and modelling are used almost everywhere. Financial models, Stock Trading models, Buildings, Cars, Spaceships, Oilrigs, Weather, etc, etc, etc, although for some reason, many Enterprises cannot understand how useful it is for Transformation.

There are two main reasons why models are used:

◆ You cannot build (or change) anything that is complex by wading in with a screwdriver - you need to understand what you are trying to build or change first.

◆ It is easier, cheaper and faster to build a model of something and then to find out it is wrong in some way, than to build the thing the model represents and then discover the problems.

What we seem to have forgotten is that Models have been used for many many years to help with Architecture and Engineering alike. Long before any computers, when technology consisted of paper, pencils, a drawing board and a chair, there was a department in many Enterprises called the **Drawing Office** and the people that worked there were called draughtsman. The only reason I have a very vague recollection of this is because my father worked in the **Drawing Office** at Rolls-Royce in the 1960's working on the design of the Olympus 593 Engine that powered Concorde. This department existed to produce and manage drawings - models. It was an extremely important and a strict change management process was in place to make sure that as the drawings were used to engineer and manufacture the engines, that any problems encountered or opportunities that were missed that meant the drawings needed to be changed, were fed back to the Drawing Office and appropriate updates were made.

This cost a lot of time and money. So why did they do it? The reasons are utterly evident and need no explanation. What does need explanation is why we are finding it so hard in the 21st century to explain to management that modelling is of crucial importance?

Imagine how Rolls-Royce would have fared if every time a change to an engine was required that the person responsible for that change had to first spend a whole lot of time wandering round the factory trying to find a drawing of the part of the engine he was going to be working on. Maybe he found one, maybe he didn't. If he found one he had no way of knowing how old or up to date the drawing was so would wander around trying to find people who knew something about it, who maybe had conflicting opinions. Then, after cobbling together a vaguely correct (who knows!) diagram of the domain of interest (that his project manager would constantly moan about him wasting his time on because that task was not on his project plan) and performing his work, the diagrams (models) of what the engine looked like before and after his changes were then left gathering dust on a shelf while he moved on to other things. Maybe the next person would find them, probably not.

This is, of course utterly ridiculous, but this is exactly what goes on in 95% of all Enterprises every single day with the resultant loss in quality of work performed, not to mention the billions of wasted money, but even more importantly the waste of time. Money maybe important, but if you lose it you can always get more of it. Once time is gone, it's gone forever.

Your Enterprise doesn't have a **Drawing Office** - but it is of crucial significance.

In the past models were drawn by hand on paper, but in today's world computers are used to streamline that process. And once a model is in a computer there are many operations and analyses that can be performed which streamlines that process even further. What-If analyses can be performed almost instantaneously to explore different scenarios and to aid selection of a final "solution".

But Enterprises seem to have forgotten the fundamentals - Fundamentals that POET is trying to highlight. IT is massively important of course, but people can fall into the trap that thinking that IT can solve all problems, forgetting that IT is only a tool and as important as a tool is, it's not a case of how big your tool is, but how you use it ;-)

Meta-Models

The word meta just means "information about" so a meta-model is information about a model. It really is that simple. You can also use the word meta in conjunction with just about anything so long as there is some benefit/reason for doing so. The word meta also can be used repeatedly for example meta-meta-model which is information about the information about a model.

Semantics

As well as giving us the structure of the information that we can model a meta-model also defines the semantics or language used. This is massively important as language is the second biggest enemy of Enterprise Transformation (after Cultural problems).

A lot of the words used in Transformation are very ill defined - from individual to individual, group to group and framework to framework. Using the same word doesn't necessarily mean the same thing and using different words doesn't necessarily mean different things. A lot of the time, people think they are speaking the same language (because they are both speaking English for example) when in fact they are not. In this environment it is easy to have a disagreement without either party being aware of it. That creates hidden problems which are the worst kind of problems. It is also easy to have disagreement when in fact both parties agree - Have you ever heard anyone say, "I think we are in violent agreement"?

Defining the meanings of the words that are used in a model is key to allowing people from multiple backgrounds and domains to be able to communicate effectively. This is one thing that a framework brings. A common set of terms, definitions and explanations of a discipline.

Semantics/Language is defined in two ways:

♦ **Words** - A dictionary or glossary, specifying definitions and the meanings of words and phrases and (more importantly) the relationships between them.

♦ **Symbols** - The Notation used on diagrams, specifying definitions and usages of shapes, lines, colours and embellishments.

These Words and Symbols form the language of Enterprise Transformation. Different people, or roles, tend to speak these different languages and dialects.

Recognising that these languages and dialects do exist is an important part of the glue between each level and in getting the whole of the Transformation stack to work holistically together.

> # KEYPOINT:
>
> Use structured data for all structural and transformational information, and generate "documents" as required.

> # ADOPTION:
>
> Management: Provide people the tools and time to model information, instead of writing it in unstructured documents.

Questions to Ponder

- Does executive management understand the benefits of modelling?
- Does your Enterprise use modelling where appropriate?
- If not, what areas could benefit more?
- What is preventing your Enterprise using modelling more?
- What things exist in your Enterprise to define a common set of words?
- What things exist in your Enterprise to define a common set of symbols?
- Does your Enterprise have a Drawing Office? Should it?

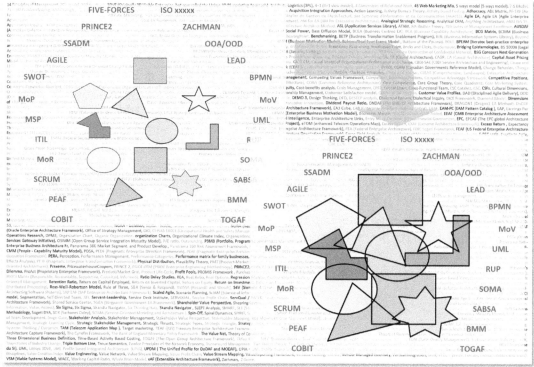

© Pragmatic 365 (2008-2021)

In relation to the Transformation of Enterprises, there are many Frameworks (**Pragmatic** is tracking over 900) that have been produced to help Enterprises deal with Enterprise Transformation in a more effective and efficient manner. These things are of various types; "frameworks", ontologies, methodologies, Notations, Architectures, Theories, Models etc, etc, etc. We use the word Framework to refer to them all.

Each of these Frameworks has been designed and engineered to operate with a specific domain or context, for example; strategic planning, project management, enterprise architecture, software design and development, service management, change management, etc, etc etc. We could categorise these Frameworks in different ways:

♦ **Domain** - Some Frameworks exist to help with Strategising or Roadmapping, while others exist to help with the design of IT systems, or a particular discipline such as Project Management.

♦ **Coverage** - Some Frameworks deal only with Structural elements of Transformation (Categories, Ontologies, meta-models) like Zachman or BMM while others deal more with Procedural elements of Transformation (Methods, Practices, Processes) like eTOM. Others encompass both like PEAF.

♦ **Depth** - Some Frameworks provide only high level concepts and guidance, others contain vast amounts of detail and very prescriptive.

♦ **Geography** - Some Frameworks exist to serve a particular country or region like The Bank of England Framework, while others are geography independent like BMM.

♦ **Industry** - Some Frameworks are Industry specific like eTOM, while others are industry agnostic like BMM.

♦ **Maturity** - How mature the framework is - (can be partly related to its age although that can also be inversely proportional!)

Like many things, these Frameworks have grown and evolved organically and expanded their scope and areas of interest as they themselves have matured. This usually happens when the framework creators realise that the problems being experienced within their domain, are being caused by immaturity in another domain (usually upstream) and therefore grow and seep into that domain to "fix" those problems. ITIL is a prime example of this.

How successful frameworks have been in morphing themselves into areas they were never designed to operate in is largely subjective, and opinion tends to be driven by allegiances and crusades. In addition, all of these Frameworks have been designed and built in isolation - to optimise specific parts rather than the whole.

So, the problem is not the lack of frameworks. The problem is the abundance of frameworks. Because of this, there are overlaps, gaps, inconsistencies and clashes. In short, total confusion. So the framework providers, whose primary aim is to provide clarity in their domain, have created confusion in the wider domain.

Consequently, people have adopted these frameworks in a similarly haphazard fashion, optimising specific parts but never considering the whole. Perhaps starting in one area and then finding themselves being subtly pulled into other areas. They have been optimising the parts at the expense of the whole.

> # KEYPOINT:
>
> Over time, frameworks have grown
>
> and overlapped.

Questions to Ponder

- How many frameworks have you heard of?
- Did you know there were so many (Pragmatic is tracking over 900)?
- Is your Enterprise using the ones most applicable to it?

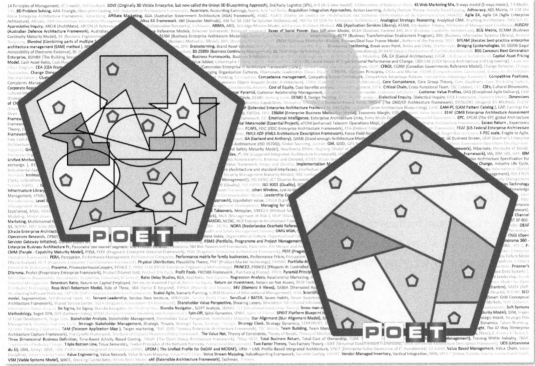

Since the whole is much much more important than the parts (Context is King™), it is important to have a cohesive and holistic Framework (meta-framework) for all the Frameworks used to aid Enterprise Transformation, to ensure that the emphasis is to use these different frameworks to optimise the whole of the Transformation domain rather than just the parts. To stop Enterprises optimising the parts at the expense of the whole, and to begin to allow Enterprises to optimise the whole at the possible expense of the parts.

POET provides this cohesive and holistic Framework and provides two main benefits:

- Firstly, and most importantly, POET provides this framework to Enterprises today - for Enterprises to be able to consider and optimise the whole of this strategically important Transformation domain. POET is the only framework in the world that does this.

- Secondly, it provides a framework to Framework Providers as a basis (a super-type if you will) to allow frameworks to begin to align themselves with this coherent and holistic environment. This will provide another benefit to Enterprises in the future because it will allow them to see much more clearly how these Frameworks relate and interface to each other in clear and straight forward ways which allow the holistic adoption of them to be much more straightforward. Of course this is likely to take a long time because framework providers tend to want to argue about their differences rather than agree on areas of similarity.

Currently, to try to understand how all these different frameworks are related is almost impossible. For all the frameworks you want to use or do use, you need to map each framework to each other framework, to try to understand how they relate.

But as framework providers begin to use POET as the context for their frameworks, and map their frameworks to POET, it will become much much easier for Enterprises and the people who are accountable for how Transformation is effected, to be able to understand how they all relate, enabling them to make more informed decisions about who needs to use what, where, why, how and when.

```
KEYPOINT:

POET provides an Ontology that you
can map all other Frameworks to.
```

```
ADOPTION:

Enterprise Architect: Map all
frameworks you currently use to
POET, in order to be able to find
your gaps and overlaps.
```

Questions to Ponder

- What Transformational Frameworks do you use?
- Are there overlaps?
- Are there gaps?
- Are there inconsistencies?
- What do you use to decide which Frameworks to use, where and how?
- What do you use to orchestrate the Frameworks you use into a holistic, coherent and cooperative whole?

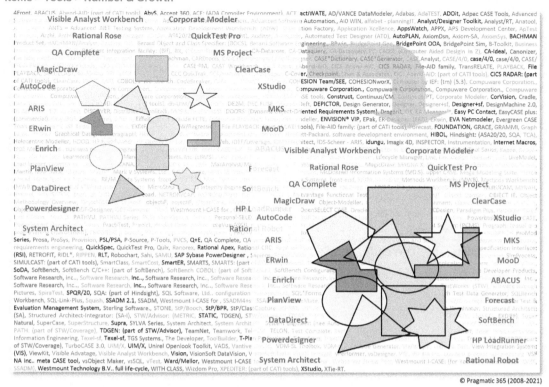

© Pragmatic 365 (2008-2021)

In relation to the Transformation of Enterprises, there are many tools (**Pragmatic** is tracking hundreds) that have been produced to help Enterprises deal with Enterprise Transformation in a more effective and efficient manner

These tools come in are of various types; Governance, Risk, Compliancy tools, Portfolio, Program, Project Management tools, Business, IT Strategy tools, Enterprise, Solution, Technical Architecture tools, Software Engineering tools, Change Management tools, Configuration Management tools, CASE tools, Test Management, Load Testing, Stress Testing tools, etc, etc, etc.

Each of these tools has been designed and engineered to operate with a specific domain or context, for example; strategic planning, project management, enterprise architecture, software design and development, service management, change management, etc, etc, etc.

We could categorise tools in different ways:

- ◆ **Scope** - Some tools exist to help with Strategising or Roadmapping, while others exist to help with the design of systems, or a particular discipline such as Project Management.
- ◆ **Type** - Some tools deal only with Structural elements of Transformation (Categories, Ontologies, meta-models) like Archimate while others deal more with Procedural elements of Transformation (Methods, Practices, Processes) like MS Project or Rational RequisitePro.

Like many things, these tools have grown and evolved organically and expanded their scope and areas of interest as they themselves have matured This has happened as the tool vendors have responded to requests from their clients for increased functionality and also as they see opportunities to expand into other lucrative areas. It's very rare that a tool vendor will tell you that their tool does not do something! Project Management tools grew into Portfolio

Management tools and vice versa, modelling tools that were created to model one thing have expanded into modelling other things.

How successful tools have been in morphing themselves into areas they were never designed to operate in is largely subjective, and opinion tends to be driven by allegiances and crusades. In addition all of these tools have been designed and built in isolation - to optimise specific parts rather than the whole.

So, the problem is not the lack of tools. The problem is the abundance of tools. Because of this, there are overlaps, gaps, inconsistencies and clashes. In short, total confusion. So the tool providers, whose primary aim is to provide clarity in their domain, have created confusion in the wider domain.

Consequently people have adopted these tools in a similarly haphazard fashion, optimising specific parts but never considering the whole. Perhaps starting in one area and then finding themselves being subtly pulled into other areas. They have been optimising the parts at the expense of the whole.

Pragmatic is currently tracking over 400 Enterprise Transformation tools. **Pragmatic** aims to categorise and compare them all. This work is currently in progress...

KEYPOINT:

Over time, tools have grown and

overlapped.

Questions to Ponder

- ♦ How many Transformation tools have you heard of?
- ♦ Did you know there were so many (Pragmatic is tracking hundreds)?
- ♦ Is your Enterprise using the ones most applicable to it?

Items > Tools > How POET Helps

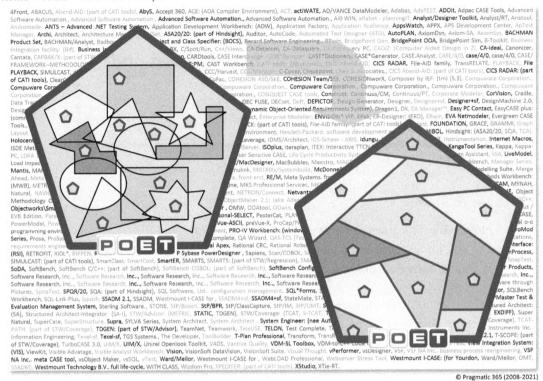

4Front, ABACUS, Abend-AID: (part of CATi tools), AbyS, Accept 360, ACE: (ADA Compiler Environment), ACT, actiWATE, AD/VANCE DataModeler, Adabas, AdaTEST, ADOit, Adpac CASE Tools, Advanced Software Automation., Advanced Software Automation., Advanced Software Automation., Advanced Software Automation., AiO WIN, alfabet - planningIT, Analyst/Designer Toolkit, Analyst/RT, Anatool, Andromede, ANTS – Advanced .NET Testing System, Application Development Workbench: (ADW), Application Factory, Application Xcellence, AppsWatch, APPX, APS Development Center, ApTest Manager, Archi, Architect, Architecture Me... ...et, ASA20/20: (part of Hindsight), Auditor, AutoCode, Automated Test Designer (ATD), AutoPLAN, AxiomDsn, Axiom-SA, AxiomSys, BACHMAN Product Set, BACHMAN/Analyst, Badbo... ...ect and Class Specifier: (BOCS), Berard Software Engineering., BPwin, BridgePoint Gen, BridgePoint OOA, BridgePoint Sim, B-Toolkit, Business Integration facility: (BIF), ...BX, C/Spot/Run, C++/Views, CA-Datacom, CA-Dataquery, CA-Dataquery PC, CADiZ: (Computer Aided Design in Z), CA-ideal, Canonizer, Cantata, CAPBAK/X: (part of STW... ...., CARDtools, CASE Interchange, CASE*Dictionary, CASE*Generator, CASE.Analyst, CASE/4/0, case/4/0, CASE/ FRAMEWORK--METHODOLO... ...E-PM, CAST Workbench, CATi tools, CAViS - Code Analysis, AID, CICS RADAR, File-AID family, TransRELATE, PLAYBACK, File PLAYBACK, SIMULCAST, ...CCC/Harvest, CCC/Manager, C-Cover, Checkpoint, Chen & Associates., CICS Abend-AID: (part of CATi tools), CICS RADAR: (part of CATi tools), ClearC... ...oFac, COHESION ASD/SEE, COHESION Team/SEE, COHESIONworX, Composer by IEF: (tm) (5.3), Compuware Corporation., Compuware Corp... ...Compuware Corporation., Compuware Corporation., Compuware Corporation., Compuware Corporation., Compuware Corporation., CONQUEST CASE tools, Construct, Continuus/CM, Continuus/PT, Corporate Modeler, CorVision, Cradle, Data Tra... ...DEC FUSE, DECset, Deft, DEPICTOR, Design Generator, Designer, Designer+sf, Designer+sf, DesignMachine 2.0, Design... ...ynamic Object-Oriented Requirements System), Dragon1, DX, EA Manager™, Easy PC Contact, EasyCASE plus: (com... ...ct, Enterprise Modeller, ENVISION: VIP, EPak, ER-Designer: (ERD), ERwin, EVA Netmodeler, Evergreen CASE Tools., ...CK: (part of CATi tools), File-AID family: (part of CATi tools) ...east, FOUNDATION, GRACE, GRAMMI, Graph Layout ... ...nvironment, Hewlett-Packard. software development ... ...HIBOL, Hindsight: (ASA20/20, SQA, TCA), Holocen... ...everage, IDMS/Architect, IDS-Scheer - ARIS, idungu... ... Instrumentation. Internet Macros, ISDE Met... ...Server. ISOplus, iteraplan, ITEX: Interactive TTC... ...AID, KangaTool Series, Kappa, Kappa-PC, LDRA ... ...er Sensitive CASE, Life Cycle Productivity Syst... ...n Assistant, liSA, LiveModel, Load Impac... ...MacDesigner, MacBubbles, Maestro, MAG... ...ench, Manager Series, Mantis, MA... ...nulink, MATRIXx/Systembuild, McDonnell... ...odelling Suite, Merge Ahead, Meta... ...s, front-end, RE/M, Meta Systems. fro... ...hods Workbench: (MWB), METR... ...ine, MKS Professional Services, MK... ...AM, MYNAH, Natural, NAVIG... ...ent, NETRON/Connect, Netvant... ...E, Object Methodology O... ...ObjectMaker 2.1: (aka Adag... ...C++, Objectworks\Sm... ...r, OMW, OOAtool, OOwin... ...ies / EVB Edition, Para... ...nal-SELECT, PesterCat, PLAT... ...ASE, PowerModel, Pow... ...Vue-ASCII, preVue-X, ProCap/P... ...al o-o programming envir... ...ent, PRO-IV Workbench: (window... ...roMod Series, Prosa, ProSys... ...omplete, QA Wizard, QAS.TCS (Te... ...ications, requirements engine... ...al Apex, Rational CRC, Rational Rob... ...nterface: (RSI), RETROFIT, RIDL*, RIPPEN, R... ...r Sybase PowerDesigner, Sapiens, Scan/COBOL, S... ...nProcess, SIMULCAST: (part of CATi tools), SmartClass, SmartCost, SmartER, SMARTS, SMARTS: (part of STW/Regression), SMF... ...SoapTest, SoDA, SoftBench, SoftBench C/C++: (part of SoftBench), SoftBench COBOL: (part of SoftBench), SoftBench Config... ...Products, Software Research, Inc.,, Software Research, Inc.,, Software Research, Inc.,, Software Research, Inc.,, Software Researc... ...earch, Inc.,, Software Research, Inc.,, Software Research, Inc.,, Software Research, Inc.,, Software Research, Inc.,, Software Resear... ...ware through Pictures, SpiraTest, SPQR/20, SQA: (part of Hindsight), SQL Software, Ltd... configuration management, SQL*Forms, ...or, SQLBench Workbench, SQL-Link-Plus, Squish, SSADM 2.1, SSADM, Westmount I-CASE, SSADM4+sf, SSADM4+sf, StateMate, STA... ...Master Test & Evaluation Management System, Sterling Software., STONE, StP/Booch, StP/BPR, StP/ClassCapture, StP/IM, StP/OMT, S... ...ured Architect, (SA), Structured Architect-Integrator: (SA-I), STW/Advisor: (METRIC, STATIC, TDGEN), STW/Coverage: (TCAT, S-TCAT, T... ...EXDIFF), Super Natural, SuperCase, SuperStructure, Supra, SYLVA Series, System Architect, System Architect, System Engineer: (nee Aut... ...Coverage), TCAT-PATH: (part of STW/Coverage), TDGEN: (part of STW/Advisor), TeamNet, Teamwork, TeleUSE, TELON, Test Complete, T... ...Instruments Inc., Information Engineering, Texel-sf, Texel-sf, TGS Systems., The Developer, ToolBuilder, T-Plan Professional, Transform, TransR... ...2.1, T-SCOPE: (part of STW/Coverage), TurboCASE 3.0, UiM/X, Unirel Openlook Toolkit, VADS, Vantive Quality, VDM-SL Toolbox, VDM-to-C++ Code ... ...est, View Integration System: (VIS), ViewKit, Visible Advatage, Visible Analyst Workbench, Vision, VisionSoft DataVision, VisionSoft Suite, Visual Thought, vPerformer, vsDesigner, VSF, VSF NA Inc... business process reengineering, VSF NA Inc.. meta CASE tool, vsObject Maker, vsSQL, vTest, Ward/Mellor, Westmount I-CASE for, WebLOAD Professional, Webserver Stress Tool, Westmount I-CASE: (for Yourdon, Ward/Mellor, OMT, SSADM), Westmount Technology B.V.. full life-cycle, WITH CLASS, Wizdom Pro, XPEDITER: (part of CATi tools), XStudio, XTie-RT.

Since the whole is much much more important than the parts (Context is King™), it is important to have a cohesive and holistic Framework for all the Tools used to aid Enterprise Transformation, to ensure that the emphasis is to use these different Tools to optimise the whole of the Transformation domain rather than just the parts. To stop Enterprises optimising the parts at the expense of the whole, and to begin to allow Enterprises to optimise the whole at the possible expense of the parts.

POET provides this cohesive and holistic Framework and provides two main benefits:

♦ Firstly, and most importantly, POET provides this framework to Enterprises today - for Enterprises to be able to consider and take a holistic, strategic and joined up view of all the Tools they use for Enterprise Transformation rather than point solutions. POET is the only framework in the world that does this.

♦ Secondly, it provides a framework to Tool Vendors as a basis (a super-type if you will) to allow Tools to begin to change and align themselves with this coherent and holistic environment. This will provide another benefit to Enterprises in the future because it will allow them to see much more clearly how these Tools relate and interface to each other in clear and straight forward ways which allow the holistic adoption of them much more straightforward. Of course this is likely to take a long time because Tool vendors tend to want to argue about their differences rather than agree on areas of similarity and demarcations.

Currently, to try to understand how all these different tools are related is almost impossible. For all the tools you want to use or do use, you need to map each tool to each other tool, to try to understand how they relate.

But as tool vendors begin to use POET as the context for their tools, and map their tools to POET, it will become much much easier for Enterprises and the people who are accountable for how Transformation is effected, to be able to understand how they all relate, enabling them to make more informed decisions about who needs to use what, where, why, how and when.

> # KEYPOINT:
>
> POET provides an Ontology that you can map Transformation Tools to.

> # ADOPTION:
>
> Enterprise Architect: Map all Tools you currently use to POET, in order to be able to find your gaps and overlaps.

Questions to Ponder

- What Transformation Tools do you use?
- Are there overlaps?
- Are there gaps?
- Are there inconsistencies?
- What do you use to decide which Transformation Tools to use, where and how?
- What do you use to orchestrate the Transformation Tools you use into a holistic, coherent and cooperative whole?

Items > Tools > Coverage

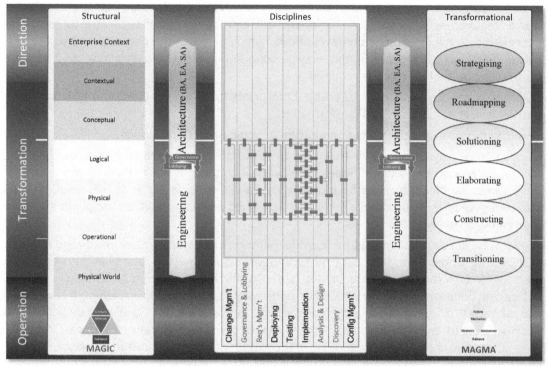

© Pragmatic 365 (2008-2021)

The use of Tools tends to grow out of the need people have to deal with the volume and complexity of the information they use to do their jobs or for people to be able to do things that they could otherwise not do. Configuration Management Tools grew out of the need to deal with the complexity and volume of the information in operations. Software Tools grew out of the complexity and volume of the information related to Software. Requirements Management Tools grew out of the complexity and volume of the information related to Requirements, etc, etc.

The Green boxes with Blue lines, indicate areas where specific tools could fit. Before we start executing projects, we are dealing with the whole Enterprise at the Contextual and Conceptual levels, and so it is logical (and possible) for us to use one tool to do so. However, as we move into project specific areas of greater detail at the Logical Physical, and Operational levels, it is more usual to use tools that are specifically designed to satisfy a particular discipline, such as Requirement Management tools, Analysis & Design tools, Testing tools, Project Management tools, Configuration Management tools, etc.

A tool could be as simple as a pen and paper but as the complexity and volume of the information rises, it is more common to use software based tools because (if used correctly, because "A fool with a tool is still a fool") they reduce the maintenance burden and can provide analysis and visualisation functions that would otherwise not be possible. The information people use to do their jobs with respect to Enterprise Transformation splits into two fundamental types, Structural information and Transformational Information as defined by MAGIC and MAGMA. In order for people performing a role at each level of the Transformation Cascade™ to be effective and efficient, they need access not only to the primary information at their level but also, in decreasing amounts, to the information at other levels.

Many Enterprises buy many tools, but these tools are usually bought as point solutions, without much consideration as to how they integrate into a whole. POET shows the scope of information that each tool requires access to, and thereby shows the large amount of overlap of information between tools. Each tool must not only be able to deal with the information that is required as an output for that phase, but each tool must also be able to relate that information to information at the level above (which provides the context) and to the level below (for impact analysis). In this way a coherent approach to selecting an integrated transformation tool portfolio is required.

POET provides the framework to enable Enterprises to take a coherent and holistic view of the Tools used for Enterprise Transformation.

This may in fact, require the sub-optimisation of some or all of the tools!

A logical view may be to use one tool for the Enterprise Architecture Model and one Tool for the Enterprise Engineering Model. However, since there is (by definition) more detail in the Engineering Model it might be more logical to use multiple Tools at that level. It would also be logical to think that those tools may be aligned more around the Disciplines and Roles used rather than levels themselves.

While these lines may be moved for individual Enterprises based on their needs and maturity, it should be noted that what is of more importance is how the interfaces between these tools work as shown by the red boxes. It is critically important that all the tools used for Enterprise Transformation work together cohesively as a whole. No information is an island, and although different roles may concentrate on working on one particular type of information and use one particular tool, what is crucially important (because Context is King™) is that people can see their information of interest, in the context of other information.

> ## KEYPOINT:
>
> Use POET to plan how all the tools you use, integrate and work together.

> ## ADOPTION:
>
> Enterprise Architect: Make sure the tools used within your Transformation capability are integrated.

Questions to Ponder

- Do the Tools your Enterprise uses for Transformation, fit together and integrate properly?
- If not, what problems does this create?
- What impact do those problems have, and how can you solve those problems?
- Which tools do you currently use?
- What domains (Structural/Transformational) do they cover?
- What disciplines utilise them?
- Are they adequate?

Items > Tools > Integration

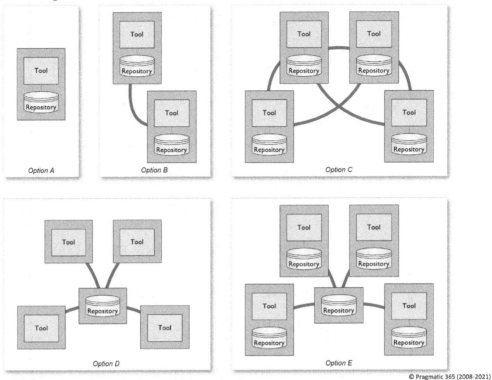

© Pragmatic 365 (2008-2021)

Each physical Tool tends to consist of two parts:

♦ A Repository that stores the information.
♦ A Tool which allows a user and other tools to manipulate that repository.

However many tools an Enterprise uses, an overriding principle should be born in mind, which is that people working within each phase need access to information not only in the level associated with that phase, but also with the information in the levels preceding and following phases. Integration of tools is therefore key - not only within a phase but also across phases.

To enable this (and to minimise integration overheads and associated synchronisation problems) it is usually advisable to minimise the number of physical tools used in any one domain (Option A), however, the number of physical tools that an Enterprise decides to buy is a personal choice and based on many things, not least the tools they already have and the tools available in the market.

If two tools are used (Option B) the integration is probably manageable, however more than two tools (Option C) can cause an integration and maintenance nightmare.

If more that 2 tools are utilised a possible solution would be for multiple tools to all sit upon and integrate with one common repository (Option D), or if that is not possible for multiple tools with their own repositories to integrate with one master repository (Option E).

Options D and E would also be beneficial for integrating all tools in the entire Transformation domain, however, these options are only possible if the Tool Vendors had had the foresight to think of them and had made the necessary investment to provide that functionality to do so - particularly for plate D.

The problem of these "interfaces" are largely of a technical nature because tool vendors need to come together to agree on a method of allowing their tools to interact. Open Service for

Lifecycle Collaboration (OSLC) is an open community trying to define a set of specifications that enable integration of Transformation tools. Its initial focus is around software development but the specifications should be (fingers crossed!) equally applicable to any set of tools that need to work together cooperatively. Their primary intention is a simple one - to make life easier for tools users and tools vendors, by making it easier for tools to work together. www.open-services.net

> ## KEYPOINT:
>
> All Transformation Tools need to be integrated to work together.

> ## ADOPTION:
>
> Enterprise Architect: Minimise the number of Tool interfaces.

Questions to Ponder

- Which of your Transformation tools exchange or reference data used in other tools?
- Which Option (A-E) best describes your approach to the integration of tools?
- How is data in different tools kept synchronised?
- How can data in one tool be related to information in another tool
- Are there any issues or problems?
- What will you do to alleviate or solve them?
- Do you have a coherent and holistic strategy for which tools you use where and for what purpose?

Culture

> # KEYPOINT:
>
> The Culture section of POET defines the roles and the culture required.

> # ADOPTION:
>
> C-Suite: Instigate a review of the Culture at play in the Enterprise's Transformation Capability, to determine if it's maturity is appropriate.

Questions to Ponder

- With respect to your Enterprises Transformation capability, what Culture exists?
- Is the Culture documented? Understood?
- Is it fit for purpose?
- Are they used? All the time? Only when it suits?
- What parts are Good? Why? Bad? Why?

Culture > Organisation Structure > Management

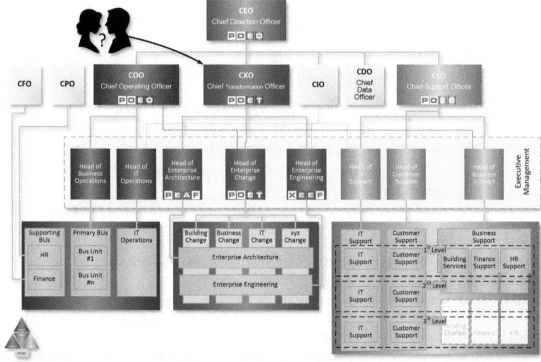

© Pragmatic 365 (2008-2021)

Here we suggest the Executive Structure required for an Enterprise based on DOTS.

The COO would have the Head of Business Operations and the Head of IT Operations reporting to them. To the COO, it doesn't matter if the business is being executed by a person or a machine. He is accountable for the execution of Operations, but also for the improvement to Operations. All of Operations.

Just as there is a COO (because the Operation part of the Enterprise is critical to its success), in the 21st century the same is true for the Chief Transformation Officer (CXO). There needs to be someone, at board/CxO level who is accountable for this strategically important part of the Enterprise, and to bang the boardroom table for resources to improve it. As well as the Head of Change, the CXO also has the key reports of the Transformation domain reporting to him – the Head of Enterprise Architecture and the Head of Enterprise Engineering.

The COO would have dotted line responsibility for the Head of Business Change.

The CSO would have the Heads of Business Support IT Support and Customer Support reporting to them. All support, regardless of the area will be initially handled by the same first line support and ticket issuing and managing system.

The COO would have dotted line responsibility for the Head of Enterprise Change.

The CFO and other CxO roles would be as normal with the continued representation of the CIO/CTO/IT Director role, although that role would have overseeing and dotted line responsibility to the Head of IT Operations, the Head of IT Change and the Head of IT Support.

In most Enterprises, the CXO role does not exist. This is the fundamental change that POET advocates for. Assuming the C-Suite has decided that a CXO is required, the obvious next question is "who will lead that domain?". Two possibilities exist, to either recruit from inside the Enterprise or from outside the Enterprise. In terms of outside the Enterprise, this may prove impossible or extremely difficult. When POET was first launched this role did not exist. Even today it is not in widespread use and its growth has not been steep. Where it does exist, it tends to be more of a carrot and tick role to drive Transformation forward (against any dissent) rather than a role that is accountable for improving the domain as well.

However, as time has gone on, more and more "experts" are beginning to tout this important role. For example, an article in Raconteur states:

> **"Chief transformation officer: revolutionary or functionary?**
> Some are visionaries, others project managers, the newest role in the C-suite is all about change…. it's not a job title that's been around for very long, emerging over the past decade or so as organisations realise the need to be more responsive to change"
>
> *- Raconteur (July 2018)*
> *https://bit.ly/2EGfCVk*

I would hope that they were inspired by POET – that has been around for, surprise surprise, since 2008!

If external recruitment is not an option, the alternative is internal recruitment which may turn out to be the most **Pragmatic** approach. So, if you were to appoint the role to an existing employee, who would that be?

You would probably want to choose someone who already spends an appreciable amount of time involved in Enterprise Transformation at a senior level, and since a large part of Transformation happening within Enterprises today is IT related it might seem reasonable to ask the CIO to expand his remit from just dealing with IT Transformation to dealing with Transformation as a whole. To be accountable for the Entire Transformation domain - Transforming the MAGIC used for Transformation not just its IT (which is a sub part of the Technology domain, which is a sub part of the Items domain, which is a sub part of the Enterprise Transformation domain).

The other important adjustment is to make this person accountable not only for the running of Transformation but for its improvement. This is a very very important point. Most CIO's today do not have that remit in their current role (or if they do, are rarely provided with the resources to do so) and therefore the move from CIO to CXO is not only a change from an IT focus to a Transformation focus (where IT is just one part), but also a change from one that is only accountable for running Transformation to one that also includes its improvement - The Transformation of Transformation. This will require the CXO to relinquish accountability for IT Operations and IT Support to the COO and CSO.

The COO has someone he can call on who is accountable for transforming Operations - the CXO, but the CXO has no one to call on who is accountable for transforming Transformation except himself, and he can only do that if he is given an explicit remit and mandate from the CEO to do so.

NOTE: It is not anticipated than an Enterprise would implement this, as-is. It is provided more as a suggestion to how an Enterprise may begin to organise itself differently in response to the strategic drivers of the 21st Century, namely Transformation and Support.

It is also important to consider the CDO role.

Some people refer to this as the Chief Digital Officer. **Pragmatic** refers to it as the Chief Data Officer. But Kevin, isn't that the CIO (Chief Information Officer) role? Errrrr! Maybe! Probably! Perhaps!!!

Here we are again. Because of IT's immaturity, even C level positions are confusing and contradictory from Enterprise to Enterprise.

So why don't we just use the CIO title, since Information ~ Data (We are not going to get intro some esoteric and academic conversation about data vs information vs knowledge). The problem with using the CIO title for someone to be accountable and an expert in Information/Data, is that most CIOs in the world are actually Technology focussed not Information focussed. Worse, a great proportion of those are actually Infrastructure Technology focussed.

The only thing that is clear, is that it's a mess! **Pragmatic**'s suggestion is to use the following

- ◆ CIO – Chief IT Officer
- ◆ CDO – Chief Data Officer

In the center at the bottom, we can see the high level department structure for the Transformation domain and the reporting structure. It illustrates the cross fertilisation and the dependencies of these departments.

Further depth of the Operations and Support areas is outside the scope of POET and handled in more detail in POEO and POES, however, for completeness we present their fundamental department structures here also.

> # KEYPOINT:
>
> Someone should be Accountable for the strategically important Transformation capability of the Enterprise.

> # ADOPTION:
>
> C-Suite: Appoint a Chief Transformation Officer (CXO).

Questions to Ponder

- ◆ Do you have a CXO?
- ◆ Who in your Enterprise will bang the boardroom table to resources to improve how Transformation is effected?
- ◆ Who in your Enterprise would be best placed to move into that role?
- ◆ Are Transformation and Support represented at the CxO level in your Enterprise?
- ◆ If not, does this cause any problems?
- ◆ What are the impact of these problems?
- ◆ What needs to happen to alleviate these problems?

Culture

Culture > Organisation Structure > Workers

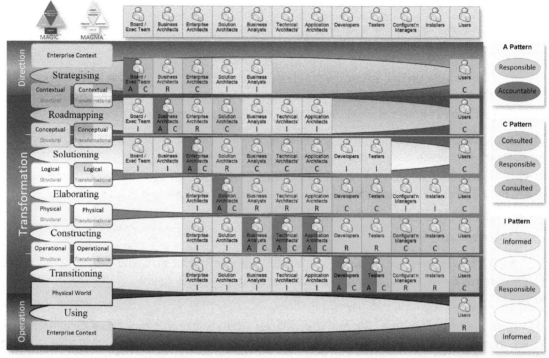

© Pragmatic 365 (2008-2021)

This view shows how the various roles of Transformation map to the different phases of Transformation. The roles shown here may differ from the names used in your Enterprise. These are not hard and fast divisions of labour but will allow us to illustrate how the simple patterns tabled here, when repeated at each level, allow the whole to work together coherently.

RACI is used here as a method of representing who is:

♦ **R**esponsible – The people who actually do the work required.

♦ **A**ccountable – The people who make sure the work is carried out correctly,

♦ **C**onsulted – The people who are consulted and can contribute while the work is being performed.

♦ **I**nformed. – The people who are informed about the work being performed as it progresses.

This does not mean that one person cannot work at more than one level. If a person does work at more than one level, that person is performing two roles, but can only wear one hat at a time.

There are three patterns here that make the whole cohesive, and each pattern guides what the A, C and I roles should be, based on the R role. As we shall see, these patterns allow use to make sure we have the right roles, doing the right things, at the right time.

First, we choose which roles are primarily Responsible for the work in each phase, and show them on the diagram in green. We now wish to add to the diagram the roles that will be Accountable and when.

To do this, we use:

- ♦ **The A Pattern** - If a role is Responsible for one phase, that role should be Accountable for the phase below.

And so we show them on the diagram in Red.

Next, we need to decide which roles will be Consulted and when.

To do this, we use:

- ♦ **The C Pattern** - If a role is Responsible for one phase, that role should be Consulted about the work happening, 1 phase above and 1 phase below.

And so we show them on the diagram in Blue. Note that Red Accountable roles are now a mixture of Accountable and Consulted (which makes perfect sense).

You will also see that we have added extra Blue Consulted roles to the User (customer), as the Users/Customer role is a special roles that needs to be consulted at all stages.

Finally, we need to decide which roles will be Informed and when.

To do this we use:

- ♦ **The I Pattern** - If a role is Responsible for one phase, that role should be Informed about the work happening 2 phases above and 2 phases below.

And so we show them on the diagram in Grey.

Towards the bottom of the diagram you will see we have added some more Grey Informed roles, as the Enterprise Architect and Solution Architect roles are special roles, that need to be kept aware of the completion and rollout of projects.

> # KEYPOINT:
>
> The Pragmatic Role and Phase patterns are key to assigning RACI to roles.

> # ADOPTION:
>
> Management: Apply the Role and Phase patterns when assigning RACI to Transformation roles.

Questions to Ponder

- ◆ Does your Enterprise have a pattern for Accountability and Responsibility, that enables the whole of the Transformation cascade to work together coherently?
- ◆ Does your Enterprise have a pattern for Consulting and Informing people, that enables the whole of the Transformation cascade to work together coherently?
- ◆ What would the diagram look like if you overlaid the people and roles that your Enterprise defines along with their RACI mappings?

© Pragmatic 365 (2008-2021)

The biggest enemy (or ally) of Enterprise Transformation, is Culture.

Do not underestimate the power of culture.

Do not underestimate the power of culture.

Let me just say that one more time.

Culture

Do not under- estimate the power of culture.

Culture Trumps Everything™ is much more than just a saying. It is a very cold hard fact, which if literally has the power to move mountains, or destroy Enterprises.

Bad culture trumps everything. Physics. Truth. Best Practice. Good Intentions. Good Ideas. Passion. Creativity. Teamwork. Trust. Common Sense. etc. It will take you good ideas, chew them up, spit them out, and then vilify you for having them in the first place. It takes passionate people and grinds them down until they can't remember why they were passionate about something in the first place. It destroys people's self-esteem. and like a cancer, eats away at the very core of an Enterprise.

You can have as many fantastic Methods as you like, define as many perfect Artefacts as you like and change the Items to use the most advanced technology and tools, but like a cork bobbing in the sea, they are utterly insignificant compared to the churning seas of bad Culture. Even when the sea appears calm there can be dangerous undercurrents and hidden dangers that can sink the unsinkable (as I have found from personal experience over 40 years of professional life). All Enterprises have to navigate the icebergs of culture, but many of them do not realise that they can only see 10% of the iceberg, or is it perhaps, that many of them do not want to see the iceberg, preferring to deal with the obvious 10% and ignore the hidden and cynical 90%.

Perhaps we should also introduce the term politics. Politics on the face of it should be a force for good – our countries are run by politicians after all - however, within an Enterprise, politics normally equates to a force for bad. Bad decisions are made because of politics. The more politics exists, the more bad decisions are made.

On the other hand, good culture also trumps everything. Incoherence. Lies. Worst Practice. Bad Intentions. Bad Ideas. Apathy. Stagnation. Loose Cannons. Distrust. Stupidity. etc. It enables and empowers people to achieve and be the best they can be. It can allow people, and therefore the Enterprise, to grow and blossom and to improve the products and services they provide and the lives of their Customers beyond recognition.

You can have as many bad Methods as you like, use as many awful Artefacts as you like and use the most basic of tools, but like a cork bobbing in the sea, they are utterly insignificant compared to the churning seas of good Culture.

KEYPOINT:

"Culture Trumps Everything"

-Kevin Smith

ADOPTION:

C-Suite: Instigate a review of the

Culture of Transformation.

Otherwise everything else is largely

pointless.

Questions to Ponder

- ♦ Does Culture trump things in your Enterprise?
- ♦ Is it a power for good or ill?
- ♦ What would you change about your Enterprises Culture?
- ♦ Who is Accountable for the Culture in your Enterprise?

Culture

$$\text{E} = \text{mc}^2$$

Enterprise Effectiveness & Efficiency = **Methods** * **Culture^2**

© Pragmatic 365 (2008-2021)

Einstein's famous mass-energy equivalence formula is possibly the most well-known formula of all time. It states that mass and energy are equivalent (mass and energy are never created or destroyed, they just change states), and the relationship is governed by a constant - the speed of light - squared.

Although the full implications of E=mc^2 don't apply to Enterprises (i.e. an Enterprise's Effectiveness and Efficiency cannot be transformed into methods, and the relationship between the two is not governed by the speed of light) it does serve as a useful way to express that an Enterprise's Effectiveness and Efficiency, while largely governed by its Methods (how it does what it does) is governed much much more by its culture - squared.

KEYPOINT:

"Culture is like the speed of light.

Very difficult to change."

- Kevin Lee Smith

ADOPTION:

C-Suite: Accept that Culture change

has much more impact than changing

anything else

Questions to Ponder

- ♦ Is your Enterprise as unsinkable as the Titanic?
- ♦ Do the icebergs of culture that you can see, mask the hidden dangers of the 90% that you cannot see?
- ♦ What are you doing to make sure that the 90% of culture that you cannot see, will not sink your Enterprise?

Source: NASA

© Pragmatic 365 (2008-2021)

Never underestimate the kind of things that a bad culture can create.

You may think there is a limit to bad culture - a point at which when the potential effects could be so catastrophic that people would pull back, but the space shuttle Challenger disaster of January 28, 1986 proves to us that the lives of seven people were naught compared with the power of culture.

The disaster resulted in a 32-month suspension in the shuttle program and the formation of the Rogers Commission, a special commission appointed by Ronald Reagan to investigate the accident. The Rogers Commission found NASA's organizational culture and decision-making processes had been key contributing factors to the accident. NASA managers had known contractor Morton Thiokol's design of the SRBs (Solid Rocket Boosters) contained a potentially catastrophic flaw in the O-rings (gas tight rubber seals between the sections of the SRBs) since 1977, but failed to address it properly. They also disregarded warnings from engineers about the dangers of launching posed by the low temperatures of that morning and had failed in adequately reporting these technical concerns to their superiors.

It is also pertinent and ironic to mention that cultural problems also surrounded the Rogers Commission itself, particularly the role of theoretical physicist Richard Feynman. His direct and apolitical style of investigating rather than following the commission schedule put him at odds with Rogers, who once commented, "Feynman is becoming a real pain".

But, even though there was an appalling disaster caused by problems deeply rooted in culture, at least the Rogers Commission and their report and recommendations would correct these failings and at last the power of culture to do massive harm would be curtailed...

Well, the power of culture is so powerful that even that was not the limit...

After another Space Shuttle disaster (Columbia in 2003), attention once again focused on the attitude of NASA management towards safety issues. The Columbia Accident Investigation

Board (CAIB) concluded that NASA had failed to learn many of the lessons of Challenger. In particular, the agency had not set up a truly independent office for safety oversight; the CAIB felt that in this area, "NASA's response to the Rogers Commission did not meet the Commission's intent". The CAIB believed that "the causes of the institutional failure responsible for Challenger have not been fixed," saying that the same "flawed decision making process" that had resulted in the Challenger accident was responsible for Columbia's destruction seventeen years later.

It is pertinent to consider how ignorance is interpreted differently in the law and in business.

In the law - "Ignorance is no defence" but in business Ignorance is the "perfect defence". You can see it used on a daily basis especially for those senior people whose job it is to be accountable, claiming ignorance of knowing the bad things "workers" had been doing and promising that they will be punished. But these are not bad people.

There are no bad people, only bad environments.

Culture is the most important environment of them all and it is Management that is responsible for setting it. Good or Bad.

KEYPOINT:

Bad Culture knows no bounds.

It can destroy lives.

And Enterprises.

ADOPTION:

C-Suite: Do not underestimate the

effects of bad culture.

Questions to Ponder

- What are the biggest "disasters" your Enterprise has faced?
- Did Culture play a part, and if so, what part?
- Were lessons learned or not?
- What are the top five Cultural problems facing your Enterprise?
- What would your Enterprise look and feel like if those problems were solved?
- What does your Enterprise do to improve Culture?
- Are they succeeding? Are they doing enough?

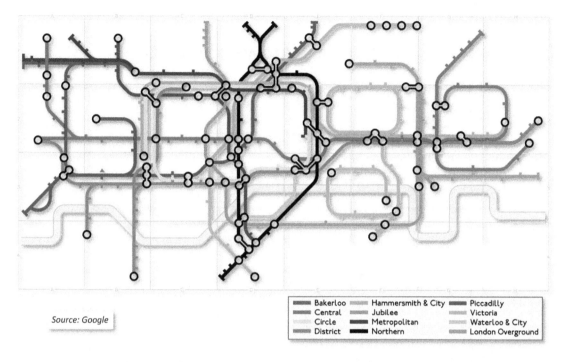

Bakerloo	Hammersmith & City	Piccadilly
Central	Jubilee	Victoria
Circle	Metropolitan	Waterloo & City
District	Northern	London Overground

Source: Google

© Pragmatic 365 (2008-2021)

Never underestimate the kind of things that a good culture can create.

A small change in culture (while perhaps more difficult to achieve) can produce literally incalculable positive benefits. Culture is what delivers a Strategy, or Culture is what destroys a Strategy. Depending on the culture, it's either the oxygen of an Enterprise's success, or the cancer of Enterprise's destruction. We can define as many processes and products as we like but it's culture that will make or break them.

Do not underestimate the kind of things that a good culture can create.

You may think there is a limit to good culture - a point at which when the potential effects could be so fantastic that people would pull back, Google proves to us that there is potentially no limit to what opportunities good culture can generate. Opportunities for the Enterprise as a whole but also opportunities for the people that work at them.

While **How** an Enterprise effects the whole of Transformation is becoming a Strategic Strength or a Strategic Weakness, where massive business opportunities can be gained or massive business problems will result, the same is true of culture. An Enterprises Culture is becoming (has become?) a Strategic Strength or a Strategic Weakness, where massive business opportunities can be gained or massive business problems will result.

Culture

KEYPOINT:

Good Culture knows no bounds.

It can lift lives.

And Enterprises.

ADOPTION:

C-Suite: Do not underestimate the

effects of good culture.

Questions to Ponder

- Do you think a change in Culture could produce large positive results?
- Could your Enterprise be more successful if Culture was changed?
- What changes would be necessary? How would they be carried out?
- Who is Accountable?

I think, therefore I might be...

We are all humans and in that respect we are all the same. Of course there are many differences between us but some things are fundamental and affect all of us. We love to think that we are intelligent. We are masters of the universe. We have created great art, we have created spectacles of construction, we have created electronic devices of amazing complexity and we have gone to the moon and back. Religion, philosophy etc, etc. We think we know a lot of stuff. And while our brains, can do some pretty amazing things, like anything else, like any tool, it has its weaknesses. Being human means we don't like to think about those weaknesses in our own brains. We (or rather our brains) prefer to ignore those weaknesses and instead concentrate on feeling smug!

Psychology tells us different. Psychology allows us to expose and understand these weaknesses, for until we expose and understand those weaknesses we will forever be ruled by them.

> "To err is human; to forgive, divine."
>
> *- Alexander Pope*

Understanding and then accepting that we are a flawed species in our thinking and in our perceptions allows us to do something about those things. Those things are problems and the first step in solving any problem is to admit that it exists.

Before an alcoholic can be "saved" they must first take the most important first step and admit they are an alcoholic.

We must accept that we will make mistakes. Many many mistakes. All of us. The number of mistakes people make is not proportional to a person's standing or seniority within an Enterprise. The CEO is liable to make the same number of mistakes as the person who cleans the toilets. What is proportional is the amount of damage that a mistake that goes uncorrected can have (in general). We must therefore accept that mistakes will happen and create an environment that allows us **all** to expose and correct those mistakes without resorting to blame. The people in your Enterprise that make mistakes and correct them (including you) are your best employees. Those that make mistakes and hide them can destroy your Enterprise. "Backtracking" or performing a "U-turn" should not be met with scorn, vilification and condemnation but instead with thanks and praise.

Those that do not make mistakes are lying.

> ## KEYPOINT:
>
> The human brain is easily fooled.

> ## ADOPTION:
>
> C-Suite: Accept that we all have
>
> mental health issues. (That are largely
>
> not under our control!)

Questions to Ponder

- Do you think Psychology is important and Why?
- Do you think you make mistakes?
- What do you do when you make small mistakes?
- What do you do when you make big mistakes?
- What do others in your Enterprise do when they make small or big mistakes?
- Are people allowed to make mistakes?
- What happens to people who expose small mistakes?
- What happens to people who expose big mistakes?
- What happens to people who hide mistakes?

Source: Washington Post

Violinist in the Metro Station

Can you see the value when there is no price tag? In 2007 world famous violinist Joshua Bell posed as a street musician in a Washington D.C. metro station to see how many people would stop and listen. Despite the fact that he was playing a $3.5 million handcrafted violin and had just sold out a concert in Boston where ticket prices averaged $100 each, very few people stopped to appreciate his beautiful performance. He made a measly $32 that day.

Sometimes the value of something is not seen until you see it in the right context.

Seeing the value in something is not necessarily as easy as "If I spend $1,000 today I will make $10,000 tomorrow". Sometimes the most valuable things crop up in unexpected places and at unexpected times. Sometimes the most important and valuable things are not dressed in $2,000 suits from Saville Row. We need to be more open to spending the time to see the value in things that we may currently think have no value at all.

> ## KEYPOINT:
>
> True value is not measured by the numbers of Clicks or Likes.

> ## ADOPTION:
>
> C-Suite: Mandate that people Invest time to see the true value of things.

Questions to Ponder

- Do people in your Enterprise know "the cost of everything and value of nothing"?
- Do people in your Enterprise only see obvious value and miss hidden value?
- Can you think of examples where this has happened in the past?
- Who were they? What was the impact? Why do you think they acted in this way?
- What needs to change to reduce the likelihood of it happening in the future?
- Who needs to drive that change?

Culture

Source: Yale University

The Milgram Experiment

Humans are trained to take direction from authority figures from very early in life. An infamous experiment conducted in 1961 by Yale University psychologist Stanley Milgram, measured this willingness to obey authority figures by instructing people to perform acts that conflicted with their morals. Participants were told to play the role of "teacher" and administer electric shocks to "the learner," who was supposedly in a different room, every time they answered a question incorrectly. In reality, no one was actually being shocked. Instead, Milgram played recordings to make it sound like the learner was in a great deal of pain and wanted to end the experiment. Despite these protests, many participants continued the experiment when the authority figure urged them to, increasing the voltage after each wrong answer until some eventually administered what would be lethal electric shocks.

Authority figures are, of course, required. But to follow them blindly or to expect people to follow you blindly is deeply damaging. Of course, in general, people in authority do not knowingly ask people to do things which are damaging. We are not suggesting that people in authority knowingly tell people to do damaging things. However, this experiment shows us that people being told what to do may know something is damaging but they will continue to do it if an authority figure tells them to. It also show that the level of "authority" needs not be holding a gun to someone's head. Wearing a white coat and telling people "you must continue with the experiment" was all that was required to make most of these people electrocute other people until they were "unconscious" or possibly "dead".

Never underestimate the capacity of people to do things that they know are deeply damaging just because you are telling them to.

What is happening in many Enterprises today is akin to how the cockpits of aircraft worked many years ago. They used to be very hierarchical with the Chief Pilot almost being revered as a god who could never be questioned. Seniority was everything and seniority was always right. Co-pilots and junior officers learned pretty fast not to question the Chief Pilot because if they did, their careers would soon be damaged.

However a number of air crashes (and their subsequent investigations) highlighted the fact that this command and control approach designed to make aircraft safe was the very thing that was crashing them. And so changes were made and the term "Cockpit Resource Management" (unfortunately the acronym is CRM!) was born. CRM's main tenet is that no person, whether, Architect, Designer, Engineer, Manager, Controller or Pilot, can perform perfectly at all times. In addition, what could be considered perfect performance in one set of circumstances might well be unacceptable in another. Therefore, people need to be seen as they really are - parts of a cooperative system.

Viewing some people or some roles as intrinsically "better" or "more correct" is worse than utterly futile, it is downright dangerous, and totally contrary to achieving the ends.

What is required, is that Enterprises begin to adopt this same CRM approach to transformation. No person, whether, Architect, Designer, Engineer or Manager can perform perfectly at all times. In addition, what could be considered perfect performance in one set of circumstances might well be unacceptable in another. Therefore, people need to be seen as they really are - parts of a cooperative system.

Viewing some people or some roles as intrinsically "better" or "more correct" is worse than utterly futile, it is downright dangerous, and totally contrary to achieving the ends.

KEYPOINT:

Sometimes the best course of action

is to not do what you are being told

to do.

ADOPTION:

C-Suite: Mandate that people are

rewarded, not punished, for

respectfully questioning authority.

Questions to Ponder

♦ Do people in your Enterprise do what they are told to do, rather than or what they should do?
♦ Can you think of examples where this has happened in the past?
♦ Who were they? What was the impact? Why do you think they acted in this way?
♦ What needs to change to reduce the likelihood of it happening in the future?
♦ Who needs to drive that change?

Culture - 275

Culture > Slaves to Psychology™ > Are You Better Than a 5 Year Old?

You Decide!

The Marshmallow Test

An experiment conducted in 1972 by Walter Mischel of Stanford University sought to determine if deferred gratification can be an indicator of future success.

Children, aged four to six, were taken into a room where a marshmallow was placed on the table in front of them. Before leaving each of the children alone in the room, the examiner told them they would receive a second marshmallow if the first was still on the table after 15 minutes. One-third deferred gratification long enough to receive the second marshmallow. In follow-up studies, Mischel found that those who deferred gratification were significantly more competent and received higher SAT scores than their peers, meaning that this characteristic likely remains with a person for life.

The children that went on to be more successful were the ones that didn't eat the marshmallow. They thought ahead. Thinking ahead requires us to not think so much about now. It means we are required to look into the future. To make some decisions now that will affect the future - which is, of course, one of the things that Architects are really good at.

This is especially pertinent for Enterprises, not from the point of view of future personal success but because two thirds of children sought short term benefits over long term benefits and will likely carry that into later life, especially when in later life the motivation they receives condones the behaviour. This is a cancer that afflicts 90% of all Enterprises today. These are not bad people however. They are just the product of Psychology and the context in which they work and the way that context motivates them.

Culture

KEYPOINT:

Short term gratification (quick wins)

most often leads to long term failure.

Delaying short term gratification,

most often leads to long term

success.

ADOPTION:

C-Suite: Mandate that people favour

future benefits over short term

gratification. If you want to pick low

hanging fruit, you first have to plant a

tree.

Questions to Ponder

- Do people in your Enterprise concentrate more on short term benefit rather than long term benefit?
- Can you think of examples where this has happened in the past?
- Who were they? What was the impact? Why do you think they acted in this way?
- What needs to change to reduce the likelihood of it happening in the future?
- Who needs to drive that change?

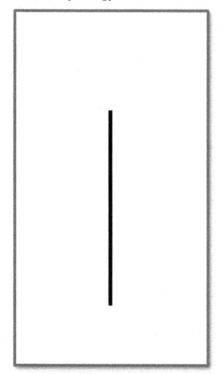
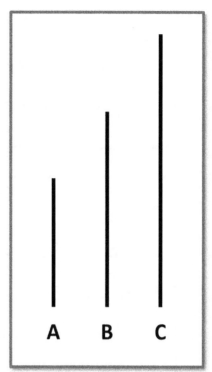

The Asch Conformity Experiment

This is a famous example of the temptation (overwhelming desire?) to conform. This series of experiments conducted in the 1950s placed one subject in a room full of actors. The person conducting the experiment held up an image with three numbered lines and asked each person in the room to identify the longest line. The actors purposely chose the incorrect line in order to determine whether the subject would answer honestly or simply go along with the group answer. The results showed that people tend to conform in group situations.

Everyone knows the tale of "The Emperor's New Clothes" by Hans Christian Andersen where it took a little child up a lamppost to point out the inconvenient truth. This can show up in Enterprises in very insidious ways. "Don't Rock the boat" or "He's a loose cannon" and similar phrases can often be used to implicitly make people conform by effectively shooting the little boy up the lamppost instead of listening to him.

Culture

> # KEYPOINT:
>
> Don't be swayed by the majority.
>
> They are wrong 80% of the time!

> # ADOPTION:
>
> C-Suite: Mandate that people are rewarded, not punished, for doing the right thing, not just because it's what everyone else does/believes.

Questions to Ponder

- Do people in your Enterprise "go with the flow" rather than speaking out?
- Do people in your Enterprise thank the "little child" or vilify him?
- Can you think of examples where this has happened in the past?
- Who were they? What was the impact? Why do you think they acted in this way?
- What needs to change to reduce the likelihood of it happening in the future?
- Who needs to drive that change?

Culture

Source: Stanford University

© Pragmatic 365 (2008-2021)

The Stanford Prison Experiment

This infamous experiment studied the psychological effects a prison setting could have on behaviour. In 1971, a mock prison was constructed in the basement of the psychology building of Stanford University and 24 male students were randomly selected to play the role of either a prisoner or prison guard for two weeks. The students adapted to their roles a little too well, becoming aggressive to the point of inflicting psychological torture. Even psychology professor Philip Zimbardo, who acted as superintendent of the experiment, proved susceptible to its effects by allowing the abuse to continue. The study was called off after only six days due to its intensity, but it proved that situations could provoke certain behaviours, in spite of an individual's natural tendencies.

Bullying

Although outlawed in every Enterprise, bullying is still rife within Enterprises worldwide.

Bullying in this context relates to the abuse of power over rational thinking.

It is also related to forcing people to do things or work in ways that they know to be wrong or inefficient. This usually goes hand in hand with blaming the same individuals for the problems that arise.

Hiding Information / Problems

This behaviour usually occurs at management levels and prevents bad news from being transported up the food chain.

It is usually the troops on the ground that can sense things going wrong first. This is usually the first sign that a project is going wrong in some way. What can happen is that these messages can get diluted the further up the food chain they go and sometimes don't make the leap at all.

Culture

Management can feel threatened as they may not understand what the troops are telling them. Management can also feel that reporting bad news to their superiors will reflect badly on them as they are ultimately Accountable for the work carried out by the people who report to them. Having started to hide or not communicate things, it can be difficult if not impossible to then begin reporting as things get progressively worse for fear of being asked "Why didn't you report this three months ago when it first started going wrong?" a phrase that I am sure many of us have heard over the years.

> "The physics definition of power is 'The ability to do work'; many social definitions of power are more like 'The ability to **avoid** work'. Therein lie **many** practical problems…"
>
> *- Tom Graves*

> ## KEYPOINT:
>
> "I hope our wisdom will grow with our power, and teach us, that the less we use our power the greater it will be."
>
> - Thomas Jefferson.

> ## ADOPTION:
>
> C-Suite: Mandate that people accept that power is the ability to do work, not the ability to avoid it!

Questions to Ponder

- Do people in your Enterprise abuse power?
- Can you think of examples where this has happened in the past?
- Who were they? What was the impact? Why do you think they acted in this way?
- What needs to change to reduce the likelihood of it happening in the future?
- Who needs to drive that change?

"Never Judge a book by its cover" is a common saying. However, humans find doing that extremely difficult. We also know the saying "First impressions count", You could say the first saying is an expression of intent, while the second is an expression of reality.

Style over substance is the idea that, far from "never Judging a book by its cover", we do generally judge a lot about a book by its cover, and first impressions are indeed extremely important. As we move past first impressions, we move into the area of Style over substance where we tend to be much more impressed by how someone says something rather than what they are saying. This Style over Substance effect can also be applied to things and is heavily used in the presentation of products as well as people, using a lot of style to either detract from or cover up the substance.

A good example is Elizabeth Holmes, who burst onto the stage in 2004. Her company, Theranos, was working to develop a blood test using only a small amount of blood, which could be run in a matter of minutes rather than hours or days. By 2004 she had managed to raise six million dollars She often tried to emulate Steve Jobs, dressing in black turtleneck sweaters and speaking in a strange deep baritone voice, that sometimes slipped towards the end of interviews as she forgot and ended up talking in a normal higher pitched woman's voice. But her claims were all a sham and in June 2018, was indicted on nine counts of wire fraud and two counts of conspiracy to commit wire fraud. Prosecutors allege that she engaged in two criminal schemes, one to defraud investors, the other to defraud doctors and patients.

Style over substance favours how things look and a general feeling of happiness over anything else. It is synonymous with the outside world where celebrity and presentation has grown to outshine any fundamental value. The whole world seems consumed with how things look.

"It's not what you say but how you say it"

This trait generally means that no one wants to rock the boat and differences of opinions and confrontations are to be avoided at all costs - regardless of the detriment to the Enterprise.

If people are mediocre, ineffective or inefficient at their jobs, then this tends to be tolerated so long as they are always happy and get on with people, smile a lot and are the "life and soul of the party" (of course there are limits but the general point stands) but if someone points this out (and by doing so annoys them) then this is not tolerated.

KEYPOINT:

"Nobody cares how much you know, until they know how much you care".

- Theodore Roosevelt

ADOPTION:

C-Suite: Mandate that people favour Substance over Style, rather than Style over Substance.

Questions to Ponder

- Do people in your Enterprise favour style over substance?
- Can you think of examples where this has happened in the past?
- Who were they? What was the impact? Why do you think they acted in this way?
- What needs to change to reduce the likelihood of it happening in the future?
- Who needs to drive that change?

The Halo Effect

The Horn Effect

© Pragmatic 365 (2008-2021)

The Halo Effect is the idea that our overall impression of a person can be based on one trait about them. However, For example, if someone has a likeable personality, people might find that person's other qualities more appealing. People may listen to them more intently, assume they are correct in what they say, allow them the benefit of the doubt, etc.

In a recent experiment, a man made two videos for a dating website. In the first video, he read the script in an upbeat manner, whereas in the second, he read the same script in a more melancholy fashion. The first video was given to a one group of girls and the second was given to another group, who watched the video in a separate room. The girls who watched the upbeat video found the man to be likeable, while the girls who watched the second video found the man to be unpleasant, even though he had read the exact same script. This can have devastating results.

For those who do not know, the picture on the left is of Jimmy Saville, who was a popular and prolific entertainer on radio and TV, in the UK, in the 60s and 70s. He also did a massive amount of fund raising, sponsorship and voluntary work. Because of his halo, people did not speak out when they had problems or worries or issues regarding him. Shortly after he died in 2011, it was discovered (or rather what was already known, was allowed to be spoken about because the halo did not protect him anymore) that he was in fact a prolific child sexual abuser. By the end of 2012, 14 police forces across the UK, were pursuing 400 lines of inquiry based on testimony from 200 witnesses. In March 2013 Her Majesty's Inspectorate of Constabulary reported that 214 of the complaints that had been made against Savile after his death would have been criminal offences if they had been reported at the time.

However, the corollary is also true, and is known as the Horn effect. If we have a negative view of someone, we are less likely to listen to them or entertain their views. We may dismiss anything they have to say as being negative and not worthy of even the time to listen to them. This can have devastating results.

For those who do not know, the picture on the right is of Stephen Christopher Yaxley-Lennon (more commonly known as Tommy Robinson) who is a person that has been vilified and character assassinated by the British News Media and Television for many years. He is always introduced by the media as "The Far Right Extremist and former leader of the EDL, Tommy Robins" instead of "Mr, Tommy Robinson". He earned this moniker because in 2009 he started an organisation called the English Defence League (EDL) after he had read a newspaper article about local Islamists attempting to recruit men outside a bakery in Luton to fight for the Taliban in Afghanistan. Unfortunately, the (real) far right infiltrated the EDL and turned it into a racist organisation. Because of this, he left it and cut off all ties to it in 2013, but note that despite this, he is still introduced as "The former leader of the EDL". It's interesting how the media cling on to that association even though he disassociated himself from them many years ago. The horns that were given to him from 2009 have continued to be attached even though he clearly states he is not racist (because Islam is not a race, it is a religion) but he believes there are teachings in Islam that are counter to English life, citing such things as death for homosexuals and apostates, and the suppression of women in society.

> ## KEYPOINT:
>
> "It's hard to see a halo when you're looking for horns."
>
> - Cullen Hightower

> ## ADOPTION:
>
> C-Suite: Initiate a review of people who have been given Halos or Horns.

Questions to Ponder

- Do people in your Enterprise wear halos?
- Who were they? What was the impact?
- What needs to change to reduce the likelihood of it happening in the future?
- Do people in your Enterprise wear horns?
- Who were they? What was the impact?
- What needs to change to reduce the likelihood of it happening in the future?
- Who needs to drive these changes?

Culture

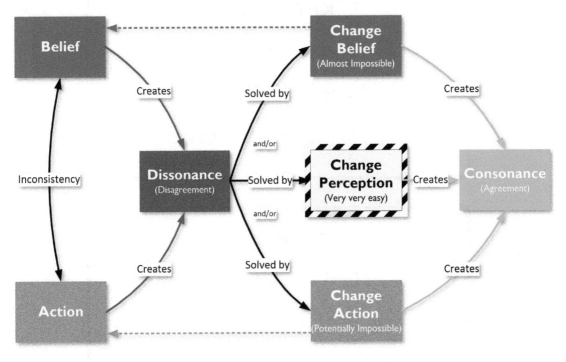

© Pragmatic 365 (2008-2021)

Cognitive dissonance theory is based on three fundamental assumptions:

♦ Humans are sensitive to inconsistencies between actions and beliefs.
♦ Recognition of this inconsistency will cause dissonance, and will motivate an individual to resolve the dissonance.
♦ Dissonance will be resolved in one of three basic ways:

	Belief	Action	Perception
1	Change	Preserve	Preserve
2	Preserve	Change	Preserve
3	Preserve	Preserve	Change

Changing ones beliefs is very hard and this very rarely happens. Changing one's actions is generally not possible - only future actions can be changed and therefore while discussions and arguments about whether the action was right or wrong can occur they are largely immaterial. Because of these two things, the dissonance (more often than not) causes the person to change their perceptions in order to justify their actions and amazingly people can change their perceptions quite easily - by lying to ourselves. Convincingly.

It's mankind's greatest achievement!

Changing one's perceptions changes the way you view/remember/perceive your action - in other words you "rationalize" your actions. For example, you might decide that the test you cheated on was for a dumb class that you didn't need anyway. Or you may say to yourself that everyone cheats so why not you. In other words, you think about your action in a different manner or context so that it no longer appears to be inconsistent with your beliefs.

In relation to Enterprises, it is not so much actions, but decisions - the decision is the action - and while an action that has occurred cannot be changed, a decision that has occurred can. However, as humans we are so used to changing our perceptions (lying to ourselves) that even though decisions can be changed we can easily fall into the routine of justifying our decisions instead of changing them.

For a decision to be changed, there first has to be a change in the context or implications or culture that was used to make that decision. That might mean the exposure and acceptance of new information, or the acceptance of information that did exist before but was not taken into account, or a change in culture.

It is often felt that there are two types of people; "Bad People" - those who know their decision to be "wrong" and use any means (including but limited to lying to themselves) to preserve it; and "Good People" - those who find out their decision was "wrong". But what makes a decision "wrong"? Who is to say what is "right" and what is "wrong"? This is where culture plays a massive part.

All people tend to be generally logical (not the same as moral) and really quite simple in the way they think (including me - and you!). Tell someone that acting strategically is monumentally important but reward them with money for acting tactically and guess what they are likely to do? There are no bad people. Only bad information and bad culture. Everything else is smoke and mirrors (created by bad culture!).

Cultural aspects never (explicitly) come into making decisions or evaluating why decisions were taken but it is exactly these cultural aspects that are the most powerful.

The effects of Cognitive dissonance can be many and varied and usually range from very bad to catastrophic. For example, incorrect decisions do not get corrected, people get demotivated and disengaged, etc.

Cognitive Dissonance is described as when someone holds two or more contradicting beliefs, ideas or values. Interestingly this is exactly what Architects do all the time and is probably what they are best at doing! Keeping conflicting beliefs or ideas in your head creates possibilities. In fact they hold intricate and complex networks of possibilities in their heads. When facts come to light or decisions are made some possibilities close down - this has a knock on effect that ripples through the remaining possibilities. Don't ask me how my brain does that - I have no idea - but that's probably a good thing!

> # KEYPOINT:
>
> "How often it is that the angry man rages denial, of what his inner self is telling him."
>
> - Frank Herbert (Dune)

> # ADOPTION:
>
> C-Suite: Mandate that people recognise Cognitive Dissonance, and they don't lie to themselves.

Questions to Ponder

- ◆ Do people in your Enterprise lie to themselves?
- ◆ Do you lie tro yourself? Convincingly?
- ◆ Can you think of examples where this has happened in the past?
- ◆ Who were they? What was the impact? Why do you think they acted in this way?
- ◆ What needs to change to reduce the likelihood of it happening in the future?
- ◆ Who needs to drive that change?

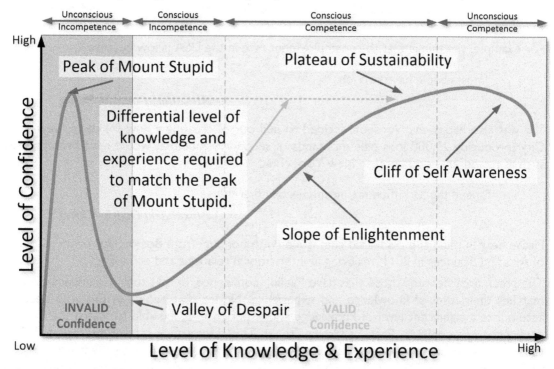

The Dunning-Kruger effect (defined by David Dunning & Justin Kruger) is a cognitive bias, where people that have a low Competence tend to have the illusion of superiority, as they do not possess the ability to assess their own ability. This means they assess their own ability as higher than it actually is. Essentially, the lack of people with low-cognitive ability, to recognise they are of low-cognitive ability - because they do not possess the cognitive ability, to assess their cognitive ability.

The less people know, the less they realise that there are things they don't know.

The more people know, the more they realise that there are things they don't know.

There is a saying:

> "If you think you understand the problem, you clearly do not understand the problem."
>
> *- Unknown*

The red area denotes those that have "Invalid" confidence. That is, their confidence largely outweighs their level of knowledge and experience. People in this area are often outspoken and passionate about what they believe, largely because they think they know everything there is to know.

Culture

A good example would be Alexandria Ocasio-Cortez, whose passion and commitment to what she says cannot be underestimated, but what she says is often confused or just plain wrong.

For example, she thinks that the unemployment rate in the USA is low because...

> "most people have two jobs."
>
> *- Alexandria Ocasio-Cortez*

She was also happy that Amazon decided to pull out of creating a new facility in New York City (producing 25,000 jobs plus thousands of secondary jobs that would have been created such as restaurants etc) because New York could...

> "spend the $3 billion tax incentives on other things."
>
> *- Alexandria Ocasio-Cortez*

Please bear in mind she graduated cum laude (with honour) from Boston University's College of Arts and Sciences in 2011, majoring in international relations and economics.

The green area denotes those that have "Valid" confidence, in that their confidence broadly matches their level of knowledge and experience. Notice that people in this area need to accumulate a significant level of knowledge and experience, to be able to match the level of confidence of people on Peak of Mount Stupid. This discrepancy can, of course, therefore cause massive problems that must be identified if they are to be dealt with effectively.

The one thing you need to be careful about is assuming that the Dunning-Kruger effect says how stupid people are. It is more about how people struggle to evaluate themselves accurately because if they are good at a task, they can see their mistakes clearly, and if they aren't good at a task, they can't see their mistakes at all. So, it is more about specific abilities than overall intelligence. {{Amber Smith}}

It should also be noted that in the original work, they noted that there was an inverse effect in the upper quadrant of those interviewed - namely, that experts who had passed the area of conscious competence and into the region you identify as the plateau of sustainability, there is often a drop in confidence as these experts tend to assess their knowledge, not against their peers, but against the knowledge they have and are aware that they don't have - often expressed as "the more I learn, the less I know" – the Cliff of Self Awareness. Thus, Dunning-Kruger also demonstrated that the more one learns, the more one becomes a master or guru - the lower they score on a self-assessment. Thus, in fact, only those in the centre - the "professional practitioners" who are consciously competent tend to be the only members who do self-assess accurately (within the usual range of error). {{Taiss Quartapa}}

> # KEYPOINT:
>
> Those who are Unconsciously Incompetent, are the one's most passionate that they are right!

> # ADOPTION:
>
> C-Suite: Mandate that passion is no substitute for evidence.

Questions to Ponder

- Do people in your Enterprise exhibit high levels of confidence, while having a low level of knowledge and/or experience?
- Can you think of examples where this has happened in the past?
- Who were they? What was the impact? Why do you think they acted in this way?
- What needs to change to reduce the likelihood of it happening in the future?
- Who needs to drive that change?

Promotions are given based on tenure or success in a previous role...

...irrespective of capacity to excel in the new position

© Pragmatic 365 (2008-2021)

The Peter Principle (developed by Laurence J Peter and published by William Morrow and Company in 1969) says that people in any hierarchy tend to rise to their "level of incompetence", because the skills required to make someone good in one job, are not necessarily the skills required for another job. For example, a good engineer would probably be a bad manager, and a good manager would probably be a bad engineer.

I had never heard the name "The Peter Principle" but very quickly after starting work in 1980, I heard a saying: "People tend to be promoted to their level of incompetence". Very soon afterwards (and throughout a professional career spanning 40 years) I have seen it happen with my own eyes.

In 2018, professors Alan Benson, Danielle Li, and Kelly Shue analyzed sales workers' performance and promotion practices at 214 American businesses to test the veracity of the Peter principle. They found that these companies tended to promote employees to management position based on their performance in their previous position, rather than based on managerial potential. Consistent with the Peter principle, the researchers found that high performing sales employees were likelier to be promoted, and that they were likelier to perform poorly as managers, leading to considerable costs to the businesses.[1]

[1] - *Benson, Alan; Li, Danielle; Shue, Kelly (February 2018). "Promotions and the Peter Principle". NBER Working Paper. 24343: 1–54. doi:10.3386/w24343. Retrieved May 22, 2018.*

Culture

KEYPOINT:

Success should not be promoted.

ADOPTION:

C-Suite: Mandate that promotions and recruitment should be based on the ability to do the promoted job, not on the success in a previous job.

Questions to Ponder

- ♦ Do people in your Enterprise promote based on success in a previous role, or the capacity to excel in the new role?
- ♦ Can you think of examples where this has happened in the past?
- ♦ Who were they? What was the impact? Why do you think they acted in this way?
- ♦ What needs to change to reduce the likelihood of it happening in the future?
- ♦ Who needs to drive that change?

Culture

© Pragmatic 365 (2008-2021)

The Matthew Effect (principle, law) is social phenomenon whereby those who have, get more and those who have not get less. It appears to be a universal truth which applies to almost anything, and while the output of its effects are clear, its cause can be less so. Whenever inequality happens, one school of thought says that it is because one group is oppressing the other group. This group tends to view everything through the simplistic prison of oppressors and the oppressed. To them, the reasons for something happening is always because some one or group has decided to oppress and exploit another group. While this thinking is virtuous, it has a fundamental obvious flaw in that sometimes the reasons things happen is not because one person or group is oppressing another, but because of natural laws of nature.

The theologians of you will no doubt know that the name of the phenomenon comes from the two parables of Jesus in the Synoptic Gospels.

The concept concludes both synoptic versions of the parable of the talents:

> "For to every one who has will more be given, and he will have abundance;
>
> but from him who has not, even what he has will be taken away."
>
> — *Matthew 25:29, RSV.*

> "I tell you, that to every one who has will more be given; but from him who
>
> has not, even what he has will be taken away."
>
> — *Luke 19:26, RSV.*

The concept concludes two of the three synoptic versions of the parable of the lamp under a bushel (absent in the version of Matthew):

"For to him who has will more be given; and from him who has not, even
what he has will be taken away"

— Mark 4:25, RSV.

"Take heed then how you hear; for to him who has will more be given, and
from him who has not, even what he thinks that he has will be taken away."

— Luke 8:18, RSV.

The concept is presented again in Matthew outside of a parable during Christ's explanation to his disciples of the purpose of parables:

"And he answered them, "To you it has been given to know the secrets of
the kingdom of heaven, but to them it has not been given. For to him who
has will more be given, and he will have abundance; but from him who has
not, even what he has will be taken away."

— Matthew 13:11–12, RSV.

But what has all this got to do with the Transformation of Enterprises? Simply that an Enterprise should be wary when bestowing accolades, awards and promotions, as those that receive them, because they have received them, are likely to receive more of them, not because they deserve them.

It should also be noted that the corollary is also true. An Enterprise should be wary when disciplining, criticising, and negatively viewing employees, as those that receive them, because they have received them, are likely to receive more of them, not because they deserve them.

Culture

> # KEYPOINT:
>
> Do not let the past, unduly affect the future.

> # ADOPTION:
>
> C-Suite: Mandate that those receiving acolades or critism should not receive them because of previous accolades or criticism.

Questions to Ponder

- Do people in your Enterprise who receive praise and accoldaes, seem to be getting more of their fair share?
- Do people in your Enterprise who receive criticism and discipline, seem to be getting more of their fair share?
- Can you think of examples where this has happened in the past?
- Who were they? What was the impact? Why do you think they acted in this way?
- What needs to change to reduce the likelihood of it happening in the future?
- Who needs to drive that change?

Culture > Slaves to Psychology™ > Prices Law

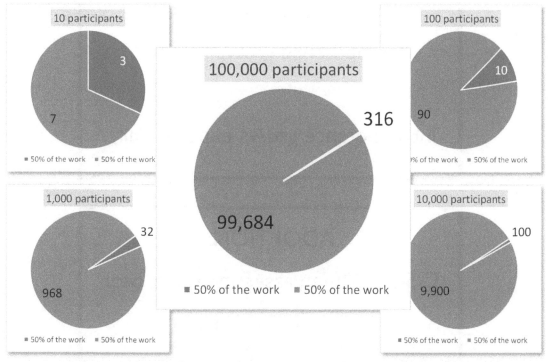

© Pragmatic 365 (2008-2021)

Price's law (named after Derek J. de Solla Price, England (1922-1983), referred to the relationship between the literature on a subject and the number of authors in the subject area. He found/stated that half of the publications come from the square root of all contributors. This phenomenon has since been show to be much more ubiquitous, in that it applies to just about any endeavour, meaning that more generally 50% of the participants in any endeavour are made up of the square root of the total number of participants.

What does this mean for Enterprises? If you are the owner or manager of any substantially sizes Enterprise, the ratio of one 50% to the other 50% can be extremely high. This has implications not only for the owners of the Enterprise as a whole, but equally importantly for the larger 50% of the workforce.

In this ultimate example here, we find that 316 people contribute to 50% of the work being done. So, these 316 people are ultra-important. But not because we should adore them. They are important because if the Enterprise loses even a small number of these people, it will be extremely difficult to replace them.

You might say that this small 50% group are obviously the executives and senior management. I would say that's dead wrong. In my experience, most Enterprise could lose 50% of their managers and rather than having detrimental effect on the Enterprise, would many times have a positive effect! I think that is borne out by many example of Enterprise that have culled the management.

This means if you happened to lose 0.1% of the people but that 0.1% was the wrong 0.1%, you would lose 15% of the work being done by the Enterprise!

So, in this example, losing the wrong 100 people could destroy the Enterprise.

Culture

KEYPOINT:

Competence grows linearly.

Incompetence grows exponentially.

ADOPTION:

C-Suite: When assessing value, bear in mind Price's Law.

Questions to Ponder

♦ How many employees does your Enterprise have?
♦ What is the square root of that value?
♦ In your enterprise, who are the people that create the most value?
♦ Are the other people somehow not useful?
♦ What puts some people in one group or the other?

I love pretending I'm not a sociopath

© Pragmatic 365 (2008-2021)

NOTE – This "problem" with culture is linked to Style Over Substance and the Dunning-Kruger Effect defined elsewhere.

If you ask people "What are the skills are required for someone to be an effective and efficient manager?" you would get a list something like this:

- Good Communication Skills.
- Ability to Delegate.
- Think Strategically.
- Empower the Team.
- Trustworthy.
- Listening to and respect for Others.
- Discipline and Focus.
- Being Organised.
- Good Time Management.
- Reliable.
- Gets Results.

Over a 40 year career, I have known many many many managers and many many many people who were not managers but aspired to be. I would also say that in my experience, at least 70% of the people who were managers, were really bad at being managers, displaying almost none of the skills associated with good managers and in many cases exactly the opposite (for example not looking at the bigger picture, not respecting and listening to other peoples opinions, not delegating but micromanaging, etc). I would also say that at least 70% or more of people who were not managers (but would like to have been), would have made excellent managers, as they displayed almost all the skills of good managers (e.g looking at the bigger picture, respecting and listening to other people's opinions, not looking to micromanage others, etc).

Culture

So what the hell is going on here?

I believe the problem is related to Sociopathy and the traits of Sociopaths.

Of course, I am no psychology expert, so what I say is not based on sound scientific evidence, however, it is based on 40 years of in the field observations and a mind that can spot patterns.

Some of the major traits of Sociopaths are the following:

- Amenable
- Likeable
- Persuasive
- Charming
- Manipulative
- Cunning
- Grandiose Sense of Self
- Pathological Lying
- Lack of remorse, shame or guilt
- Shallow emotions
- Callousness/Lack of Empathy

Research into the kinds of jobs that Sociopaths are interested show time and time again that the first place on the list goes to Capitalist positions of leadership (Managers, CxO's, etc) offer power, autonomy, command, and status.

These traits largely affect how one person can manipulate other people. For example, for a Manager, whether it is people below them (report to them), on the same level (other managers) or above them (CxOs).

It is also very difficult for people to separate the charming, amenable, likeable and charming traits of someone from other, perhaps more valid traits — aka traits more specific to a particular job.

Until Enterprises recognise this as a serious problem which can cause other and numerous knock-on problems, we will continue to have people rising to positions of power that are exactly the opposite of the people that we need in those positions.

KEYPOINT:

"The trouble with Sociopaths, is that they are very, very nice people!"

- Kevin Lee Smith

ADOPTION:

C-Suite: Recognise that the traits required to gain promotion, are no necessarily the traits required to execute the job.

Questions to Ponder

♦ Are there any Sociopaths in your Enterprise?
♦ Have you seen any sociopathic traits?
♦ Who were they? What was the impact? Why do you think they acted in this way?
♦ What needs to change to reduce the likelihood of it happening in the future?
♦ Who needs to drive that change?

Culture

Culture > Slaves to Psychology™ > Personality Traits

Belbin

Belbin® Team Role Summary Descriptions

For more information.
+44 (0)1223 264975 | www.belbin.com

BELBIN

Myers Briggs

		Temperament	Role	Role Variant
Abstract or Concrete?	Cooperative or Utilitarian?	Directive or Informative?		Expressive or Attentive ?
Introspective (N)		Idealist (NF) Diplomatic	Mentor (NFJ) Developing	Teacher (ENFJ): Educating
				Counselor (INFJ): Guiding
			Advocate (NFP) Mediating	Champion (ENFP): Motivating
				Healer (INFP): Conciliating
		Rational (NT) Strategic	Coordinator (NTJ) Arranging	Fieldmarshal (ENTJ): Mobilizing
				Mastermind (INTJ): Entailing
			Engineer (NTP) Constructing	Inventor (ENTP): Devising
				Architect (INTP): Designing
Observant (S)		Guardian (SJ) Logistical	Administrator (STJ) Regulating	Supervisor (ESTJ): Enforcing
				Inspector (ISTJ): Certifying
			Conservator (SFJ) Supporting	Provider (ESFJ): Supplying
				Protector (ISFJ): Securing
		Artisan (SP) Tactical	Operator (STP) Expediting	Promoter (ESTP): Persuading
				Crafter (ISTP): Instrumenting
			Entertainer (SFP) Improvising	Performer (ESFP): Demonstrating
				Composer (ISFP): Synthesizing

© Pragmatic 365 (2008-2021)

Although we all like to think of ourselves as individuals (and that's a good thing) it is possible to create categories or "types" of people traits, based on certain criteria. Having created these categories, it is then possible to compare and contrast these traits to understand how one person relates to (or should relate to?) another person.

This is a bit of a minefield though, as you will find proponents and detractors alike that hold very firmly held beliefs about the accuracy or otherwise of such methods. Personally, I think they are wonderful methods for understanding yourself, other people, how you interact with other people and how other people interact with you. Anything that makes understanding and communication better, and easier has got to be a good idea!

People test their own personality traits using these links

♦ www.16personalities.com
♦ www.123test.com

The Belbin website is www.belbin.com and the MBTI one is www.myersbriggs.org

Highlighted in red are the categories I fall into for Belbin and MBTI.

In Belbin I am categorised as a plant and a shaper, while in MBTI I am categorised as a Mastermind and an Architect.

The reason I fall into two categories, is because for some people they are truly a merging of two distinct but related types. For example, I have long thought of myself as an architect and an engineer. Two roles that are fundamentally different, and yet could be considered to be two sides of the same coin.

> # KEYPOINT:
>
> People with different personality traits are required for different roles

> # ADOPTION:
>
> C-Suite: Initiate an evaluation of everyone's personality traits vs the traits required to do their job.

Questions to Ponder

- ◆ What are your MBTI or Belbin results?
- ◆ Do you agree with them?
- ◆ What are the MBTI or Belbin results of your colleagues?
- ◆ Does your Enterprise use personality trait measurement?
- ◆ If not, do you think it would be beneficial?

Culture

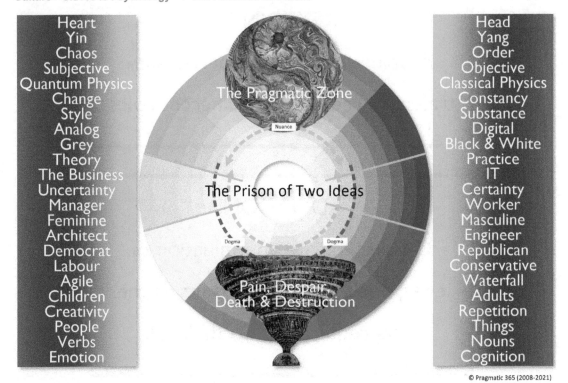

© Pragmatic 365 (2008-2021)

First of all, I need to make something very very clear.

Chaos is not inherently bad, and Order is not inherently good. Both have the capacity for good and bad. Whoever thought of those names initially made a big big mistake because in most civilisations, the connotations are that chaos is bad and order is good, which spikes any conversation from the get-go. So let's put those connotations in a box right at the start.

What we can say (because history teaches us) is that 100% Chaos is inherently bad and 100% Order is inherently bad. So, it is plainly obvious that a mixture is required.

You may think of that as a kind of battle where one "wins" out over the other, and in a way this is true, but this mixture happens, not by one overruling the other so to speak, but by one inhibiting or limiting the other more than the other inhibits them. So one "wins" by taking away from the other. Amazingly this is exactly what very intelligent people now say about the left-brain right-brain debate. It is now said that each hemisphere is actually the same, containing both left brain and right brain features in old money. One hemisphere "wins out" over the other by disabling parts in the other hemisphere.

One interesting thing I have observed though is that, one trait of the "left" is feeling an accomplishment when they have caused the other to fail rather when they have succeeded, while an observed trait of the "right" is a feeling of accomplishment when they have succeeded, rather when the other has failed.

So, with the good/bad connotations put firmly in the bottom of a locked filing cabinet stuck in a disused lavatory with a sign on the door saying "Beware of the Leopard.", *(ref. Douglas Adams)* we can move on.

I am not going to spout the usual stuff about Taoism and Chaos Theory. Much more has already been written by much better people than me.

But I am going to speak about is the patterns of chaos and order I have, without my awareness, observed over 40 years or so, and have only just coalesced in my mind and come forward from my subconscious to my conscious mind..

We can slice and dice people and Enterprises into many groups and subgroups, some overlapping, some not, but I have realised a correlation between the items I list on the left and which I list on the right. It is common for people (because we are all individuals) to sit in camps that are on the left and the right. For example, it is quite likely to find a business worker who is a woman, trained in Engineering, that votes Democrat in the US (Labour in the UK), who thinks like and adult and prefers agile over waterfall. It is also quite likely we could find an IT manager, who is a man, trained in architecture, that votes Republican in the US (Conservative in the UK) who thinks like a child and prefers waterfall to agile. And of course, many permutations in between.

Having said all that, I have personally witnessed a general trend that forms these two groups, so while there are exceptions at either end of the bell curve, there is a pronounced alignment in the middle.

Why am I prattling on about all this? Because in order for groups of people to work together harmoniously and productively they need to understand each other and understanding each other is fundamentally about understanding how the other side thinks. I would also say, "and why", but I am not sure why they think the way they do is important. They do, you will not change them and so the best we can achieve is understand them.

As we move further clockwise, our views become more extreme and our thoughts become more entrenched. If this continues, we stray into "The Prison of Two Ideas" *(ref. Greg Gutfeld)*. This is where both sides are held captive by their own views and actively dismiss anything that does not conform to their current beliefs. This is a precipice. A Precipice that the US political world is currently standing on (as of April October). Many Enterprises are also standing on this precipice.

Ultimately both sides taken to the extreme usually results in large numbers of people dying. (e.g Stalin or Hitler).

Once we have entered "The Prison of Two Ideas" it is extremely difficult to move back to the centre without a lot of pain. Whatever direction you take, it results in more pain, either to your opponent or to you. And since humans tend to always choose the least painful option, the most likely outcome is a further descent towards Pain, Despair, Death and Destruction. However, a return to the centre may be so painful that a descent into the abys is required, at which point, it doesn't really matter what you do because either route will be less painful.

There is certainly conflict between each of the pairs listed and is often spoke of in terms of X vs Y. E.g. Management vs Workers, Business vs IT, Architects vs Engineers, Agile vs Waterfall. For an Enterprise to increase effectiveness and efficiency in anything, these conflicts need to be exposed, understood, and accommodated. Or is that my Order side telling me to apply order to the problem when in fact, applying Chaos is the solution? Perhaps applying both is the key!

Either way, a descent into the abys helps no one.

> # KEYPOINT:
>
> "In all chaos, there is a cosmos.
>
> In all disorder, a secret order."
>
> - Carl Jung

> # ADOPTION:
>
> C-Suite: Mandate that people seek to balance Chaos with Order. Never to remove Chaos or Order.

Questions to Ponder

- Where do you fit into this diagram?
- Does it change if you consider professional vs private life?
- Does it change upon situations? If you are angry or calm?
- Can you think of examples of your yin and examples of your yang?
- Does change always bring chaos into order, or can it also bring order into chaos?
- Which areas of your Enterprise have a good balance of chaos and order?
- Which areas have too much chaos?
- Which areas have too much order?

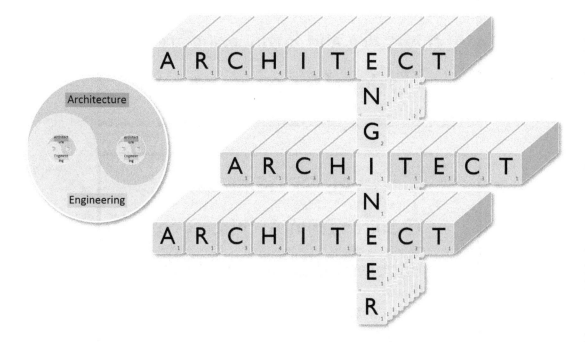

© Pragmatic 365 (2008-2021)

It seems everyone these days works on solutions. Thinking about one solution or another, solving problems, discussing or arguing with others on which is the right solution or not. People tend to concentrate on solutions because a solution to a problem is the end goal. There is also a psychological aspect to it - whoever's solution is adopted proves their solution was superior (supposedly - in my experience that's not always the case!).

It is human nature to answer questions - to create solutions.

Of course. The Architecture Paradigm™ is also about providing solutions and dealing with their complexity, but the approach focusses much more on understanding the problem - for when you truly understand a problem, solutions tend to be:

   a)   much easier to see and
   b)   much more effective and efficient.

However, The Architecture Paradigm™ also recognises that the approach must integrate with work that is to come later, namely Engineering.

Architecting is more concerned with WHY we need a solution which largely involves asking questions and understanding things. Engineering is more concerned with HOW the solution will be made real which largely involves creating solutions and talking.

It could be said that Architecting and Engineering are two sides of the same coin.

Culture

KEYPOINT:

Architecture and Engineering are two

sides of the same coin.

ADOPTION:

C-Suite: Train Architects to

understand Engineers. Train

Engineers to understand Architects.

Train Management to undertstand

both.

Questions to Ponder

- ♦ Do the Management in your Enterprise, know the difference between Architecture and Engineering?
- ♦ Do the Workers in your Enterprise, know the difference between Architecture and Engineering?
- ♦ Does your Enterprise use Architecture and Engineering appropriately?
- ♦ If not, what problems are created?

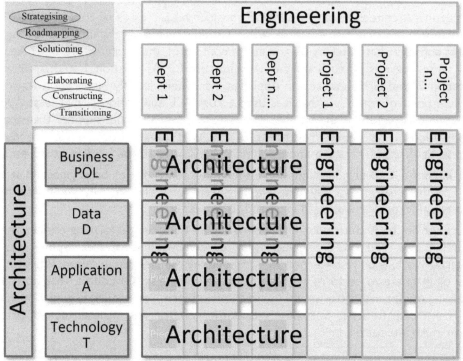

© Pragmatic 365 (2008-2021)

A fundamental confusion that people have when people try to explain or advocate the Architecture of something, is that just because an Architect is talking about the **whole**, it does not mean they are advocating building the whole, or building the whole immediately. By definition, Architecture (**fundamentals)** are **high level**, and by definition, the **whole** is **big**. Comments such as

> "Yes that's all very good but it's all **high level**, and it's just **too big**, we
>
> can't do it all (in a short space of time), so we won't do anything at all"

illustrates that confusion. Architecture, by definition, is **high level** and is **big.** So, the next time someone says that something Architectural is "**high level** and **big**" as a means to dismiss it, you should say...

> "Yes, it is! If it were not high level and big, it wouldn't be Architecture!
>
> And it is precisely because it is high level and big, that it is important."

When we say Architect horizontally, it means that Architecture tends to (should) consider the fundamental structure of something large and complex (If it were not large or complex there is little need for Architecture) and for that you have to (should) consider the whole. We also say horizontally because Architecture tends to (should) layer things and is concerned with systemic qualities and capabilities such as Process, Organisation or Locatgion – as a whole, or Data – as a whole, or Applications – as a whole, or Technology – as whole.

Because Architecture tends to (should) consider things from a Contextual and/or Conceptual and/or Logical perspectives this allows us to consider the whole.

The phases mostly concerned with Architecture work are during the Strategising, Roadmapping and Solutioning phases of Transformation.

Whenever we perform Architecture work (Business Architecture, Enterprise/Transformation Architecture, Solution Architecture, Application Architecture, Data Architecture, Infrastructure Architecture, etc) we MUST consider **ALL things of that type** NOT just the Architecture of a piece. For example, when considering the Architecture of an Application, we must consider that in terms of, and in the context of, the Architecture of all Applications. In this sense, there is no such thing as Architecture for Application 1, and Architecture for Application 2, and Architecture for Application n. There is only Application Architecture - the whole point of which is - that it is used across ALL applications, or at least Applications of a certain class, and that the number of classes is a much smaller number than the number of Applications. This applies regardless of the type of architecture we are considering (Business, Enterprise/Transformation, Solution, Application, Data, Infrastructure, etc).

This is in contrast, to Engineering, where the whole tends not to be engineered at the same time. For this reason, we say that we Engineer vertically, that is, we utilise horizontal Architectural Structures but build in an end to end fashion.

In direct conflict to Architecture, Engineering MUST consider performing engineering **ONLY for that piece**, and NOT Engineering of all other things of that type. Why, because engineering work, is only concerned with engineering the piece in question. It has no remit or budget or mandate to perform engineering on anything else. Of course, that does not mean engineering cannot use patterns and lessons learned form performing Engineering in the past, but this use of patterns is not the same as the creation and maintenance of patterns we perform in Architecture work.

Thus…

We Architect horizontally, systemically.

We Engineer vertically, specifically.

KEYPOINT:

Think (and Plan) Strategically (Architecture), Act Tactically (Engineering)..

ADOPTION:

C-Suite: Mandate that people Architect horizontally and Engineer vertically.

Questions to Ponder

♦ Do the Management in your Enterprise, know the difference between Architecture and Engineering?
♦ Do the Workers in your Enterprise, know the difference between Architecture and Engineering?
♦ Does your Enterprise use Architecture and Engineering appropriately?
♦ If not, what problems are created?

Culture

Architecture

WHY. Understanding. Asking Questions. Thinking.

Finishes when there is nothing more to take away.

Engineering

HOW. Creating Solutions. Talking. Doing.

Finishes when there is nothing more to add.

© Pragmatic 365 (2008-2021)

In practice, there is of course an overlap between Architecture and Engineering. The overlap may be small or may be large depending on the problem in hand. This tends to decide whether one person is required to perform both roles or if two people who specialise in each are required.

In this day and age, thinking about things seems to be viewed as a very bad thing as no discernible progress is being made. It should be noted that all the major advancements since time began have come from people thinking about things rather than doing - at least initially. This is not to say that everyone should sit around thinking about things and not doing anything. Doing things informs thinking and thinking informs doing. This is the yin and yang where balance must be achieved for best results and progress. No one ever suggested that people should stop doing things, but it is common for people to suggest that people should stop thinking about things "Just do it!" - not explicitly because when you say it explicitly, as I have just done, it sounds ludicrous in the extreme, but in practice, in life, in the day to day run of things, thinking is routinely put on the back burner as the next urgent (but probably unimportant) thing becomes the focus.

One of the differences between doing and thinking is that doing things has many limitations. Thinking has no literally no limitations. It is hardly surprising therefore that innovation and progress comes more from thinking than doing, albeit you do not see the fruits until something is built. For example, the fantastic smartphones we have today did not come from doing things, they can from thinking about what could be done. Thinking created the catalyst and doing made it happen. They had to be envisaged first. In that way, engineering places limitations on architecting however, architecting pushes those limitations and boundaries and thereby advances Engineering.

KEYPOINT:

The line between Architecture and Engineering is a blurred one.

ADOPTION:

C-Suite: Instigate training so that people recognise that Architecture and Engineering overlap.

Questions to Ponder

♦ Do you agree that Architecture is more about Why, while engineering is more about How?
♦ What do other people in your Enterprise believe?
♦ If there is not a common understanding, does this create problems?
♦ If so, what is the impact of those problems?

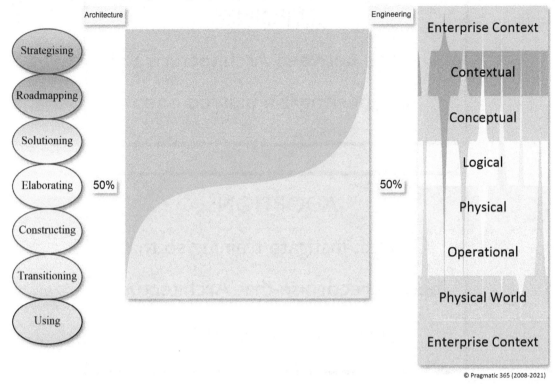

© Pragmatic 365 (2008-2021)

From the perspective of the entire Transformation domain, Architecture is performed more at the top of the stack and less at the bottom. Conversely Engineering is performed more at the bottom of the stack and less at the top.

The further down the stack we go the more concrete things become, and the further up the stack we go, the more abstract things become. This does not mean we are saying that there is no Engineering happening at the top and there is no Architecture happening at the bottom.

Culture

> ## KEYPOINT:
>
> Architecture is performed largely in the early phases of Transformation, while Engineering is performed largely in the later phases.

> ## ADOPTION:
>
> C-Suite: Instigate training so that people recognise that Architecture is performed largely in the early phases of Transformation, while Engineering is performed largely in the later phases.

Questions to Ponder

- ♦ Does your Enterprise recognise that people working towards the top of the Transformation stack are more Architects than Engineers?
- ♦ Does your Enterprise recognise that people working towards the bottom of the Transformation stack are more Engineers than Architects?
- ♦ If not, does this create any problems?
- ♦ Does this create any opportunities for education?

Culture

Culture > Architecture & Engineering > Overlap > Intra Phase

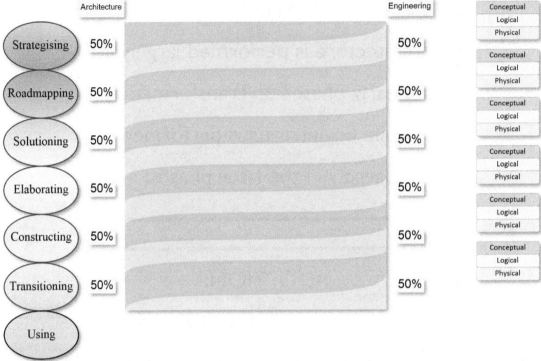

© Pragmatic 365 (2008-2021)

Architecture and Engineering map on to the fundamental phases of Transformation, and within each phase (depending on the Complexity of the information being worked upon).

Consequently the reality is a (potentially confusing) mixture of Architecture and Engineering which probably goes a long way to explain why there is such confusion and debate about how they are related and where they fit into the Transformation cascade. The truth is, they fit everywhere!

KEYPOINT:

Architecture and Engineering can be performed within any phase.

ADOPTION:

C-Suite: Instigate training so that people recognise that Architecture and Engineering are skills that can be applied anywhere.

Questions to Ponder

♦ Considering each phase of Transformation, do people who work there think of themselves primarily as Architects or Engineers or a mixture?

♦ Which phase of Transformation do you primarily work in?

♦ Do you consider yourself to be primarily an Architect or Engineer or a mixture?

Culture > Architecture & Engineering > Overlap > Overall

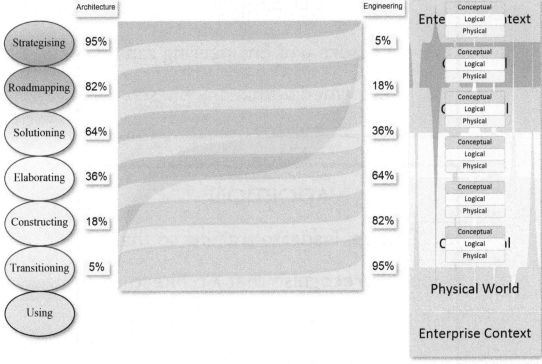

© Pragmatic 365 (2008-2021)

In many ways, the key to Transformation happening in a coherent, holistic fashion is the Architecture and Engineering Disciplines working together in harmony.

It is natural that the drive is always towards Engineering because it is Engineering that actually produces the tangible things that people want, but this overwhelming desire must be tempered and balanced by Architecture where appropriate. And while it is true that Architecture without Engineering is pointless, it is also true to say that Engineering without Architecture is foolhardy at best and at worst downright dangerous. And this risk increases as complexity and volatility rises.

The yin and yang of Architecture and Engineering is built upon the concept of the Thinking Mind-set and the Doing Mind-set. Research by psychologists Arie Kruglanski, Tory Higgins, and their colleagues suggests that we have two complementary motivational systems: the "thinking" system and the "doing" system - and we're generally only capable of using one at a time.

Think about how you best generate new ideas. Often, you "brainstorm" or try to come up with as many ideas as possible. That is called diverging and requires our thinking system. At other times, you need to evaluate those ideas and figure out which ones are best. That is called converging, and it requires the activation of the doing system.

> # KEYPOINT:
>
> The relationship between Architecture and Engineering as we move from the top to the bottom phases is complex.

> # ADOPTION:
>
> C-Suite: Instigate training so that people recognise that the application of Architecture and Engineering can be useful in any phase.

Questions to Ponder

- Are the Architecture and Engineering disciplines recognised in your Enterprise?
- Are they working in harmony or not?
- If not, what will you do to increase the harmony?

Culture

Architect	Engineer	Consultant
A person who knows very little, about a great deal,	A person who knows a great deal about very little,	A person that starts out knowing practically everything about everything,
and keeps knowing less and less about more and more,	and keeps knowing more and more about less and less,	but ends up knowing nothing about anything, due to his association with architects and engineers.
until he knows practically nothing about everything.	until he knows practically everything about nothing.	

- Aglaia Daae

© Pragmatic 365 (2008-2021)

{{Abdul Aziz}}

This is a little joke, but like all jokes, there is usually some grain of truth in it. In this case, there's a whole bag of rice and contains an important message!

Architects are generalists who look at the big picture. Since no one has the bandwidth to know everything about everything, an obvious side effect is that the more things they know about, the less bandwidth they have to drill into the details of those things.

Engineers are of course, the opposite, being specialists, who look are the small detailed picture. Since no one has the band width to know everything about everything, an obvious side effect is that the more detail they know about some thing, the less bandwidth they have to look at the bigger picture.

This intensely important distinction is imperative for the management of Enterprises to understand, not only from the point of view of needing both, but from the point of view of making people happy in the roles they perform and the effectiveness and efficiency by which they perform them.

Putting someone with an Architects brain in an Engineering job, or someone with an Engineers brain in an Architecture job, will make both feel hopelessly lost and depressed, which is guaranteed to make their work ineffective and inefficient. The Enterprise loses, the employee loses.

Culture

> ## KEYPOINT:
>
> Know and exploit the fundamental difference between Architects and Engineers.

> ## ADOPTION:
>
> Management: Ensure that Architects are give Architects jobs and Engineers are given Engineering.

Questions to Ponder

- ◆ Are you more of an Engineer or an Architect or are you both?
- ◆ Who in your Enterprise is an Engineer in an Architect's role?
- ◆ Are they happy?
- ◆ Who in your Enterprise is an Architect in an Engineer's role?
- ◆ Are they happy?
- ◆ How can your Enterprise exploit the differences between Architects and Engineers?

Culture

Culture > Architecture & Engineering > Comparison

Architecture tends to be more about...	Art	About	Science	Engineering tends to be more about...
	Why	Looking	How	
	The Problem	Understanding	The Solution	
	Outside-In	Think in terms of	Inside-Out	
	Whole	Focus	Parts	
	Why > What	Translation	What > How	
	Uncertainty	Deal in	Certainty	
	Opportunity	Impossible is a	Constraint	
	Abstraction	Function	Elaboration	
	Nothing more to Remove	Finished when	Nothing more to Add	
	Eraser / Mind	Important Tool	Pencil / Hands	
	Thinking	Work	Doing	
	What is yet to come	Consider	What has been	
	Engineer	Best Friend	Architect	
	Client	Driven by	Architect	
	Breadth, Big Picture	View	Depth, Big Detail	
	Paints Them	Pictures	Takes Them	
	Long Term	Wins	Short Term	
	Impossible	Cost Justification	Possible	
	Intangible	True Value	Tangible	
	Love it	When they are wrong	Hate it	
	Creativity	Change	Innovation	
	Lines	Focus	Boxes	
	Immortal / Permanent	Sustainability	Mortal / Temporary	

© Pragmatic 365 (2008-2021)

It is not easy (Impossible? – But that's why I like it!) to just state what Architecture and Engineering are. The relationship between these two disciplines is complex and more grey than black and white. And so, the best way to more fully understand them is to compare and contrast them in various dimensions.

Architecture tends to be more **art** than science.	Engineering tends to be more **science**, than art.
Architecture is more about looking up (**Why**) than looking down (**How**).	Engineering is more about looking down (**How**) than looking up (**Why**).
Architecture is more about understanding the **Problem**.	Engineering is more about understanding the **Solution**.
Architects tend to think in terms of **outside-in**.	Engineers tend to think in terms of **inside-out**.
Architects are aware of the parts of a system, but tend to **focus on the whole**.	Engineers are aware of the whole system, but tend to **focus on the parts**.

Architects tend to be more concerned with the **why > what** translation with a little of the **how**.

Engineers tend to be more concerned with the **what > how to** translation with a little of the **why**.

Architects tend to deal in **uncertainty**.

Engineers tend to deal in **certainty**.

Architects tend to see **impossible** as an **opportunity**.

Engineers tend to see **impossible** as a **constraint**.

Architecture is more about **omission**, **composition**, **generalisation** and **idealisation**, than it is about inclusion, decomposition, specialisation or realisation.

Engineering is more about **inclusion**, **decomposition**, **specialisation** and **realisation**, than it is about omission, composition, generalisation or idealisation.

An Architect knows their job is done when there is **nothing more to take away**.

An Engineer knows their job is done when there is **nothing more to add**.

The most important tool for an Architect is their **eraser**.

The most important tool for an Engineer is their **pencil**.

Architects tend to **think**.

Engineers tend to **do**.

Architects tend to consider things from the perspective of **what is yet to come**.

Engineers tend to consider things from the perspective of **what has been**.

An Architect doesn't get **what** they want until an Engineer Builds it.

An Engineer doesn't know **what** to Build until an Architect specifies it.

An Architect doesn't know **why** to Architect something until a Client specifies it.

An Engineer doesn't know **why** to build something until an Architect tells specifies it.

To "do" Architecture you need **breadth**, to see the **big picture**.

To "do" Engineering you need **depth**, to see the **big detail**.

Architects **paint pictures**. An interpretation of reality.

Engineers **take pictures**. A record of reality.

You Architect **long term wins**.

You Engineer **quick wins**.

You **cannot** cost justify Architecture.

You **can** cost justify Engineering.

The true value of Architecture is **intangible**.

The true value of Engineering is **tangible**.

Architects tend to **like** to find out when they are wrong.

Engineers tend to **hate** to find out when they were wrong.

Architects tend to be more about unleashing the potential of the mind to conceive new ideas (**Creativity**).

Engineers tend to be more about introducing change into relatively stable systems (**Innovation**)

Architecture is more about the lines (**Relationships**) than the boxes

Engineering is more about the boxes (**Objects**) that the lines.

Architecture tends to be immortal and permanent.

Engineering tends to be mortal and temporary.

> # KEYPOINT:
>
> Architecture and Engineering, bring important things to the table, and makes the whole much more than the sum of its parts.

> # ADOPTION:
>
> C-Suite: Instigate training so that people recognise the differences between Architecture and Engineering, and use both appropriately.

Questions to Ponder

- Are you more of an Engineer or an Architect or are you both?
- How much time are you allowed to spend "thinking" rather than "doing"?
- If you were given the space to think more, would you be better at your job?
- How many Architects does it take to change a light bulb?
- (None - It's an Engineering problem ;-)
- Does your Enterprise use Architects and Engineers in an appropriate way?
- Can you think of other ways that Architects and Engineers contrast each other?

Culture

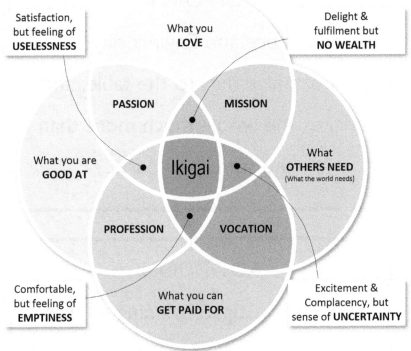

© Pragmatic 365 (2008-2021)

Are you an Architect in an Engineers job? A manager in an Architects job? An Engineer in an Architects job. An Engineer in a Managers job?

While others may decide or confer titles on you, we suggest you look into yourself, your soul, and decide first and foremost who the real you is, and then make any changes necessary, so that the real you shines through.

Here we discuss a diagram from a book called "The Japanese Secret to a Long and Happy Life" by Francesc Miralles and Hector Garcia. Like most models, it is a powerful aid to thinking about yourself (and others) and can help you decide if you are in the right job, or if you are doing the right things for the right reasons.

It considers that there are 4 main areas:

- ♦ What you **LOVE** - This equates to what you like to do. What gets you out of bed in the morning. What you would choose to do if there were no other restrictions.

- ♦ What you are **GOOD AT** - This equates to what you are good at. There will be some things you are good at, and like doing, There will be other things you are good at, that you do not like doing.

- ♦ What **OTHERS NEED** - This was originally titled "What the world needs" but the word "world" puts a domain constraint on the question that need not be there. To one person "the world" may literally be the world. To others "the world" may mean their family, or the company they work for. As we have learned before "Context is King"™ and therefore you need to place the context you wish on the model to be able to answer its questions.

- ♦ What you can **GET PAID FOR** – This equates to getting something of value that you can exchange for other things you need, aka money.

Since you are in control of the context, it allows you to utilise the model in different contexts. For example, one to represent your home life where "the world" is your family and "what you can get paid for" is the respect of your family (and the "payment" of your family achieving their Ikigai) and another to represent your working life where the company you work for is "the world" and the "payment" is your salary.

Where these primary domains overlap is where happiness (and sadness) lies.

At the intersection of what you are good at, and what you need lies your **PROFESSION**.

At the intersection of what you are good at, and what you love, lies your **PASSION**.

At the intersection of what others need, and what you need lies your **VOCATION**.

And, at the intersection of what others need, and what you love, lies your **MISSION**.

The other intersections illustrate areas of partial Ikigai where three of the four aspects are fulfilled but one is not.

- Satisfying what you love, what you are good at, and what you need, leaves a feeling of **USELESSNESS**, because you are not doing what **OTHERS NEED**.
- Satisfying what others need, what you love, and what you are good at, means you have **NO WEALTH**, because you are not doing what you can **GET PAID FOR**.
- Satisfying what you need, what others need, and what you love, leaves you with a sense of **UNCERTAINTY**, because you are not doing what you are **GOOD AT**.
- And, satisfying what you are good at, what you need, and what others need, leaves you with a feeling of **EMPTINESS**, because you are not doing what you **LOVE**.

Ikigai, is that perfect balance where you balance what you need, with what others need, with what you are good at, with what you love.

It would be nice if people can truly achieve Ikigai, but for the most part, many of us do not. From my professional life context (at this point in time – because things always change) I would say that I exist in the "Delight & fulfilment but no WEALTH. That is:

- I am doing what I truly love to do (maturing the Transformation domain of Enterprises).
- I (believe) I am good at it.
- I (believe) I am supplying what others need – others being Enterprises all over the world (even though they may not realise they need it)

So, I feel delight and fulfilment, but have no wealth. For me this is fine, because I place a much higher value on doing things I enjoy, that I am good at, and that help others, than any monetary gain. Money is not what gets me out of bed in the morning. The other three together do.

> # KEYPOINT:
>
> A happy productive person, balances what they are good at, with what they love, what others need, and what they want.

> # ADOPTION:
>
> C-Suite: Initiate a review to allow people to balance what they are good at, with what they love, what others needs are, and what their needs are.

Questions to Ponder

- ◆ What do you love and what are you good at? Are they the same things?
- ◆ If not, what are you going to do about that?
- ◆ What can you get paid for and what do others needs that you can provide? Are they the same things?
- ◆ If not, what are you going to do about that?
- ◆ How does your home life Ikigai map, compare to your professional life Ikigai map?
- ◆ If you were only able to satisfy 3 out of the 4 primary areas, which ones would you chose and why?

Culture

Culture > The Architect > Secrets

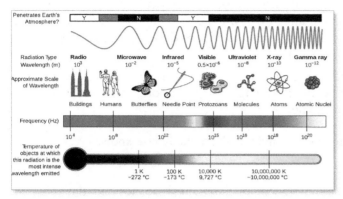

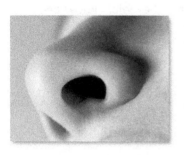

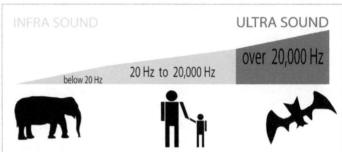

One of the curses ("my name is Legion, for we are many") of being an Architect is that they often can see things, as plain as day, that others who are not Architects cannot see. This does NOT mean that Architects are in some way superior or more important. It just means they are different. It's like everyone else can only see visible light, but Architects can see the full spectrum from infrared to ultraviolet and beyond. Architects can hear what others cannot hear, feel what others cannot feel, smell what others cannot smell and taste what others cannot taste.

But there is another curse far worse than all of these. And that is that Architects can see into the future. I don't mean, of course, that they can tell you the winner of the 4:15 as Ascot! What I mean is that they have the uncanny ability (some may call it a sixth sense) to be able to foresee things, to think ahead. In fact it's more than a sense, it is almost what defines them to be Architects in the first place. Ignore an Architect because he is talking about things in the future and there is no point in employing him in the first place!

Actually, although everyone knows and is taught that there are five senses, this is in fact wrong (as are many things taught in school!). The five senses we commonly know about come from Aristotle who also got it wrong when he said that there are only four elements (Earth, Fire, Water, and Air). Today, it is thought that there are actually anywhere from nine to twenty one senses, for example; Pressure, Itch, Thermoception, Proprioception, Tension Sensors, Nociception, Equilibrioception, Stretch Receptors, Chemoreceptors, Thirst, Hunger, Magnetoception and Time.

Architects do not necessarily discover new things, more they discover new ways of seeing existing things. Putting things "in a new light".

"New Light through Old Windows"

- Chris Rea

Architects expose things that can provide new insights into existing things. When people see **New Light through Old Windows** it can change fundamentally how they see and approach things, the decisions they take and why. This is one thing that POET helps to do, but it's a difficult thing to see - hence the references to SEPs and the Magic Eye picture at the beginning.

Since Architects can see, hear, taste, feel, and smell things that others cannot and also have the ability to peer into the future, they therefore know things that others do not know. Some may say, secrets. And as someone once said:

"The secret of business is to know something that nobody else knows".

- Aristotle Onassis.

It may be surprising to people, that the leaders of Enterprises do not see the value that Architects can bring to all domains rather than just IT. In time they will. I know because I am an Architect and I can see into the future ;-)

> ## KEYPOINT:
>
> "The secret of business is to know something that nobody else knows."
>
> - Aristotle Onassis

> ## ADOPTION:
>
> C-Suite: Mandate that people should exploit the fact Architects should be exploited to easily see things that others find difficult or impossible to see.

Questions to Ponder

- Would you like to see things others cannot?
- Would you like know things others do not?
- Do you think seeing into the future is valuable?
- We are very happy to use animals that have super-senses like the dogs to sniff out drugs and explosives, so why do people shy away from using that strange "animal" called an Architect?
- Does your Enterprise shy away from Architects?

Culture

"Impossible is just a big word thrown around by small men who find it easier to live in the world they've been given than to explore the power they have to change it. **Impossible is not a fact. It's an opinion.** Impossible is not a declaration. It's a dare. Impossible is potential. Impossible is temporary. Impossible is nothing."

- Muhammad Ali
Boxer

"It always seems impossible until its done."

- Nelson Mandela
Revolutionary / Politician

"To believe a thing impossible is to make it so."

- French Proverb

"Everything is theoretically impossible, until it is done."

- Robert A. Heinlein
Science Fiction Writer

"We would accomplish many more things if we did not think of them as impossible."

- Vince Lombardi
American Football Player

"Never tell a young person that anything cannot be done. God may have been waiting centuries for someone ignorant enough of the impossible to do that very thing."

- G. M. Trevelyan
Historian

"Every noble work is at first impossible."

- Thomas Carlyle
Philosopher

"So many of our dreams at first seem impossible, then they seem improbable, and then, when we summon the will, they soon become inevitable."

- Christopher Reeve
Actor / Activist

Impossible is why Architects get out of bed in the morning. But even though they strive to achieve "impossible" things, their job is, in itself also "impossible".

Being an Architect could be looked on more as an affliction - a cross to bear. Architects can't stop being Architects (which tends to really irritate people who are not Architects!). Being an Architect is a state of mind, a way of being. For an Architect 1+1 often equals 3, or more likely 1+1 equals blue! Architects tend to break the rules. For when you break the rules, you change the game.

Architects know and accept that there are things that they do not know about and go looking for them (remember Donald Rumsfeld?). Most of these things do not magically appear to them, they appear to them because they go looking for them. They wheedle them out from all the background noise. While most people bask in their knowledge and experience, an architect knows there are things he does not know about and actively goes about trying to find them. An architect is much more interested in what he doesn't know that what he knows. He is often surprised by what he finds, but never bored.

Because an Architect tends to see things (and find things) others cannot, they tend always to be in a position of exposing things that were not known, and therefore not taken account of, when decisions were made. This puts them in a position of seemingly to always be challenging decisions and wanting those decisions changed or in some cases reversed. This is not something that is generally welcomed, especially by the type of people who are responsible for making those decisions.

Humans are good at spotting patterns - our brains are hardwired for visual pattern recognition. However Architects are different for two reasons. Firstly, because they are more adept at seeing patterns in concepts and thoughts, and secondly, because they can see patterns based on sparse or very limited volumes of information. If the volume of information is large (like a hi resolution photo) anyone can spot the pattern, but if the volume of information is low (like a pixelated photo) only an architect can "squint" with his brain and still see things of value.

It's not so much about people not understanding what an Architect is saying, but more about people finding it difficult to see the thing the Architect is talking about in the first place. Most people do not (are not allowed to) spend the time to do so.

An Architect is an investigator (like Judge Judy!) and one of the tools of an investigator is cynicism - he doesn't believe anything until he can prove it or at least not have any feeling that he is not getting the whole truth. The yardstick of that is understanding. When an Architect gets an answer to a question and the answer doesn't make sense (a big part of that is common sense) he asks more questions. This irritates people who are hiding things or do not know what they are talking about and then begin to call the Architect "confrontational" or "rude" or "inappropriate" or any other of a number of vague negative words. When that happens, an Architect knows he is onto something.

Many many people go through life unchallenged. Talking about things that they do not really understand - possibly just repeating what they heard someone else say, saying things that while not bare-faced lies, could be considered to be economical with the truth. Many more people go through life also hearing things that perhaps they think are wrong or do not make sense but they do not say anything. They do not question and they do not challenge. The reason for this is not because they are bad people, but is rooted in psychology and man's deep desire to "not upset the applecart" and to be friends and get on with everyone. Architects do not think or work like that. In a way, they could be thought of being socially inept which can easily come across as being rude, confrontational, arrogant or disrespectful. This is not because they are bad people that should be controlled or ignored. The more you try to control or ignore an Architect, the more vocal he is likely to become. Paying them lip-service or trying to placate them is like adding fuel to a fire and is usually a recipe for disaster.

Another problem with Architects is that they tend to be in a minority. Perhaps less than 1% of all people are intrinsically an Architect. Add to this the fact that they tend to see things that others cannot see, and it tends to mean they are also in a minority in terms of their views and ideas and there is great scope for the majority to ignore them as it is usually thought that the majority must always right - "You are the only one that thinks that" - aka you must be wrong because the majority must be right.

Another problem with being an Architect (and making a difference) is that we, by definition, **only see and only raise fundamental problems.** By definition this either means a big grand plan needs to be changed or if the work has been going on that a lot of work has to potentially be thrown away. Both of these things can (and usually do) create massive political problems as the onus is usually on someone "important" having to either change something big he/she previously announced or admit they already wasted a whole lot of money, time and resources. That's why Management should involve Architects in matters as early as possible. It's almost a case of - "if you don't involve us early enough, you better not involve us at all because you probably won't like what we are going to say!"

Architects can often be accused of living in a "perfect world". This is really just a perception problem. Because they can see things clearly that others cannot see, or cannot easily see, or do not want to see, they can see those things are achievable while others think they are not.

In general, people see disagreements as confrontations - and people in general really hate confrontations and tend to do anything and everything to avoid them. That, of course, does not mean that they do not tell anyone, it just means they tell the "wrong" people. How many times have you received bad service in a restaurant or from a call centre but didn't say

Culture

anything at the time, but then complained to your friends about it later? There is a saying in retail - a happy customer will tell one friend, an unhappy one will tell ten.

> "A wise man gets more use from his enemies than a fool from his friends."
>
> *- Baltasar Gracian*

Of course, with the advent of the internet, social media and YouTube, if you are unlucky, one unhappy customer will tell thirteen million people - as happened with the famous "United Breaks Guitars" case. United Airlines concentrated on saving $1,200. Their stock price fell 10% four days after the YouTube video was posted wiping $180 million off the company's value. The resulting bad publicity cost them unimaginably more.

But we digress. The bigger the disagreement, the greater the perceived confrontation. There is also an element that the person who believes they hold the most "power" tends to see the other person as confrontational rather than the other way round. If the disagreement is about something small or of no real significance the confrontation is very small, but if the disagreement is about something of fundamental importance then confrontation can be huge. Bearing in mind that Architects only talk about things of fundamental significance, it could be said that appearing to be confrontational is not only possible, it is mandatory!

> "As an Architect, if you aren't annoying someone, you aren't doing your
> job properly"
>
> *- Pragmatic*

The new light Architects expose (through the old windows of peoples existing perceptions) is very challenging for many people as this basically takes them out of their comfort zone. Big time. Most people do not like that at all. Most people are happy to continue to live their lives, in their familiar comfortable pond, and they react in all manner of negative ways when someone tries to explain there is life outside their pond, especially when it impacts their pond in a big or fundamental way. They are not bad people.

So, where do architects "fit"? The simple answer is, nowhere and everywhere. They don't really fit anywhere! This is why many architects always have an uneasy feeling of being different and misunderstood.

> "When green is all there is to be
> It could make you wonder why, but why wonder?
> Why Wonder, I am green and it'll do fine, it's beautiful!
> And I think it's what I want to be."
>
> *- Kermit the Frog*
> *It 'ain't easy, being green.*
> http://youtu.be/hpilWMWWVco

> ## KEYPOINT:
>
> "Every noble work is at first,
>
> impossible."
>
> - Thomas Carlyle

> ## ADOPTION:
>
> C-Suite: When asking an Architect a
>
> question, do not expect an
>
> Engineering answer.

Questions to Ponder

- ♦ How do you react when an Architect talks about unknown unknowns?
- ♦ How do you react when you cannot see what an Architect is trying to explain?
- ♦ How do you react when an Architect is in the minority?
- ♦ How do you react when an Architect exposes (fundamental) things that may cause you to change a previous decision or cause you to "throw away" work?

Culture

"Our job is to give the client ... not what he wants, but what he never dreamed that he wanted; and when he gets it, he recognizes it as something he wanted all the time."

- Sir Denys Lasdon

Some notable quotes that I believe illustrates what an Architect does,

> "Architecture at all levels provides the Landing strip of intent for any viable implementation to touch down on."
>
> *- {{Gareth Llewellyn}}*

> "An Architect knows his job is done, not when there is nothing more to add, but when there is nothing more to take away."
>
> *- Based on a quote from Antoine de Saint-Exupéry, Airman's Odyssey*

> "The architect must be a prophet... a prophet in the true sense of the term... if he can't see at least ten years ahead don't call him an architect."
>
> *- Frank Lloyd Wright*

> "The most important tool for an Architect is his eraser."
>
> *- Frank Lloyd Wright*

> "Every great architect is - necessarily - a great poet. He must be a great original interpreter of his time, his day, his age."
>
> *- Frank Lloyd Wright*

> "There is nothing more uncommon than common sense."
>
> *- Frank Lloyd Wright*

> "All fine architectural values are human values, else not valuable."

- Frank Lloyd Wright

"Early in life, I had to choose between honest arrogance and hypocritical humility. I chose honest arrogance and have seen no occasion to change."

- Frank Lloyd Wright

"Form follows function- that has been misunderstood. Form and function should be one, joined in a spiritual union."

- Frank Lloyd Wright

"A great architect is not made by way of a brain nearly so much as he is made by way of a cultivated, enriched heart. "

- Frank Lloyd Wright

"Our job is to give the client ... not what he wants but what he never dreamed that he wanted; and when he gets it, he recognizes it as something he wanted all the time."

- Sir Denys Lasdon

"A good Architect can't sleep because a piece of the puzzle is missing. A bad Architect can't sleep because his conscience won't let him."

- Unknown

> # KEYPOINT:
>
> "Architecture provides the Landing strip of intent, for any viable implementation to land on."
>
> - {{Gareth Llewellyn}}

> # ADOPTION:
>
> C-Suite: If you know what you want, but don't know what you need, ask an Architect.

Questions to Ponder

- Do you agree with Sir Denys Lasdon?
- If not, how would you describe the job of an Architect (of any domain)?
- What do others in your Enterprise believe?

Culture

© Pragmatic 365 (2008-2021)

How can you tell the difference between an Architect and a Charlatan?

DO NOT TURN THE PAGE.
YET….

Please take some time to consider an answer to this question.

Think about the kinds of things an Architect and a Charlatan might say.

Think about how you would determine (from how they speak and what they say) which one was an Architect and which one was a Charlatan?

Then, turn the page to find the shocking answer….

You can't!

Both talk of future benefit that is impossible or difficult to quantify and understand.

- The Architect speaks in this way because it's true.
- The Charlatan speaks in this way to draw you in.

Both say that they will have fantastic effects.

- The Architect speaks in this way because it's true.
- The Charlatan speaks in this way to draw you in.

Both say they can see into the future.

- The Architect speaks in this way because it's true.
- The Charlatan speaks in this way to draw you in.

Of course, from the perspective of what they do, they are very different, but from the perspective of someone who doesn't know if you are a Charlatan or not, they are almost indistinguishable by the things they say. It all sounds a bit like "smoke and mirrors".

So, as an Architect, don't be surprised if people look at you as a potential Charlatan.

That is the way an Architect looks to many people - especially the kind of people Architects are "selling" to, such as Leaders, Executives, Managers, CxO's, Directors etc. These kinds of people have spent many many years listening to the claims and promises of hundreds of vendors who all want to sell them the next bottle of snake-oil and will promise anything just to make the sale.

Architects need to accept that inconvenient truth and deal with it.

Face it.

Talk about it.

Openly.

Because if you don't, many people will view you as a Charlatan, whether you like it or not, whether you realise it or not.

They are not bad people, they are just a product of the Context they operate in. A context that consists of a never ending supply of salesman and vendors telling them that their offering is the next big things that has will solve all their problems.

KEYPOINT:

"The value of Architecture is intangible.

If it were tangible, it would be Engineering."

- Kevin Lee Smith

ADOPTION:

C-Suite: When asking an Architect a question, do not expect a tangible answer.

Questions to Ponder

♦ Do you or your Enterprise view Architects as Charlatans, promising snake oil that will cure all ills?
♦ Do you or your Enterprise view Architects as people that talk in future promise that cannot really be objectively quantified?

Culture > The Architect > The Pragmatic Architect Creed

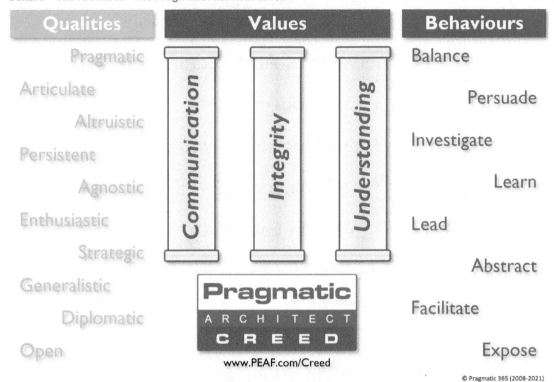

© Pragmatic 365 (2008-2021)

The **Pragmatic** Architect Creed (PAC) is a set of values, qualities and behaviours that an Architect in any domain should abide by. It effectively defines the culture of a **Pragmatic** Architect.

If a **Pragmatic** Architect is asked to do something which conflicts with the Creed, or is aware that another **Pragmatic** Architect is acting in conflict with the values, he or she should raise a concern within their own department. Their department should investigate their concern. If the **Pragmatic** Architect remains dissatisfied following the outcome of the investigation, they may bring a complaint to the **Pragmatic** Architect Commission. In some cases, the Commission may also hear a complaint direct.

You can sign the **Pragmatic** Creed at www.Pragmatic365.org/creed

Pillars

The creed defines of 3 main values:

♦ **Communication** – Recognising that open, honest and direct communication is key to both understanding and being understood.
♦ **Integrity** – Recognising that being a trusted advisor is key to being believed by our clients.
♦ **Understanding** – Recognising that understanding client's minds and getting clients to understand our mind is the backbone of what we do.

For each of these values, there are statements that a **Pragmatic** Architect should be able to recite, with their hand on their heart.

Communication

♦ I believe that communication is crucially important as an architect.

♦ I believe that communication is key to me understanding other people and getting others to understand me.

♦ I believe that without good communication, no relationship can survive or thrive.

♦ I evangelise the value of Architecture and its benefits.

♦ I strive to create a "safe environment" where people are free to express their views without fear of punishment or recrimination.

♦ I relate new things that people do not know to things that people already know.

♦ I can vehemently agree with someone about subject/point "A" when I have only recently vehemently disagreed with the same person about subject/point "B".

♦ I commit whatever time is required to explain and convince others when I am right.

♦ I can always explain the reasoning behind my views.

♦ I can clearly communicate contextual, conceptual, logical and complex issues and trade-offs to any audience.

♦ I am comfortable talking and presenting to large groups or individuals at any level.

Integrity

♦ I believe that integrity is crucially important as an architect.

♦ I believe that an architect's biggest asset is the trust he is afforded by the people he works for and the people he works with.

♦ I believe that without trust, no relationship can survive or thrive.

♦ I ensure the interests of the Enterprise as a whole are addressed even if they appear to conflict with immediate management.

♦ I stand up and give an unpalatable truth when no one else will, even though it may mean I lose my job.

♦ I will seek to terminate a consulting engagement early if it transpires that the customer can get no or little value by continuing.

♦ I always tell the truth.

♦ I never hide or disguise things.

♦ I tell clients what they need to hear, not what they want to hear.

♦ I welcome being proved wrong and if I am, admit it as soon as possible.

♦ I suggest only appropriate solutions - even if that is a 'pen and paper solution'.

Understanding

♦ I believe that understanding is crucially important as an architect.

♦ I believe that if we do not understand something, people cannot form opinions or solutions to problems.

♦ I believe that without understanding, no relationship can survive or thrive.

♦ I believe that the primary responsibility of an architect is to enable informed decision making.

♦ I believe that the most important question to ask is - Why?

♦ I see patterns and structure in everything from traffic congestion to Pop music and flowers.

♦ I spend more time understanding a problem domain than determining a solution.

♦ I spend more time asking questions and listening than I do talking.

- I can see disagreement between people when those people think they are in agreement and vice versa.
- I can abstract anything or idea to a logical and conceptual level.
- I constantly self-analyse what I do and how I do it to determine how to improve myself and my work.
- I know the difference between Architecture & Engineering.
- I know the difference between types of abstraction (Omission/Inclusion, Composition/Decomposition, Generalisation/Specialisation, Idealisation/Realisation) and when and how to use them effectively.
- I know the difference between types of Idealisation/Realisation (Contextual, Conceptual, Logical, Physical, Operational) and when and how to use them effectively.
- I know the difference between a model, a meta-model, and meta-meta-model.

Qualities

	Description	Rationale
Pragmatic	They are always looking to understand what the perfect solution can be but tempering that with a more commercial and tactical view that relates to the realities of getting things done.	Architects need to be able to see the long term perfect solution but they need to be able to temper that unattainable goal with the tactics of getting things done.
Articulate	They are at home communicating with everyone from the board to the graduate programmer or claims clerk and in scales from one to one to speaking to hundreds at conferences.	Communication is a major part of an Architects role. Being able to listen, ask the right questions, and explain things in words that people can understand from CEOs to the tea lady.
Altruistic	They are selfless, and always focused on what is best for the Enterprise not what is best for them.	Architects are 100% focused on the Enterprise they work for. Even if this means losing their own job.
Persistent	They will not be steamrollered and will stand up for what they believe in.	A good idea or a worthy point that needs to be made for the benefit of the Enterprise, needs to be made regardless of an environment that may not let that happen.
Agnostic	They see all things from Supercomputers to paper, pencils and people as possible solutions to business problems and will propose the most appropriate for any given context not what their favourite is.	Architecture is all about providing business value, not about and Architect's "favourite" things.
Enthusiastic	They are passionate and enthusiastic about what they do and how they do it.	Enthusiasm is an inspiring trait and Architects need to inspire others in order to affect and guide the culture of an Enterprise.
Strategic	They are focused on long term and lasting benefits rather than short term benefits which compromise long term objectives.	Long term and lasting benefits are more important strategically to an Enterprise.

Culture

Generalistic	They have a broad base of technical and business experience.	Architects deal with breadth rather than depth, and therefore need a broad range of business and technical skills.
Diplomatic	They are sensitive to other people's drivers and the political context.	Architecture is more to do with people and culture than anything else. Architects therefore need to be able to discuss often difficult and controversial subjects and truths with tact and sensitivity.
Open	They are open to critique, happy to be proved wrong, and will assimilate and apply new information as it arises.	Architects do not have all the answers. They need to be open to criticisms and open to adjusting their views as new information is exposed or the environment changes.

Behaviours

	Description	Rationale
Balance {{Tamás Nacsák}}	They balance a multitude of different and often competing factors in order to arrive at solutions that make the best of	The problems Architects solve are "wicked problems". Such problems do not have simple answers. Indeed, the questions they answer are also not simple.
Persuade	They persuade others of their views and the way forward rather than dictating.	Architects rely on others to achieve their aims and as such people must be persuaded of an approach. When people buy into an idea or approach they are much happier and much more productive.
Investigate	They have a nose to seek out things that don't make sense or could pose threats and risks, and the ability to get to the bottom of them.	Things that don't make sense are usually problems or opportunities. Either way, Architects need to be able to dig into things where necessary to expose them so that they can be addressed.
Learn	They pick up and assimilate new information quickly and easily and are always open to new ideas, businesses, technologies and processes.	Business and the world is an ever-changing place. New things are happening all the time and Architects need to quickly understand them and how they impact the business.
Lead	They lead, motivate, inspire and enable others to reach their potential and create the environment where people want to follow them.	Architecture is all about culture, and therefore to adopt and make the cultural changes required, Architects need to be able to take individuals and the Enterprise on a journey and that journey must be by mutual consent not by dictation.
Abstract	They abstract levels of detail to higher levels to aid understanding and to see hidden relationships and patterns.	Architecture is a lot about seeing structure and patterns. In order to do this an Architect needs to be able to see and synthesise these higher-level structures from underlying information that can be very detailed and/or incomplete.
Facilitate	They guide discussions and workshops in order to get the best out of people.	Architecture is a lot about communication and also about liberating information from others. It is also important to be able to guide discussions and to bring people together where there is agreement and to facilitate valued discussed where there are differences.

Culture

Expose	They seek to expose pertinent information to business leaders to enable them to make more informed decisions.	Decisions will get made regardless of whether full and/or pertinent facts are known. Architecture is all about making sure people who make decisions are fully aware of the risks, issues and implications before the decision is made.

```
┌─────────────────────────────────────────────┐
│                                             │
│               KEYPOINT:                     │
│                                             │
│   The Pragmatic Architects Creed™           │
│                                             │
│   sorts the wheat from the chaff.           │
│                                             │
└─────────────────────────────────────────────┘
```

```
┌─────────────────────────────────────────────┐
│                                             │
│               ADOPTION:                     │
│                                             │
│   C-Suite: Mandate the use of the           │
│                                             │
│   Pragmatic Architects Creed™ to            │
│                                             │
│   recruit Architects.                       │
│                                             │
└─────────────────────────────────────────────┘
```

Questions to Ponder

- Would these Qualities and Behaviours be beneficial to your Enterprise?
- If so, in what parts of your Enterprise and in what roles?
- what happens to people who exhibit these Qualities and Behaviours in your Enterprise?
- Do you evaluate your current employees or new hires using these Qualities and Behaviours
- If not, which Qualities and Behaviours do you actively look for?
- Will you sign the Creed?

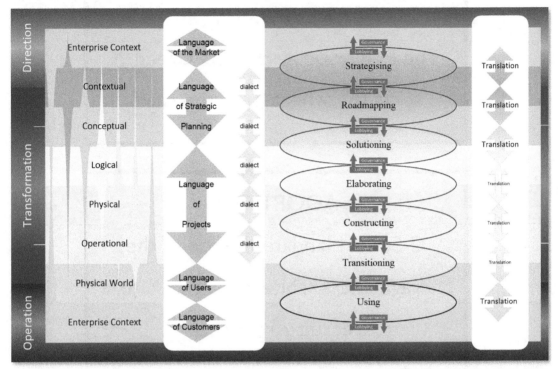

© Pragmatic 365 (2008-2021)

Although we all speak our native tongue fluently, the same cannot be said about the language we use to talk about things in relation to the Transformation of Enterprises. Different people use different words to mean different things at different times. This is a massive problem which makes understanding anything anyone says at best impossible and at worst apparently possible. People, including me, get attached to the meaning of the words we use and defend those meanings passionately. This is totally understandable because the meanings we attach to words is the absolute basis for our understanding things.

It is therefore extremely pertinent to understand how roles communicate with other roles at the same level, between levels in the same area and between each area. Languages correspond to the overall areas of The Market, Strategic Planning, Projects, Users and Customers. People within those areas can use slightly different words but they are more akin to dialects. Recognition of these different languages and dialects is important but more importantly is the realisation that people who operate in the various phases of the Transformation Stack need to be able to speak at least two different languages (if not three) and therefore also need to be able to translate between them depending on who they are talking to or what information they are dealing with.

There are five fundamental languages:

♦ **The Language of The Market** - The language used by senior executives and the board to communicate with The Enterprise Context (Regulators, Investors, Competitors, Suppliers, Customer Segments, Communities, Governments, Non-clients, Non Suppliers, Anti-Clients, The Media, etc)

♦ **The Language of Strategic Planning** - The language used by senior executives and the board to formulate the Enterprise Strategy as it relates to the Enterprise Context, and to create Strategic Plans, Project Portfolios and Roadmaps to execute any Transformation required to deliver the Strategy.

- ◆ **The Language of Projects** - The language used by all those working on Transformation projects while executing individual projects.
- ◆ **The Language of the Users** - The language used by those operating parts of the Enterprise that Transformation is delivered into.
- ◆ **The Language of Customers** - The Language used by those operating the business to relate to and communicate with Customers.

It is particularly important to pay attention to Governance and Lobbying where the fundamental Language barriers are. If the people performing those functions do not understand each others language, the whole Governance and Lobbying discipline will break down, and take the rest of the Transformation capability with it.

One thing a Framework or Ontology brings (hopefully!) is a common and consistent language. The importance of which should not be underestimated.

> ## KEYPOINT:
>
> For each phase of the Transformation cascade, people speak either a different dialect or language from the phases above and below.

> ## ADOPTION:
>
> C-Suite: Instigate an initiative to educate people on the different languages used in all areas of the Enterprise.

Questions to Ponder

- What Languages does your Enterprise use for Enterprise Transformation?
- Do people recognise when they are talking a different language?
- What happens when people say "we are talking a different language"?
- Are different languages taught?
- If not, how do you expect people to be able to communicate effectively?

APPENDIX

> # KEYPOINT:
>
> The Appendix section contains
>
> information on the background of
>
> PF2, POET, PEAF and the author.

WHY?	• We Care About Enterprises • We Care About the People who Direct, Operate, Transform and Support Enterprises
WHEN?	• PEAF 2008 • POET 2014 • PTMC 2018
WHERE?	• Born from Observing Failure
HOW?	• 150,000 Hours of Thinking • 20,000 Hours of Creating
USING WHAT?	• Architecture, Engineering, Altruism • Honesty, Integrity, Persistence, Passion • Common Sense, Logic

© Pragmatic 365 (2008-2021)

Why Were They Created?

Because I care. Because I care about Enterprises. Because I care about the people who **Direct**, **Operate**, **Transform** and **Support** Enterprises. Because I am angry about how much time is wasted. Because I am angry about how much money is wasted. From the Afghani to the Zloty, I guarantee you are wasting it. Big time!

This work was inspired by all those who seek to make the world a better place rather than those that seek to own it.

When Were They Created?

PEAF was initially launched in November 2008 and POET in 2014.

Where Did They Come From?

All **Pragmatic** Ontologies and Frameworks were created from observing failure. That is:

- ◆ Seeing why people fail
- ◆ What problems they encounter
- ◆ Providing things to reduce the risk of others failing in the same way
- ◆ Providing things to alleviate the problems people have.

Around 2002 I began to be interested in something called "Enterprise Architecture". The term started to appear more in publications and people started to talk about it more - although from listening to them there never seemed to be a concrete definition of what it actually was that everyone agreed with (some say that's still the case today!). Using logic and common sense I could surmise that it was not Project level Architecture (because that already had a name - Solution Architecture) and therefore it must be something at a "higher level" - not just bigger. Something related to:

♦ What goes on before projects execute and before Solution Architects start working on those projects.
♦ Enterprise Centric, or more specifically Enterprise Transformation Centric, rather than Project Centric and/or IT Centric.

At that time it all seemed to be a bit of a black art (some say it still is!) and so, being an Architect and not wanting to reinvent the wheel (others call it being lazy!), I surmised that there must be something out there (a bit like Prince or ITIL or MSP for example) - a framework - that might help people to "do" EA by:

♦ Helping people understand what EA was.
♦ Helping people increase the maturity in how an Enterprise "does" EA.

So, I consulted the mighty Google (sorry Oracle!). Google told me about something called Zachman and something called TOGAF. And so I went off to investigate further.

From what I could tell, Zachman's message seemed to resonate well with me in terms of general thinking I had built up over the preceding 20 years, namely:

♦ You can't change what you can't see - hence the need to model things - in a structured way.
♦ There must be Phases involved in Transformation to get from Strategic intent at the top down to real physically deployed things at the bottom.

These basic messages haven't changed and are as valid today as they always were - although the important distinction between Enterprise Architecture and Enterprise Engineering that **Pragmatic** makes today was not (and still is not) recognised in Zachman (despite my attempts to do so). But, whilst these fundamental things (modelling and phases/levels) were a good start, they were much too high level to provide any practical help in using them (which is what a framework is supposed to do) and so I invested more time looking into the much more detailed TOGAF.

As I looked into TOGAF, the first thing that struck me was "Where the hell do I start?". The material was immense, complex, confusing, very dry, hard to consume and offered no guidance about how to adopt it. So, assuming it was my ignorance that was the problem I booked myself on a TOGAF course. Within the first 2 hours of the first day it became clear that it was centred around Project level IT centric Architecture.

Nothing wrong with Project level IT centric Architecture, but not Enterprise Architecture.

Fantastic for those Enterprises that had still not figured out that the complexity of the IT landscape had grown to such a level that using Architecture as a discipline on IT Projects (Solution Architecture) was almost mandatory (unless you wanted to waste a shed load of money and deliver a shed load of bad IT to customers), but not Enterprise Architecture.

Great for those Enterprise that wanted to formalise their Solution Architecture discipline, but not Enterprise Architecture.

Great for those Enterprises that wanted to continue to treat "The Business" as a second class citizen to "IT", but not Enterprise Architecture.

At least not the Enterprise Architecture that logic and common sense dictated to me.

Anyway, I got through the course, passed the exams and became TOGAF Certified. Over the next few years I worked at various organisations and my TOGAF certification served me well in terms of getting me job interviews and most of the subsequent contracts. Having got a contract (because I was TOGAF certified) I then endeavoured to first discover how much and what parts of TOGAF were being used. The conversation (over many days, sometimes weeks) usually went something like this:

> K: "Hi Allen, I'm new here. I've been told that you use TOGAF, can you tell me what parts you are using and which you aren't?"
>
> A: "Hi Kevin, Errrmm, Yeah sure - you need to talk to Steve, he's the one that did the training."

<time passes....>

> K: "Hi Steve, I'm new here. I've been told that you use TOGAF, can you tell me what parts you are using and which you aren't?"
>
> S: "Hi Kevin, Errrmm, why are you asking me?"
>
> K: "Allen told me you did the training and you would know."
>
> S: "Err yeah, but I was only one of the twenty people who did it, I wasn't the main person. Listen - I'm a bit busy on this CRM project at the moment, can you go and ask James about it - I think he was the main guy."

<time passes....>

> K: "Hi James, I'm new here. I've been told that you use TOGAF, can you tell me what parts you are using and which you aren't?"
>
> J: "Hi Kevin, Errrmm, why are you asking me?"
>
> K: "Steve told me you did the training and you were the main guy so you would know."
>
> J: "Err yeah, but I was moved off that onto this ESB project. Listen - I'm a bit busy at the moment, Dave took over that TOGAF thing - go talk to Dave."

<time passes....>

> K: "Hi Dave, I'm new here. I've been told that you use TOGAF, can you tell me what parts you are using and which you aren't?"
>
> D: "Hi Kevin, Errrmm - why are you asking me?"
>
> K: "James told me you did the training and you're now the guy in charge of TOGAF adoption."
>
> D: "Err No! That's Chris, you need to talk to Chris"

<time passes....>

> K: "Hi Chris, I'm new here. I've been told that you use TOGAF, can you tell me what parts you are using and which you aren't?"
>
> C: "Hi Kevin, Errrmm, why are you asking me?"
>
> K: "James told me Dave did the training and he was the guy in charge of TOGAF adoption, but that Dave says it wasn't him, it was you"

> C: "Err Yeah - well I went on the course, but to be honest we never did
>
> anything about if after that, you should go talk to Allen, he knows what's
>
> going on"

In every case, after being passed from pillar to post, it always transpired that no one was actually using TOGAF at all.

So, I began to build up my own intellectual capital (documents, checklists, presentations, spreadsheets, ideas, concepts, processes, products, etc) so that I could bring them to bear as a set of quick start artefacts for subsequent contracts.

During 2008 it suddenly dawned on me that all this intellectual capital that I had built up, actually constituted what I thought an EA framework should contain. So, in addition to cleaning up and structuring the material so others could adopt and use it easily, I had to choose a name. So, I thought, what one word would sum up my approach? A core of fundamental things - the 20% that would give 80% of the benefit - that would reduce or remove 20% of the risks that cause 80% of the failures. Cutting through all the smoke and mirrors and Cutting EA to the Bone. And so the name **Pragmatic** chose me.

How Were They Created?

POET and PEAF have taken more than 10,000 hours to produce in terms of physical work, born from approximately 150,000 hours of thinking. The graphics were not just drawn - like most good things they evolved - and while many of them look quite simple, it took an awful lot of work and pain to get to those simple graphics. To an outside observer, those diagrams could appear as if someone just sat down and drew them but each one has had many versions as it has evolved, coalesced, fragmented, reconstituted, gone down the wrong track, fragmented, coalesced again and then finally thrown away, only to be resurrected when a light bulb went on somewhere in the deepest darkest recesses of my feeble brain.

Elegance and simplicity takes a lot of hard work to achieve but, anything **Pragmatic** must be so.

> "Je n'ai fait celle-ci plus longue que parce que je n'ai pas eu le loisir de la
>
> faire plus courte."
>
> *- Blaise Pascal ("Lettres Provinciales", 1657)*

Which loosely translates to

> "If I Had More Time, I Would Have Written a Shorter Letter"

In fact, the amount of things and work I have thrown away greatly outweighs what now exists.

I believe that POET and PEAF have achieved elegance and simplicity to some degree but, of course, "we don't live in a perfect world" (as so many Managers I have worked for in the past have reminded me on so many occasions) and there is always more work to do. POET and PEAF will evolve, as everything must do, but for now, it is good enough.

With the benefit of time to think of a suitable response to those Managers, my response now would be:

> "We don't live in a perfect world?
>
> I know - Believe me I know!
>
> If we did, we wouldn't be having this conversation ;-)"

What Was Used to Create Them?

Basically, common sense. It has always amazed me, how many things in business (and in life) do not seem to adhere to any common sense at all, which probably explains why a lot of things that are created to help people improve or mature something, contain a lot of common sense. In addition I have a brain split into two parts (Architecture and Engineering) that work together but also conflict a lot of the time. But it is from this conflict that progress lies.

Methods

♦ Architecture, Engineering, Logic.

Artefacts

♦ Input - Air, Water, Nespresso, Earl Grey, Toast, Ham Eggs & Chips, Bombay Sapphire (Tonic), Johnny Walker Black Label (Coke Zero), Whiskers, Paper, Ink, Blood, Sweat, Tears.

♦ Output - PF2 Book, POET Book, PEAF Book, **Pragmatic365**.org Website

Guidance

♦ Common Sense, W.E. Deming, J. Zachman, T. Graves.

Items

♦ Biological Technology - Kevin - Generally all of him, but mostly his brain, eyes and hands. (His stomach, colon and bladder put in an appearance occasionally, with his posterior providing a supporting role :-), Murphy the cat.

♦ Mechanical Technology - 25 Buttermere, Braintree, Essex, CM77 7UY, UK, Desk, Chair, Whiteboard (Pens and Eraser).

♦ Electrical - Challenge Fan Heater, Creative GigaWorks T40 Series II 2.0 PC Speakers

♦ Information Technology

  ♦ Hardware - Dell Latitude E6520 (Intel i7-2760QM @ 2.4GHz, 8GB RAM), 2 * 32in 2560x1600 LED Monitors, 2 * 24in 1920x1200 LED Monitors, HP Officejet Pro X576, Samsung Galaxy Note 8.

  ♦ Software - MS Windows 10, MS Visio, MS Word, MS Excel, MS PowerPoint, Paint.NET, Integromat, CognitoForms

  ♦ Languages – VBA, VBscript, Javascript, SQL, ASP, HTML, CSS

  ♦ Data – (mp3) David Bowie, Pet Shop Boys, Dean Martin, Chris Rea.

Culture

♦ God, Honesty, Integrity, Pragmatism, Altruism, Persistence, Passion, Psychology

> # KEYPOINT:
>
> Use POET and PEAF to make sure
> you don't make the mistakes that
> cause 90% of all EA initiatives to fail.

Questions to Ponder

♦ Do you think that observing failure is a good way to figure out how to improve things?

♦ What failures have you witnessed in the past?

♦ What does that tell you about how to improve it?

- # Kevin Lee Smith

- # 40 Years in all phases of Enterprise Transformation

- # MBTI: (INTJ) Mastermind, (INTP) Architect

- # DISC: (7414) Result-Oriented

- # Belbin: Plant, Shaper

Who Created The Pragmatic Family of Frameworks (PF2)?

A simple man.

My career began at the age of 16 in 1978 as an Electrical and Electronic Apprentice with Marconi Radar Systems (Blackbird Road, Leicester, UK) At that time I was really into electronics and had been playing with little circuits for a few years. It was really exciting. I spent my time between college and "The Factory" where I got the chance to work in many different departments. It was really exciting. Around 1980 I ended up in a Department (New Parks, Leicester UK) called TEPIGEN (**TE**levision **PI**cture **GEN**erator) who had built the visual system for a ship simulator. Six million Pounds of custom built hardware (that had less processing power than the CPU in the phone that's in your pocket) consisting mainly of four racks of "Picture Processors" (Motorola 68000s) driven by a PDP11. It was really exciting. The output was on three channels each delivering 40 degrees field of view which drove three large Barco projectors. Interestingly at one point there were black speckles that kept appearing on the displays, moving about in random patterns and appearing and disappearing in the same apparently random fashion. After months of software and hardware investigation the problem was identified. It was a test Radar across the apron from where our Portacabins where located that was spraying us periodically with microwaves! It was really exciting.

I began my time there hand entering the data which described the terrain and buildings and which fed the picture processors, and wrote my first program in DEC BASIC. Over the next four years or so my programming skills grew, and I moved from BASIC to FORTRAN and then to PASCAL. It was really exciting. The ship simulator turned into a flight simulator which meant it was the biggest video game in the world. It was really exciting. So much so that I would work late into the night (sometimes 48 hours at a stretch) and go into work on Saturdays or Sundays. Right from the beginning it wasn't so much the code I wrote that I got excited about it was more HOW I wrote the code that interested me. I would often spend hours writing a program and finally get it working, only to tear it to pieces and rewrite it in a new and elegant way, often with more features, less code and more opportunity to reuse things later. It was really exciting. Even at that time I spent more time throwing things away than I spent creating things. I believe this is where progress comes from. Sounds totally counter-intuitive I know, but most things of value are counter-intuitive!

Around 1986 the plug was pulled on TEPIGEN and I moved to another department (Fleet, Hampshire, UK) who produced a system called TELEVIEW (an improvement on Teletext and a forerunner of "The Web") for Singapore's Telecom Company (SingTel). I had moved on to C as a programming language. The most elegant and powerful language I have ever used. It took me a while to understand it but after reading the perfect "The C Programming Language" (Kernighan and Ritchie) the penny dropped. It was really exciting.

A brief spell at SD Scicon (1989-1991) was followed by three years working for Deutsche Bank (Singapore) where I found the best food in the world and where my architectural tendencies came to the fore. It was really exciting. While there I created and sold a numerical analysis package for lottery numbers called Mega4D. Returning in 1994 I spent six years working for Eurobase Systems (Chelmsford, UK) doing Application Architecture and creating Architectural and programming frameworks.

From 2000 to 2011 I spent my time working for various Enterprises as a contractor. While interesting, it wasn't very exciting, but all the time, whatever domain I worked in I was always interested in improving it. Each time this met a limit and the limit was always as a consequence of things being done less than effectively and less than efficiently in the preceding step. Hence my roles moved from Application Architecture, Data Architecture and Technology Architecture into Technical Architecture (a bit of a misnomer!) then Solution Architecture then Enterprise Architecture and finally the entire Transformation domain.

Since 2011 I have devoted my time to **Pragmatic**. It is really exciting.

Whilst I have never been an academic person, and never went to university (I have always preferred to "go out and do stuff") I have recognised over the last year that Psychology plays such a vital role in Enterprise Transformation (for good or bad) and so in February 2014 I began a BSc (Honours) Psychology degree with The Open University. It is really exciting.

MBTI

My MBTI is a split between **INTJ** and **INTP**.

INTJ - Sometimes referred to as the "Architect," or the "Strategist," people with INTJ personalities are highly analytical, creative and logical.

Strengths: Enjoys theoretical and abstract concepts. High expectations. Good at listening. Takes criticism well. Self-confident and hard-working.

Weaknesses: Can be overly analytical and judgmental. Very perfectionistic. Dislikes talking about emotions. Sometimes seems callous or insensitive.

INTP - People who score as INTP are often described as quiet and analytical. They enjoy spending time alone, thinking about how things work and coming up with solutions to problems. INTPs have a rich inner world and would rather focus their attention on their internal thoughts rather than the external world. They typically do not have a wide social circle, but they do tend to be close to a select group of people.

Strengths: Logical and objective. Abstract thinker. Independent. Loyal and affectionate with loved ones.

Weaknesses: Difficult to get to know. Can be insensitive. Prone to self-doubt. Struggles to follow rules. Has trouble expressing feelings.

DISC

My DISC Profile is 7414 and categorised as **Result-Oriented.**

Result-Oriented people display self-confidence, which some may interpret as arrogance. They actively seek opportunities that test and develop their abilities to accomplish results. Result-Oriented persons like difficult tasks, competitive situations, unique assignments, and "important" positions. They undertake responsibilities with an air of self-importance and display self-satisfaction once they have finished.

Result-Oriented people tend to avoid constraining factors such as direct controls, time-consuming details, and routine work. Because they are forceful and direct, they may have difficulties with others. Result-Oriented people prize their independence and may become restless where involved with group activities or committee work. Although Result-Oriented people generally prefer to work alone, they may persuade others to support their efforts especially when completing routine activities.

Result-Oriented people are quick-thinkers, and they are impatient and fault-finding with those who are not They evaluate others on their ability to get results. Result Oriented people are determined and persistent even in the face of antagonism. They take command of the situation when necessary, whether or not they are in charge. In their uncompromising drive for results, they may appear blunt and uncaring.

Belbin

Belbin categorises me as a **Plant** (Creative and inventive individuals, Plants are the ones in the team most likely to come up with new ideas and suggestions. The name comes from Dr Belbin's original research. It was discovered that there was no initial spark of an idea in a team unless a creative person was "planted" in each team) and a **Shaper** (Shapers are people who challenge the team to improve. They are dynamic and usually extroverted people who enjoy stimulating others, questioning norms, and finding the best approaches for solving problems.).

Putting MBTI, DISC and Belbin together just about sums me up to a tee.

Different people have different profiles, and different profiles fit into different roles in different ways. We all kind of know this but do we ever take it into account?

> # KEYPOINT:
>
> Use people for the type of person they are, not the type of person you want them to be. If we were all the same, nothing would ever get done.

Questions to Ponder

- What are the MBTI, DISC and Belbin profiles of the people in your Enterprise?
- Do they all suit their roles?
- Have you ever found someone to be a "difficult person" or a "loose cannon"?
- If so, did their MBTI/DISC/Belbin profile taken into account?

The only constant is the ACCELERATION of change. POET helps you cope with the punishing G-Force, by driving the Transformation of Transformation™.

The Adoption section of POET defines 'HOW' it should be adopted and used.

Designing Changes allows you to decide what to change from POET to your own XOET.

Use POET to design your own XOET.

Developing Changes allows you to create your own XOET.

Use P3 to develop your own XOET.

Rollout Changes allows you to rollout your own XOET for people to use.

Use P3 to train your staff in your own XOET

The Methods section of POET defines 'WHAT' should be done, 'HOW' and 'WHEN'.

The seven phases of transformation (Strategising, Roadmapping, Solutioning, Elaborating, Constructing, Transitioning, Using) are connected with the Governance & Lobbying discipline.

Business Architecture feeds Enterprise Architecture feeds Solution Architecture feeds Enterprise Engineering.

99.9% of Enterprises are happy to spend money on improving Engineering, but are very reticent to spend money on improving Architecture.

Strategising is what the C-Suite does.

Roadmapping is "doing" Enterprise Architecture.

Solutioning is "doing" Solution Architecture.

Do not constrain Solution Architecture in executing projects.

Elaborating, Constructing and Transitioning is "doing" Projects.

Use the Transformation cascade to link the phases together.

Understand how common artefacts relate to the Phase cascade.

The Disciplines are used to a greater or lesser extent in each phase.

The Disciplines form the Capability Model for the Transformation Capability of the Enterprise.

MAGIC relates to the Structural information and MAGMA relates to the Transformational information that each phase consumes and produces.

The 6 main disciplines are: Discovery, Requirements Management, Analysis & Design, Governance & Lobbying, Modelling and Decision Making.

Use discipline Orchestration to guide the overall work going on in a Phase.

Requirements provided to a phase, will never by sufficient for that phase.

Finding information to perform a job is just as important as performing the job.

Architecture and Engineering lie at the heart of Analysis and Design.

1. Only model things to answer a question. 2. Treat model population as a Data Migration exercise. 3. Integrate/remove source data.

1. Only model things to answer a question. 2. Treat model population as a Data Migration exercise. 3. Integrate/remove source data.

"The crucial differences which distinguish human societies and human beings are not biological. They are cultural."
-Ruth Benedict

"Too many cooks spoil the broth"
"Many hands make light work"

"Unless we embrace changing decisions, we will always be stuck with bad ones."
- Kevin Lee Smith

Pushing the Red Button is not recommended.
It is a necessity.

"Making decisions too quickly, is as bad as making them too slowly."
- Kevin Lee Smith

Recognise that Governance & Lobbying are inextricably linked.

It is imperative that Governance is balanced by Lobbying.

Utilise Governance and Lobbying to synchronise Transformation.

Technical Debt is the future problems created when we write "bad" code. (Ward Cunningham)

Transformation Debt™ is applying the principle of Technical Debt to all Guidance, all Phases and all Levels of Transformation.

The future cost of Non-Compliance and Remediation will always be bigger than the current Cost of Compliance.

If you do not control Transformation Debt™ it will control you.

Managing Transformation Debt™ can save huge amounts of money, and (probably more importantly) time.

The Artefacts section of POET defines 'WHAT' information is consumed and produced and 'WHEN'.

The seven levels of transformation (Enterprise Context, Contextual, Conceptual, Logical, Physical, Operational, Physical Stuff) sit in between the seven phases of Transformation.

Business Architecture, Enterprise Architecture and Solution Architecture information are closely related.

Structural information (MAGIC) needs to exist at different levels of abstraction (Idealisation/Realisation).

Methods act on Artefacts that are executed by Culture (people) or Items (Technologies).

Transformational information (MAGMA) needs to exists at different levels of abstraction (Idealisation/Realisation).

The Motivation drives the creation of Actions and the production of Guidance (which guide those Actions), all of which are Assessed against the Measures.

In the past, people only saw part of the picture – they considered only Structural information.

In the past, people only saw part of the picture – that Structural information needed Strategy information.

In the past, people only saw part of the picture – that Structural information and Strategy information needed to be bridged by execution information.

In the past, people only saw part of the picture – that Strategy and Execution were the top two levels of abstraction and Structure was the conceptual, logical, physical and operational levels.

There are two fundamental domains of information (Structural & Transformational) that exists at ALL levels of abstraction.

POLDAT provides for Structural information at mostly conceptual, logical and physical levels, and no Transformational information.

BMM provides for Transformational information only relating to Strategising, and no Structural information.

EBMM covers most Structural and Transformational information but only at the top two levels.

All levels of the Enterprise Transformation model are used in all phases.

Information from all levels are used in each phase.

Ensure that the Logical and Physical levels are populated over time as a deliverable of executing projects.

Be aware that there are two main Whys: 1. Why are we doing it. 2. Why are we doing it this way.

For each phase, be aware that Context comes from above, and levels below Operationalise it.

MAGIC defines Structural information at points in time, MAGMA defines Transformational information between them.

This is the complete map of information required for Transformation to be executed in an Effective, Efficient, Agile and Durable way.

Enterprise Strategy is the Business Motivation and Capability models, set in the context of the Business Model. Transformation Strategy is the Roadmap and Operating models, set in the context of the Capability and Business Motivation models'

There is no single metamodel, that covers all the information required for Transformation.

The Guidance section of POET defines what information is used to guide people in their decision making.

Context is King™ because context can fundamentally change how something is viewed and therefore the basis of the decisions that are made about it.

The Context of something is comprised of Requirements, and Structural and Transformational constraints.

The Items section of POET defines 'WHAT' tools and frameworks are required, 'WHERE' and 'WHEN'.

X Architecture, is the fundamentally important structure of the whole of X, set in the context of things outside of X, that affect X, or are affected by X.

Any "good" Architecture ONLY EXISTS to fulfil a customer's needs.

Structural Complexity is a function of the number of things something is composed of, and the number of relationships between them.

Transformational Volatility is the rate of change of something.

Transformational Complexity is a function of the Structural Complexity and Transformational Volatility of something.

Contextual Volatility & Complexity is defined as the Structural Volatility & Transformational Volatility of the context of something.

The Architecture Paradigm™ is only applicable when Structural Complexity and Transformational Volatility are high enough.

As Transformational Complexity rises, use of the Architecture Paradigm™ becomes mandatory, to preserve your ability to transform, and manage the cost of transformation.

As the need to utilise Architecture increases, the appetite to do so will decrease.

The short term value of Architecture is overestimated.
The long term value of Architecture is underestimated.

Why is the most important question.

There are 4 types of Abstraction / Elaboration.

The relationships between things rises in a polynomial fashion.

Lines (relationships) are an order of magnitude more important than the boxes.

Look for patterns in everything.

Use structured data for all structural and transformational information, and generate "documents" as required.

Over time, frameworks have grown and overlapped.

POET provides an Ontology that you can map all other Frameworks to.

Over time, tools have grown and overlapped.

POET provides an Ontology that you can map Transformation Tools to.

Use POET to plan how all the tools you use, integrate and work together.

All Transformation Tools need to be integrated to work together.

The Culture section of POET defines the roles and the culture required.

Someone should be Accountable for the strategically important Transformation capability of the Enterprise.

The Pragmatic Role and Phase patterns are key to assigning RACI to roles.

"Culture Trumps Everything"
-Kevin Smith

"Culture is like the speed of light.

Very difficult to change."

- Kevin Lee Smith

Bad Culture knows no bounds.

It can destroy lives.

And Enterprises.

Good Culture knows no bounds.

It can lift lives.

And Enterprises.

The human brain is easily fooled.

True value is not measured by the numbers of Clicks or Likes.

Sometimes the best course of action is to not do what you are being told to do.

Short term gratification (quick wins) most often leads to long term failure. Delaying short term gratification, most often leads to long term success.

Don't be swayed by the majority. They are wrong 80% of the time!

"I hope our wisdom will grow with our power, and teach us, that the less we use our power the greater it will be."
- Thomas Jefferson.

"Nobody cares how much you know, until they know how much you care".
- Theodore Roosevelt

"It's hard to see a halo when you're looking for horns."
- Cullen Hightower

"How often it is that the angry man rages denial, of what his inner self is telling him."
- Frank Herbert (Dune)

Those who are Unconsciously Incompetent, are the one's most passionate that they are right!

Success should not be promoted.

Do not let the past, unduly affect the future.

Competence grows linearly.

Incompetence grows exponentially.

"The trouble with Sociopaths, is that they are very, very nice people!"
- Kevin Lee Smith

People with different personality traits are required for different roles

"In all chaos, there is a cosmos.
In all disorder, a secret order."
- Carl Jung

Architecture and Engineering are two sides of the same coin.

Think (and Plan) Strategically (Architecture), Act Tactically (Engineering)..

The line between Architecture and Engineering is a blurred one.

Architecture is performed largely in the early phases of Transformation, while Engineering is performed largely in the later phases.

Architecture and Engineering can be performed within any phase.

The relationship between Architecture and Engineering as we move from the top to the bottom phases is complex.

Know and exploit the fundamental difference between Architects and Engineers.

Architecture and Engineering, bring important things to the table, and makes the whole much more than the sum of its parts.

A happy productive person, balances what they are good at, with what they love, what others need, and what they want.

"The secret of business is to know something that nobody else knows."
- Aristotle Onassis

"Every noble work is at first, impossible."
- Thomas Carlyle

"Architecture provides the Landing strip of intent, for any viable implementation to land on."
- {{Gareth Llewellyn}}

"The value of Architecture is intangible.
If it were tangible, it would be Engineering."
- Kevin Lee Smith

The Pragmatic Architects Creed™ sorts the wheat from the chaff.

For each phase of the Transformation cascade, people speak either a different dialect or language from the phases above and below.

The Appendix section contains information on the background of PF2, POET, PEAF and the author.

Use POET and PEAF to make sure you don't make the mistakes that cause 90% of all EA initiatives to fail.

Use people for the type of person they are, not the type of person you want them to be. If we were all the same, nothing would ever get done.

All Pragmatic books contain a Keypoint section.

www.Pragmatic365.org is the official source for all PF2/POET/PEAF related materials, and is constantly evolving.

Pragmatic EA is a non-profit research company, dedicated to developing Best Practice in relation to the structure and transformation of Enterprises.

Sources

- Book cover: Tropical Storm Lee - NASA/NOAA GOES Project Science Team.
- Stereogram used on "Hitting the Wall" produced by Easy Stereogram Builder - www.easystereogrambuilder.com
- "Brain Function with gears and cogs" used on the "Slaves to Psychology" graphic from BigStock - www.bigstockphoto.com/search/digitalista
- Technical Debt - www.wikipedia.org/wiki/Technical_debt
- Zachman Framework - www.wikipedia.org/wiki/Zachman_Framework
- TOGAF (The Open Group Architecture Framework) - www.opengroup.org/togaf/
- Business Motivation Model - www.omg.org/spec/BMM/
- Enhanced Business Motivation Model - www.MotivationModel.com
- ITIL (IT Infrastructure Library) - www.itil-officialsite.com
- COBIT (Control Objectives for Information and Related Technology) - www.wikipedia.org/wiki/Cobit

Resources

- www.Pragmatic365.org is the official source for all **Pragmatic** related materials.

Here is listed various sources and references to things referred to in the **Pragmatic** Frameworks.

You can always access the most up to date material online at www.Pragmatic365.org.

KEYPOINT:

www.Pragmatic365.org is the official source for all PF2/POET/PEAF related materials, and is constantly evolving.

Pragmatic 365

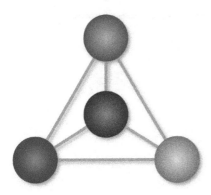

CONNECTING THE DOTS

KEYPOINT:

Pragmatic EA is a non-profit research company, dedicated to developing Best Practice in relation to the structure and transformation of Enterprises.

Lightning Source UK Ltd.
Milton Keynes UK
UKHW051851070421
381614UK00002B/24